LIKE A
HURRICANE

Like a Hurricane:
An Unofficial Oral History
of Street Fighter II

Written by Matt Leone

With 55 illustrations

Like a Hurricane

FOREWORD

→ JAMES CHEN
Street Fighter series commentator

It's interesting how a simple decision can change your life. In this instance, it wasn't even my decision; it was my older brother Jeff's. He was finishing high school, and he'd applied to two colleges, both in California where we lived: the University of California, Berkeley and the University of California, Los Angeles. He'd gotten into both, but since we'd grown up in southern California, he decided to go to UCLA. And that was it: that was the decision that changed my life.

I didn't know it at the time, but back in the '90s, UCLA had one of the best arcades in southern California, called simply the UCLA Gameroom. It was huge, well maintained, and always up to date with the latest games (alongside some classics). As my brother started at UCLA, he regaled me with stories of how he was getting better at games, being able to finish *Strider* on one credit and *Teenage Mutant Ninja Turtles* on three.

Then everything changed one day when a little game called *Street Fighter II* showed up at the arcade. My brother called me immediately. 'It's crazy, all the CPU characters that you fight in the game, you can use them, too!' He described the wild yellow monster (to this day I think of Blanka in *SFII* as more yellow than green), the karate guys, the big Russian wrestler, the Chinese girl, and the stretchy Indian guy who spits fire.

Now granted, at this time – even though I'd seen Super Nintendo games and arcade games looked even better – the visual that popped into my head was about five years out of date. I remember picturing the NES game *Renegade*, a pretty janky side-scroller. I had this image of an all-blue subway-esque background with a short pixelated Japanese guy fighting a short pixelated Indian guy on an isometric stage.

Wrong as that was, my brother's stories kept piling up. And eventually, on one of his weekend visits home, we decided to look for the game. Now, there weren't many arcades near where we lived, but there was one called Laser Blast in San Bernardino that we never went into as kids. It was a shady looking joint and our parents never let us go, but we were on a mission and old enough at this point. So we called — they had it. And when we walked in, everything changed for me.

The butterflies were palpable, but could the game live up to my brother's hype? Well, the original vision in my imagination vanished in the face of what I can only describe as one of the most beautiful videogames of its time. Bright, colourful, detailed fighters were displayed with detailed facial expressions, clearly defined muscles, scars, necklaces made of tiny skulls ... and there was a Chinese fighter that, for her time, looked far less sexualized than most. Back then, fighting games always tended to have scantily clad women, like Angel from *Pit-Fighter* or Poison and Roxie from *Final Fight*. But I digress: the graphics, the characters, the music, the sound effects, the voices … everything fit together so perfectly to bring together a masterpiece of a game unlike anything I had seen before. So yeah. It lived up to the hype.

At the time, we didn't really think of *SFII* as a competitive game; we mostly played against the CPU. But that changed pretty quickly, as we became friends with many of the *SFII* fanatics that frequented Laser Blast. We eventually journeyed to our first tournament at a mini-golf arcade where a friend, my brother, and I took 1st, 2nd, and 3rd place respectively. We thought we were the best. We soon learned how little we actually knew.

Eventually, we were visited by two players: Tony Chung and Tomo Ohira (yes, that Tomo, of legendary fame). They were driving around southern California to hand out flyers advertising a tournament they ran at a comic book shop called World's Finest. And let me tell you, those two destroyed me and everyone else who thought they were the best at our arcade. We took the flyer, and decided to go to their third-ever tournament, as advertised. The comic shop was tiny and barely had room for three cabinets, but people found a way to cram in there. There were so many players and they were all so skilled at the game. It was like those scenes in old James Bond movies where Bond walks into

Q's laboratory and sees all the ridiculous gadgets on display. My brother and I were amazed as we saw things we never thought were possible.

That's when the world opened up and I started to understand what competitive *Street Fighter II* was all about. From that point on, it became a mad scramble to become one of the best at the game. It wasn't about being the best at your local arcade anymore. There was a veritable proving ground at World's Finest in Pico Rivera. Our friends drove there repeatedly, each time bringing back new tricks and strategies.

And I just never stopped playing.

I still remember the day *Champion Edition* showed up in southern California. It was at a bowling alley and I was sick that day, home from school. But I forced my weak body out of bed and my brother and I made our way there just to see the game. Everyone we knew from the county we lived in was there. It was the sort of huge meet-up that players today take for granted, and everyone was so giddy with excitement at using the boss characters, at the fact that Ryu and Ken fought differently, at the ability to use the same character against the same character. It was euphoric!

I would go to visit my brother every year and stay with him for a week during spring break just to play at the UCLA Gameroom, where the skill level was always very high. They had a row dedicated solely to *Street Fighter II* head-to-head cabinets. It was the only time, according to the manager of the arcade, that they ever had to collect the quarters out of the machines twice a week. Otherwise, *Street Fighter II*'s quarter bucket would overflow and the machine would stop working.

Here's the thing that people today might not understand: *Street Fighter II* wasn't just a popular videogame. It was a cultural phenomenon unlike anything we'd seen since *Pac-Man*. While games like *Super Mario Bros.* and *The Legend of Zelda* had massive fanbases, they were still considered kids' properties. Videogames still had the stigma of being a waste of time. Adults did not take videogames seriously. But *Street Fighter II* appealed to everyone.

And because of its wide appeal, you could find it everywhere: liquor stores, gas stations, pizza joints, VHS rental stores, bowling alleys, etc. Every place you visited, it was like a virtual kumite: the locals there would stare you down to see just how good you were. Because every location had their top players, and pride meant they couldn't lose to outsiders. I was definitely lucky to be in southern California, where we had a particularly robust scene, but Street Fighter was everywhere. Even people who didn't know a thing about videogames knew what *Street Fighter II* was. To this day, when I travel across the country for big Street Fighter tournaments, my rideshare drivers still know exactly what game I mean when I say I'm there for 'Street Fighter', with them often mimicking Ryu's original muffled vocal, 'Hadouken!' while putting their hands out in the classic pose.

This wasn't just a game that changed my life; it was a game that changed many people's lives. Yoko Shimomura's music has inspired people to become composers. Akira Yasuda's art has inspired people to become illustrators. A lot of people I know have gone into game development to make their own fighting games ... because of Street Fighter. And millions of fans haven't stopped playing fighting games, with many still attempting to be the best in the ever-growing competitive scene we now know as the Fighting Game Community.

A character yells, 'Hadouken!' in the movie *Shazam!*, and a *Champion Edition* cabinet shows up in *Captain Marvel*, movies that came out nearly 20 years after *SFII* debuted in arcades. Guile's theme music became a popular meme decades after its release. Comedian Pete Holmes did a comedy sketch series about *Street Fighter II* in 2014 for a TBS show. Even when Ryu showed up in *Fortnite*, the trailer for the reveal used the classic *Street Fighter II* cabinet instead of referencing any of the myriad sequels that have come out since. *Street Fighter II* still burns strongly in the hearts of so many people.

Street Fighter II wasn't just a game. It was a comic book. It was a board game. It was a terrible movie. It was a terrible game based on that terrible movie. It was a toy tie-in with G.I. Joe. It was a cartoon. It was a pinball game. It was a kids' book based on *Where's Waldo?* that, yes, I still own. It marked the start of an entire genre of games and spawned countless rip-offs. But most of all, it was a cultural phenomenon. It defined a period of time so many people from my generation will never forget.

That's what makes the game so special. That's why a book like this exists. I hope this evokes some nostalgia for you, or gives you a glimpse of what has made *Street Fighter II* so much more than just a videogame. Enjoy ... like I have been for 30 years.

Like a Hurricane

CHAPTER 01

STREET
FIGHTER

On 12 May 1987, Capcom gathered arcade distributors from across the US at a Philadelphia gym. The company had rented out the Cambria Boxing Club, known for its appearance in *Rocky*, and staged an exhibition with local boxers, kickboxers, and a ring girl to entertain the crowd of rowdy onlookers.

Earlier that day, Capcom had shown their action game *Bionic Commando* at the airport Marriott, but that wasn't why everyone was in town.

At Cambria, Capcom vice-president of sales and marketing Bill Cravens worked the room. A popular figure known for his towering presence and reputation for showmanship, the tuxedo-clad Cravens was gearing up for his big moment. After watching 12 rounds of fights, as reported by industry trade magazine *RePlay*, Cravens walked over to a brown paper package, tore off the paper, and laid bare why everyone was gathered in a gym.

Beneath the wrappings was *Street Fighter*, a new competitive fighting game with buttons that looked like punching bags and a boxer bearing a slight resemblance to Mike Tyson. No Rocky Balboa, but Cravens lived in Philadelphia, so he took certain liberties with the venue choice.

For Capcom, *Street Fighter* was an experiment. It wasn't just a game but an initiative to sell an elaborate, expensive arcade cabinet. Up to that point, Capcom had made their name on software that arcade operators could swap into existing cabinets, and *Street Fighter* was supposed to be the big, flashy example that would convince those operators to pay twice as much for the full thing.

As the crowd of distributors watched, they saw a game that fit the sales pitch, with large characters, creative mechanics and custom controls. In 1987, before it picked up the baggage of 30 years of sequels that made it look clumsy in comparison, *Street Fighter* was cutting edge.

From the start, Capcom positioned the Street Fighter series to be a breakthrough that would move the company in a new direction. And a few years later, the series did exactly that, just not in the way Capcom intended.

A GAME OF IDEAS

Thirty-plus years after its release, *Street Fighter* is a template, a high-level blueprint for what fighting games would become. The game's legacy has become less about how well it holds up, and more about its mechanics. From the international cast of characters, to the joystick motions that triggered special moves, to Ryu and Ken's trademark attacks, the game established the formula for competitive fighting games right out of the gate.

Behind the scenes, it started with someone bored in a meeting.

→   TAKASHI NISHIYAMA
       Street Fighter director, Capcom Japan

I actually remember it very clearly, even now. One day at Capcom, we had a meeting between the development staff and the sales team, and this particular meeting happened to run very long – I think it was about two hours. Personally, as someone on the development side, I found it very hard to stay interested during these meetings, so I tended to daydream and think about games. And I remember not really paying attention and jotting down some ideas on paper. Then there was just this one moment where the idea for *Street Fighter* popped into my head, and I drew it out on a piece of paper during the meeting. I was sitting next to [Capcom producer Yoshiki] Okamoto and I asked him what he thought about it, and he said it looked very interesting.

I guess, concretely speaking, the idea was inspired by *Spartan X* [an action game known as *Kung-Fu Master* in the US and Europe], which I worked on at Irem. I was thinking about the boss fights in that game, and thought it could be interesting to build a game around those. I think you could say *Spartan X* was the basis of the whole idea for *Street Fighter*.

So yeah, the notes I wrote during that meeting were all very rough, but I used those to put together a design document to convince the higher-ups at Capcom to greenlight the game. And I ended up showing that document to [Hiroshi] Matsumoto, and he's the one who ended up refining the ideas after that. [...] Everything after that was basically all his doing. I oversaw things, but you can say it was really Matsumoto's game.

→   HIROSHI MATSUMOTO
            Street Fighter planner, Capcom Japan

After Nishiyama came up with the basic concept, I thought about what kinds of characters we should have, what kinds of moves they should have, what kinds of fighting styles they should have. [...] At the time, I was very interested in martial arts and – just as a hobby – I had studied and read up on them extensively. So I was excited.

→   TAKASHI NISHIYAMA
            Street Fighter director, Capcom Japan

I think *Street Fighter* was a bit of a unique game at the time because it had story and character elements to it that weren't very common in other popular games, like shooters or racing games. And what was interesting about *Street Fighter* was we had characters with different fighting styles in it. We had boxing, kickboxing, bojutsu, shorinji kempo, etc. If you're trying to make a competitive fighting game, if you have just two boxers facing up against each other, that might be very simple, right? And not terribly remarkable. But if you pit a boxer, for example, against a kickboxer or someone who knows bojutsu or someone who knows shorinji kempo, you get all these very interesting combinations. So Matsumoto and I ended up coming up with these ideas together, to give the game deeper story and character elements. And I think it became a trend to incorporate these kinds of elements into games. A lot of the characters ended up in multimedia projects like movies and novels, which was great.

The other thing that I really liked about *Street Fighter* was how we set up the joystick motions and button presses to generate special moves that you couldn't have done otherwise. I think it was through these ideas that the competitive fighting genre was born.

DEVELOPMENT CHALLENGES

While *Street Fighter* established a framework that went on to generate billions of dollars in revenue, it was also a game built on limitations. With twitchy movement, a limited number of playable characters, and special moves that required extreme precision to perform, fights didn't feel like the gracefully choreographed battles they would become in later instalments.

Before Capcom could worry about things like character balance and deep gameplay mechanics, they had to build the foundation. And what they came up with was a game that showed promise, but one that lacked the level of polish necessary to overwhelm the marketplace.

As Nishiyama and Matsumoto recall, many of the biggest challenges they faced came down to the resources available at the time, and how much of the game Matsumoto had to implement by himself.

→   HIROSHI MATSUMOTO
    Street Fighter planner, Capcom Japan

The most difficult aspect of making that game, as far as I'm concerned, was the fact that the main programmer wasn't originally a game programmer. I don't think he'd come to Capcom as an official employee, but had been dispatched from another company. And he was a systems engineer, not a game programmer, so he had no idea how to make games. So I think the toughest hurdle was trying to communicate with him and trying to teach him how to make games, because no matter how we tried to explain it, he just didn't seem to understand even the most basic concepts.

I had learned a few things while working on [overhead shooter] *Legendary Wings*, so it got to the point where I had to do some of his work myself to speed things up. It was just faster for me to do it than for me to teach him how to do it. Today we use programming and tools to animate graphics, but back then, we had to use a table to look up every frame of animation for every character. We used an old Hewlett-Packard computer for that, and it was very tedious work, delineating each frame manually by hand. If you wanted an animation to go from point A to point B, you had to manually enter all that data. And revisions meant doing the same thing all over again.

It wasn't my job, officially, to do that, but we had no choice. It would have been much faster to just do it all myself.

→   TAKASHI NISHIYAMA
         Street Fighter director, Capcom Japan

I think the most regrettable experience of the game was the fact that, you know, we had all these ideas for different playable characters that we wanted to put into the game, but due to budget concerns, scheduling concerns and whatnot, eventually that got whittled down to just having Ryu and Ken in the game. And I would have loved to have more playable characters, but unfortunately we were only able to put in the two of them.

→   HIROSHI MATSUMOTO
         Street Fighter planner, Capcom Japan

Because we only had so much time on our hands – you know, time is not infinite, right? – I couldn't do everything that I wanted to do. I remember wanting to put a bunch of different characters into the game, but Okamoto would come to me and say, 'Hey, we don't have time to put these in, so we have to cut them.' I thought that was pretty unfortunate.

Okamoto had actually taken an interest in the *Street Fighter* project even though he wasn't directly involved in it. [...]

He had been interested enough in *Street Fighter* that he had been involved in some of the discussions regarding the pressure sensor that we used in the arcade cabinet [which players would hit to generate weak, medium or strong attacks]. I remember one day he wanted to test out how that would work, and we ended up making a prototype of that sensor using a rubber band and a button. And we both ended up testing how the pressure would work by banging it a bunch of times. So we both ended up with scratches on our fists.

CAPCOM'S EXPERIMENT

As it turned out, the prototype wasn't the only setup that hurt players' hands.

> When *Street Fighter* arrived in arcades, it came in a crescent-shaped 'deluxe upright' cabinet with a joystick and two large, pneumatic, pressure-sensitive buttons on each side – one for punches and one for kicks. Capcom was attempting to move into the high-end arcade cabinet business, where they could sell a bigger machine with a custom interface for more money, and the gimmick of pressure-sensitive buttons set the game apart from the hundreds of games using standard control setups.

RePlay magazine called Capcom's contraption 'a pricey but extremely inventive item combining interactive video competition with the physical demands of a mole whacker'.

→   TAKASHI NISHIYAMA
      Street Fighter director, Capcom Japan

Back in the day, I think the biggest arcade cabinet manufacturers were Sega and Namco. Capcom did most of their business selling printed circuit boards that you could plug in to other machines. But Sega and Namco specialized in selling large cabinets, and they made a lot of money doing that. Once Capcom found out, they wanted a piece of the pie, so they wanted to sell their own cabinets.

> The thing is, though, Capcom didn't know what they were doing – they didn't specialize in mechatronics or know how to build those sorts of cabinets. So Capcom thought, *Maybe we could make a simpler cabinet that we could sell?*

That's why we came up with the pneumatic buttons, and the idea tied directly in to how we designed *Street Fighter*. The idea was that, ideally, the sensor would be able to detect how strongly or how weakly you pressed it, and that would translate into the kinds of moves you'd perform in the game, because a simple arcade stick couldn't accurately replicate a human's complex movements, right? We wanted to kind of offset that shortcoming.

It basically came down to two particular objectives, two missions here. The first was to come up with some kind of an arcade cabinet that the sales department could sell to their customers, and the other was coming up with a way to improve the game and offset the shortcomings of an arcade stick.

But it was very difficult to develop a pressure-sensitive sensor, and that was a technological issue that Capcom never quite ended up overcoming. So we ended up working with Atari, and we worked together to develop the sensor, since they're the ones who had the knowhow to make that happen.

→ ALDO DONNALOIA
Street Fighter Western regional sales manager, Capcom USA

I was the liaison between Atari and our engineering group that came over, so I did some translation for the engineers. And back then, Atari built the highest-quality cabinets, so we went to them to build this cabinet for us. [...] You know, it took some time, but both Capcom engineers and Atari figured it out. I do remember it was kind of like a quarter-moon-shaped cabinet. Yeah, it was a fantastic cabinet.

→ ZENJI ISHII
Editor-in-chief, Gamest magazine

I remember seeing it for the first time and seeing how big the cabinet was, and that it had the pressure-sensitive buttons, and I remember thinking how different and impressive it was from other arcade games at the time.

→ TAKASHI NISHIYAMA
  Street Fighter director, Capcom Japan

The problem was, during location tests, we realized that it was very tiring to hit the sensor over and over. It was basically like exercising. The whole point of monetizing this business was to get people to become repeat customers, where they would put in 100 yen coins over and over again so we could make money. And when you're getting tired from playing the game, that's not going to happen.

→ TODD CRAVENS
  Son of Capcom USA vice-president Bill Cravens

You had to beat the hell out of it. I remember playing it for the first time and being absolutely exhausted. Everyone was kind of like, 'Oh my goodness. It's gonna be hard to get the second and third quarter on this.' [...] They were doing a big unveiling of this at a gym in Philadelphia for the US distributors, and they had boxers there who [played the game], and even those guys were tired afterwards.

→ ALDO DONNALOIA
  Street Fighter Western regional sales manager, Capcom USA

It just was too radical.

→ JOE MORICI
  Street Fighter II console vice-president, Capcom USA

I remember when I first saw it — it had those big rubber [pads] that you punch with your fists. That had to come off the market because everybody was getting injured.

→ JEFF WALKER
  Street Fighter II vice-president of sales and marketing, Capcom USA

What we were hearing was everyone was getting bloody hands, it wasn't working too well, and yadda yadda yadda.

→   TOMOTAKA SUZUKI
Street Fighter II series combo video creator

I hurt my hand a few times. There were times when I had to use my elbow.

→   ZENJI ISHII
Editor-in-chief, Gamest magazine

There's a way you have to press the buttons. You shouldn't slam down on them from high. You have to use your palms to press them gently.

→   TODD CRAVENS
Son of Capcom USA vice-president Bill Cravens

I think one of the other concerns they had was just the hold-up of it, right? You know, you just keep punching something over and over again; how often are you going to have to replace these parts?

→   ALDO DONNALOIA
Street Fighter Western regional sales manager, Capcom USA

I think we were worried about getting sued as well.

→   TAKASHI NISHIYAMA
Street Fighter director, Capcom Japan

We ended up changing the control panel so it would have six buttons instead of the pressure-sensitive sensor. It wasn't really the sort of success Capcom was looking for.

→   TODD CRAVENS
Son of Capcom USA vice-president Bill Cravens

They were kind of looking around like, 'OK, we think we have a good game here, but the controls are going to have to be modified back more to a more standard type of deal, otherwise no one's gonna play this game for more than five minutes.'

→   TAKASHI NISHIYAMA
          Street Fighter director, Capcom Japan

We also ran into a big issue with the six-button layout on the control panel, because most games back then had two buttons and the eight-way directional arcade stick, right? But we wanted to go with six buttons, and we got a lot of pushback from the sales department because they were concerned that people wouldn't be able to figure out how to play six-button games. But we managed to put in the six buttons in the end, and we ended up getting a lot of positive consumer feedback to that. So we were able to shut the sales department up.

> I was very focused on trying to carefully navigate company politics, working with the sales department to get the game out the way we wanted it to be.

→   ALDO DONNALOIA
          Street Fighter Western regional sales manager, Capcom USA

We decided to forgo this idea of pneumatic buttons and switched over to the six buttons, and I think we were the first with six buttons. And that's when *Street Fighter* began to take off, you know?

A MIXED SUCCESS

More than 30 years after the fact, we don't know exactly how well *Street Fighter* sold. Capcom hasn't released official numbers, trade magazines from the 1980s only show operator survey results, and no one we spoke to for this book had specific data. Perhaps more notably, many of those people estimate the numbers differently from one another, and interpret them differently as well.

→   ALDO DONNALOIA
          Street Fighter Western regional sales manager, Capcom USA

Nishiyama was a great guy, and this is what he always told me. He said, 'Hey Aldo, the part of R&D that I engineer, they do not try to hit a home run, you know? I'm happy with a double.' Whereas the other guy, I think his name was Okamoto. He wanted to hit a home run every time. [...] And of course, Nishiyama's *Street Fighter*, you know, hit the home run.

→   TAKASHI NISHIYAMA
          Street Fighter director, Capcom Japan

From my perspective, I think the most difficult part of making the game was that we initially came up with a game that was built to sell arcade cabinets, right? And I think that we did fail in that regard.

      Thinking about the numbers, though [...] I think it was actually a pretty decent hit, so I guess it was a success. Probably more so in the US than in Japan.

→   HIROSHI MATSUMOTO
          Street Fighter planner, Capcom Japan

I remember there was this industry newsletter called Game Machine, and around the end of the year, I think president [Kenzo] Tsujimoto got a copy and saw Street Fighter's ranking and was happy with it. It seemed like the game had sold a lot of units.

[Ed. note]   The deluxe upright version of *Street Fighter* peaked at #3 on Game Machine's Upright/Cockpit Videos list in October 1987. A cheaper cocktail table version of the game went to #1 on the Table Videos list in January 1988. Both left their respective charts in mid-1988. These rankings came from opinion polls surveying arcade operators about the earnings of games on location in Japan.

In the US, *RePlay* magazine ran similar operator opinion survey charts. In December 1987, the game peaked at #10 in *RePlay*'s Upright Videos charts and then gradually fell down the list until it left the top 25 in mid-1989. In the US, these rankings included both the original deluxe upright cabinet and a standard cabinet produced later.

→   RYAN CRAVENS
        Son of Capcom USA vice-president Bill Cravens

It was popular, but obviously it wasn't *Street Fighter II*.

→   TODD CRAVENS
        Son of Capcom USA vice-president Bill Cravens

It was not huge. [...] I don't want to take a stab because I don't really know, but it was not really a commercial success, I don't think.

→   JEFF WALKER
        Street Fighter II vice-president of sales and marketing, Capcom USA

They removed the punch pad, they put buttons on it, but they only sold ... I want to guess 2,500 to 3,000 units, period.

→   TAKASHI NISHIYAMA
    Street Fighter director, Capcom Japan

I think we sold around 1,000 cabinets with the pneumatic buttons. [...] For the version with the six-button controls, I don't have the exact numbers. It might have been 50,000 units. But it was definitely in the tens of thousands.

→   PAUL WIEDERAENDERS
    Street Fighter II Midwest regional sales manager, Capcom USA

Well, I mean both [Walker's and Nishiyama's] numbers could be correct, although I think the 2,500 is a little low. The original *Street Fighter*, when it came out in a dedicated game, I'm pretty sure the sales of that were well into 10,000 or 15,000. But the problem was, in those days there was a lot of pirating of boards out of Korea. And so, if you take that into account, there could be 50,000 boards, conceivably, because nobody knew how many pirated boards were being produced and sent into the United States and into Europe and into Australia.

→   ALDO DONNALOIA
    Street Fighter Western regional sales manager, Capcom USA

They did not sell too many of the quarter-moon cabinets due to people hurting their wrists. I am estimating a couple of hundred units of this type. Once they went to a normal cabinet with six push buttons per joystick, Capcom's orders started to go up. I am guessing nearly 10,000 units sold.

→   BRIAN DUKE
    Street Fighter II Western regional sales manager, Capcom USA

Everyone was talking about the reason why it did not reach the level of success Capcom expected, and the controls were the main problem, I heard. [...] It wasn't until later that customers and players started saying that the six-button [version] worked and earned much better than the units with original pads – and if we had only chosen to market it that way from the beginning, *Street Fighter* probably would have been the number one game of the year.

There was a lot of interest in a sequel.

THE EXODUS

Before getting to a sequel, Nishiyama threw a spanner in Capcom's plans.

> Shortly after *Street Fighter*'s release, a headhunter approached Nishiyama and convinced him to leave Capcom and join nearby studio SNK. Nishiyama took Matsumoto and most of his team with him, abandoning the Street Fighter IP. The move carried baggage, both because of the scale of the exodus and because the two companies had a history.

In the years that followed, word of a rivalry built up around the pair, with both developing similar games and occasionally referencing one another in those games.

> While researching this book, we spoke to more than ten former Capcom and SNK employees about the dynamic between the two companies in that era. They all say that development staff on both sides got along well; many of them went to the same schools and arcades, and hung out after work. In at least one case, a developer at SNK married someone who worked at Capcom.

As some of them point out, though, that doesn't mean there weren't issues at the top.

[Ed. note]   Capcom declined an interview request with founder Kenzo Tsujimoto for this book. We were unable to locate SNK founder Eikichi Kawasaki.

→ NORITAKA FUNAMIZU
Street Fighter II series producer, Capcom Japan

I remember why SNK and Capcom were rivals. It's because the presidents didn't get along with each other, Kawasaki and Tsujimoto.

→ TAKASHI NISHIYAMA
Street Fighter director, Capcom Japan

Yeah, I think there was a rivalry in the 1980s. Capcom's Tsujimoto and SNK's Kawasaki originally were friendly with each other, but apparently something happened and they ended up having a falling out. What happened to cause that, I'm not sure myself. I've heard a lot of different things from different people, but yeah, something happened.

→ HARUMI FUJITA
Composer, SNK Japan

There was a lot of gossip around the office. Kawasaki, actually, his original profession was as a boxer. He's got this, you know, very tough, intimidating look to him. I remember hearing that he would often complain and badmouth Tsujimoto and Capcom back in those days.

→ NORITAKA FUNAMIZU
Street Fighter II series producer, Capcom Japan

I think the bad blood existed even before I joined the company [in 1985]. I remember thinking the game *Ikari Warriors* may have had something to do with it ... hmm ... there was a ninja game ... actually, I think Harumi Fujita might have been the reason why. I think maybe the two didn't get along because Capcom headhunted her. The companies were trying to steal employees from one another. That might be the reason why things weren't so friendly at the beginning.

→ HARUMI FUJITA
Composer, Capcom Japan

Yeah, I think Funamizu is right. It wasn't just me. It was me and two people who worked on international sales, for the US market. Capcom hired them away from SNK, and the president of SNK at the time got upset about that and actually sued Capcom. The official story – I guess it's OK to talk about this nowadays – was that we joined Capcom after leaving SNK, but the reality is, we had made our decisions before officially resigning. So yeah, because of the headhunting issue, Capcom and SNK got into a legal battle.

[Ed. note] According to Fujita, her hiring came about after she bumped into a friend on a train – the friend happened to work at Capcom and mentioned the company was hiring. Fujita says she doesn't know the details of the legal claim.

→ TAKASHI NISHIYAMA
Street Fighter director, Capcom Japan

I remember hearing something about that. There was a rumour floating around about a lawsuit because Capcom headhunted Harumi Ihara, as she was known at the time, away from SNK.

→ HARUMI FUJITA
Composer, Capcom Japan

I didn't go to court myself. I was asked a lot of questions about how, exactly, Capcom hired me. SNK and Capcom's legal departments apparently reached a settlement about it at some point, and they decided to keep the details private. So I don't actually know the specifics of what happened.

NORITAKA FUNAMIZU
           Street Fighter II series producer, Capcom Japan

So SNK taking Nishiyama might have been revenge for Capcom
taking Fujita, right?

→   HARUMI FUJITA
           Composer, Capcom Japan

Yeah, it felt like payback. I mean, some of Capcom's main people had
just gone to SNK, so that was a pretty big incident.

→   AKIRA YASUDA
           Street Fighter II planner, Capcom Japan

I think SNK headhunting Nishiyama played a big part in why the
two companies were rivals.

→   DARRYL WILLIAMS
           Technical manager, Romstar

You know, it wasn't a big rivalry thing, but obviously it was egg on
your face if somebody – you know, Japan's really big on reputation
and respect – stole one of your staff.
              From my understanding, everybody knew who everybody
          was, the players knew who the players were, so it would
          have taken someone being aggressive on one side to get
          an employee from the other side. You know, the employee
          didn't just get up and go. Someone would have had to
          chase him down and make him an offer he couldn't refuse,
          long story short. And I think at that time, the offer was,
          [Nishiyama] gets his own division.

[Ed. note]   Fujita's and Nishiyama's groups weren't the only
                    staff to jump between Capcom and SNK in the
                    1980s. In one case between those two, SNK hired
                    Capcom USA president Paul Jacobs to run their
                    US office. Jacobs says he left because Capcom

wanted him to work exclusively on NES sales and he was 'a coin-op man at heart', and that he was aware of certain hires made in Japan, such as Nishiyama, but he wasn't aware of a rivalry: 'If that was happening in Japan, it didn't affect our US operations at SNK.' Nishiyama says there was no legal action following his departure.

→   TAKASHI NISHIYAMA
                Street Fighter director, Capcom Japan

I think this is just something that we often see in the videogame industry. I don't know if anyone was trying to get revenge on anyone else. To go back even earlier, I worked at Irem with Tsujimoto. And apparently some things happened at Irem and Tsujimoto ended up quitting and forming Capcom instead. And Tsujimoto headhunted me from Irem, right? Then afterwards, Kawasaki headhunted me from Capcom to go to SNK. So I think in this industry, not just in Japan but in America as well, I think this kind of thing is just inevitable. You know, people have various reasons for leaving companies and going elsewhere. I don't think a lot of these things are necessarily motivated by revenge. I think that sounds like a joke Funamizu would make. He wouldn't really know about this in detail.

→   ZENJI ISHII
                Editor, Gamest magazine

I remember conducting an interview with Nishiyama, Okamoto, [*Ghosts 'n Goblins* creator Tokuro] Fujiwara, and the president of Capcom at the time, actually just a little bit before the release of *Street Fighter I*. [...] I remember observing how different Nishiyama, Fujiwara, and Okamoto were, and I could kind of tell that there was this rivalry between the three of them because they all had different approaches to creating games. I was able to feel that just from the interview itself. I don't know if they'd admit that, but I could feel it. So when I heard that Nishiyama had left to go to SNK, I felt like maybe it seemed like a natural next step or inevitable, if anything.

→   AKIRA YASUDA
      Street Fighter II planner, Capcom Japan

Nishiyama was the oldest planner in Capcom at the time, but Nishiyama's team hadn't been able to produce a big hit. *Street Fighter* did OK; it sold a small amount.

>   Okamoto liked Nishiyama as a person, but he didn't like his games, and he would order me and others to fix them. I remember one time when Okamoto asked me in front of everybody to pick apart Nishiyama's [action game *Avengers*] and talk about what was wrong with it. Nishiyama's games weren't really selling well but Okamoto's games were. So, yeah. As far as I saw it, Nishiyama had pretty much lost his standing in the company, so it didn't feel like his team going to SNK was a big surprise.

→   TAKASHI NISHIYAMA
      Street Fighter director, Capcom Japan

This is honestly very, very hard to talk about, but to explain why I ended up leaving Capcom, it's because I didn't get along with my boss at the time, and I had hit a point where I was wondering if I could continue to stay at the company despite such a situation. I was very close with Tsujimoto, the president, and I'd had a relationship with him ever since I worked at Irem. I was close enough with Tsujimoto to the point where he actually spoke at my wedding. So I had a good relationship with him and I didn't hate the company. But it was my particular boss who I was unsure if I could get along with.

>   And it just so happened that SNK asked me to join them. So I got the offer and I ended up going there. But there were people that I had worked closely with at Capcom, including Matsumoto. So I ended up basically taking a bunch of them with me.

There was a lot of friction between SNK and Capcom at the time, with my quitting and taking employees with me, and then after that, the Neo Geo came out, which caused a lot of problems in the industry. I'm not even sure now if I should be talking about this openly. It's been a while, so maybe it's fine.

> I remember Tsujimoto saying, 'I'm never going to forgive you for quitting.'

But I mean now, obviously, we've moved past that. Dimps [the studio Nishiyama formed years later] developed *Street Fighter IV,* and I think we have a very good relationship with Capcom. I also believe Tsujimoto probably knows why I ended up leaving the company, and I think he understands the reasoning behind it. So we get along quite well now.

Like a Hurricane

CHAPTER 02

STREET
FIGHTER II

In 1985, artist Akira Yasuda showed up to a Capcom job interview dressed in pyjamas and a tie. He left his portfolio at home, saying fans stole his work because it was too good. Asked why he chose pyjamas, he replied that he wanted to look presentable and that was the only thing he owned with a collar.

Capcom producer Yoshiki Okamoto sat on the other side of the room, amused by Yasuda's antics. Okamoto, himself known for outlandish behaviour, liked Yasuda's work.

Yasuda got the job.

That same year, Okamoto – who ran one of Capcom's arcade development teams – brought on Noritaka Funamizu, a designer with an art background who took a high-level view of game production.

The next year, Okamoto hired Akira Nishitani, a young game designer who had written for the game magazine *Beep* and understood technical play mechanics on a deeper level than many developers at the time.

Without realizing it, Okamoto was recruiting a team that, in 1990, would oversee one of the biggest games of the decade: *Street Fighter II*. The Street Fighter franchise would go on to sell more than 45 million units. It would become a cologne. For kids of a certain generation, it was the most important game series in the world.

HOW IT HAPPENED

From a certain perspective, *Street Fighter II* was inevitable. Despite the exodus of Nishiyama and most of the original *Street Fighter* development team following its release, talk of a sequel continued to float around Capcom. This manifested in several forms – some of which made it public.

In their September 1988 issue, US arcade industry trade magazine *Play Meter* ran a 'Street Fighter II' logo on their cover, yet didn't mention the game inside the issue. In 1989, Capcom USA ran a 'Street Fighter II' logo in a sales catalog, advertising it as an NES game. That same year, side-scrolling brawler *Final Fight* appeared at an arcade trade show under the name 'Street Fighter '89' – a title briefly given to the game by Capcom's sales staff. Then in 1990, Capcom released *Street Fighter 2010: The Final Fight* – a console action game with loose Street Fighter story connections.

Intentionally or not, Capcom was priming the market for a proper *Street Fighter* sequel.

While all this was happening, Okamoto had continued to build his development staff, pairing up Nishitani and Yasuda to lead projects. In 1987, their side-scrolling shooter called *Forgotten Worlds* – the first game on Capcom's custom CPS-1 arcade hardware – earned critical acclaim but underperformed. In 1989, their big follow-up, *Final Fight*, became one of the most successful games of the era.

What happened next is a story that's up for some debate. We know that Nishitani and Yasuda moved on to head up *Street Fighter II*. Over the years, though, the key figures involved with the game have told different versions of how the project came about behind the scenes.

As Nishitani and Funamizu tell it, after the release of the original *Street Fighter*, Capcom USA's sales department asked Capcom Japan to develop a sequel. Funamizu remembers the request coming from Bill Cravens specifically, and that Cravens was excited about the potential of a *Street Fighter* follow-up.

Despite the request, Nishitani said in a 2014 *Polygon* article that the team in Japan saw the success of Technōs' side-scrolling brawler *Double Dragon*, so they decided to develop a similar game: *Final Fight*. Then, he said, after *Final Fight* came out, Capcom USA asked again for a *Street Fighter* sequel, and the team in Japan thought the timing seemed right.

Okamoto's version of the story starts similarly to Nishitani's, with the request for a *Street Fighter* sequel and *Double Dragon*'s popularity convincing the team to develop *Final Fight* instead, though he remembers the request coming from the sales team at Capcom Japan. In the same 2014 Polygon article, he said the idea for *Final Fight* came after seeing players huddled around *Double Dragon* arcade cabinets in the US, and that after the team started making the game, his bosses told him he needed to put the Street Fighter name on it or it wouldn't sell (thus 'Street Fighter '89') – though after taking the game to a convention in Japan and receiving feedback that the name seemed misleading, he went with the name *Final Fight* instead. Then, following *Final Fight*'s release and success, Okamoto said the sales team came back with a new request: to make a sequel to *Final Fight*. He said he again chose not to listen to them, portraying himself as someone who doesn't like to do what he's told, and thinking a head-to-head game would solve the economic challenge of trying to get multiple players on an arcade cabinet simultaneously without making the game seem like it was cheating players out of their money.

Funamizu's story branches off earlier in the timeline. He says a translation error led to a misunderstanding about what Cravens wanted in a *Street Fighter* sequel, so Capcom Japan decided to make *Final Fight*, as it loosely fit under the broader 'fighting' umbrella. Then, Funamizu says, after Cravens saw *Final Fight*, he said that he actually wanted a head-to-head *Street Fighter* sequel, so Funamizu took that information back to Okamoto, which kicked off the development of *Street Fighter II*.

Yasuda, meanwhile, says he doesn't think requests from Capcom USA had much to do with it, saying that *Final Fight* and *Street Fighter II* came about because of the hardware available at the time. He says that after the original *Street Fighter* came out, he started putting together a plan for a sequel – coming up with the idea to expand the roster to eight playable characters, but not diving into any proper production work. He adds that he realized the team couldn't do the game properly at that point because of a memory chip shortage, so they ended up making *Final Fight* in the interim – and when the shortage lifted, they got around to making *Street Fighter II*.

When asked about these discrepancies, Funamizu says he doesn't think Okamoto's story about the request to make 'Final Fight 2' is correct, and that Okamoto was going off the same mistranslated information that he was when the team decided to make *Final Fight*, though he's open to the possibility that Okamoto heard Cravens' initial feedback and ignored it. Funamizu defers to Okamoto, though he adds that Okamoto 'wasn't always straight with people', which he says may have been why Cravens told Funamizu and Nishitani about his request for a *Street Fighter* sequel directly after seeing *Final Fight*, rather than only telling Okamoto.

Yasuda says he thinks aspects of all the stories are probably true, adding that he recalls the plan to make *Street Fighter II* being set in place before the team finished *Final Fight*, so it wouldn't have been possible for the team to make a decision based on feedback following *Final Fight*'s release. Yasuda also notes that Funamizu wasn't heavily involved in the original *Street Fighter II*, saying that he worked out of a different building at the time, so he's sceptical that Funamizu would know the full story – though he speculates that the details of Funamizu's story are most likely true, just not the primary reason for Capcom making the decisions they did.

Takashi Nishiyama and Hiroshi Matsumoto, who often spoke to Cravens and worked briefly at Capcom after finishing the original *Street Fighter*, say they recall Capcom USA giving feedback on what types of games were popular in the West, but they don't recall any specific conversations requesting a sequel.

Cravens' son Ryan says he doesn't know the full story, but recalls hearing that after *Street Fighter* came out, Bill expected to see a 'Street Fighter II' and was surprised to see a side-scrolling beat-'em-up instead. Ryan also says he heard that Bill gave feedback saying Capcom shouldn't use the Street Fighter brand for *Final Fight* because the game felt different. Ryan, his brother Todd, and multiple former co-workers of Bill's say that Capcom USA didn't typically pitch game ideas to Capcom Japan and that the US office usually only gave notes on localization changes, such as censoring an exposed breast in *Strider* or a pentagram in *Magic Sword*. But, they say, if there was someone in the US office who would have given that sort of advice, it would have been Bill.

[Ed. note]   Nishitani, Okamoto and then-Capcom USA president George Nakayama declined to participate in this book, and Capcom declined interviews on behalf of sales staff who may have had input on the decisions. Yasuda also points to former Capcom executive Akio Sakai, who has since passed away, as being a key figure in the decisions. Bill Cravens died in 2007.

So ... we don't really know.
Factor in limited communication between international offices, 30-year-old memories, the passing of certain key figures and multiple people wanting to take credit, and it all gets a bit jumbled – a theme that comes up many times in this book. When you dig into the making of the game itself, the decisions become a lot more clear.

MAKING THE GAME

At a conceptual level, *Street Fighter II* didn't stray far from Capcom's *SFI* template. It pitted two characters against each other in best-of-three matches, featured a cast of fighters from around the world, and again starred Ryu and Ken – each with the same set of special moves.

On an execution level, the game marked one of the biggest steps forward a sequel has taken in the game industry. *Street Fighter II* brought a more detailed art style that highlighted the personality of each character, an exciting and catchy soundtrack, six distinct new playable characters, smoother controls, and an overall pace, feel, and balance that let players feel like their successes were earned and their mistakes were their fault.

While Capcom assigned dozens of team members to the project, many give the bulk of the credit to planners Yasuda and Nishitani, who took on the game following their success with *Final Fight*. Yasuda had seniority and spent much of his time on the game's visuals, while Nishitani was establishing himself as someone with an eye for precise game mechanics.

→   ZENJI ISHII
      Editor-in-chief, Gamest magazine

I think to begin, I need to explain a little bit about the history of the arcade game scene in Japan even before *Street Fighter I* and *II* came along. I know games like *Pac-Man* were popular in America, and the same was true in Japan. After Namco released [space shooter] *Xevious*, the number of fans visiting arcades saw a huge spike. They would compete with each other for the highest scores, and in a way, you could call it the esports of that generation. This boom mainly occurred between 1984 and 1991, though it extended a little bit past that too. And it was during those years that a lot of people who began as arcade game fans eventually found their way into videogame development.

> For example, you had Nishitani, who now runs Arika, and he made *Street Fighter II*. Another one would be Satoshi Tajiri from Game Freak, who ended up making *Pokémon*. There's many more, but yeah, they all got their start playing at game centres. I was one of them too, but I ended up going in the whole game magazine direction. Nishitani lived in Tokyo and he spent a lot of his time going to arcades there, trying to get high scores. Back then, we called those people 'scorers'.

I'd also like to add that, in Japan at the time, people who went to game centres were seen as delinquents. The laws and regulations on game centres were very strict too. It wasn't just game centres either; there was a lot of criticism of videogames in general then. People would say that if you played videogames as a kid, you wouldn't grow up to be a responsible adult. So I think that a lot of the game developers who came up in that era and went on to be game developers, they had to have an especially strong will and love of games given the adverse environment and negativity from society at large.

→   TAKESHI TEZUKA
             X-Men: Children of the Atom planner, Capcom Japan

I wasn't directly involved in any of the Street Fighter games of the 1990s. However, I sat next to Nishitani, so I was able to see what was happening regarding the development of those games.

> I think the most amazing or profound thing I could say about observing *Street Fighter II*'s development at the time was that ... basically, the project was spearheaded by two people. There was Akira Nishitani and Akira Yasuda, or Akiman as he's known. And Nishitani was

the planner and Yasuda was kind of the main lead or the director of the game.

[Ed. note]   Both appear in the game's credits as planners.

And I realized that they were both very talented creators and they were both very skilled and knowledgeable. But what they were particularly good at was their ability to incorporate ideas from all members of the development team. Nishitani sat next to me so I often got to see other staff approach him. They'd bring him their suggestions for new moves, things like that. And the amazing thing was how, in almost every case, he would right there, on the spot say, 'That sounds cool. Let's do that!' It was almost like 'let's do that!' was a personal catchphrase of his or something, the way he was able to so quickly decide on incorporating a new idea. It's something I've always remembered about him, that talent he had for quickly recognizing and including others' ideas.

→   YOKO SHIMOMURA
      Street Fighter II composer, Capcom Japan

Nishitani really, really loves games. He's always thinking about the game he's making. He's always tweaking the details and just really seriously thinking about how to make the game better. So when someone's like that, you might think they have a very narrow vision – just concentrating on the game from his point of view. But it wasn't like that. When I had a suggestion I thought, 'Maybe he won't take me seriously', or 'Maybe he's not going to like this.' But I just gave it a shot and he would usually say, 'Yeah that's a great idea. Let's do that.'

→   JAMES GODDARD
      Street Fighter II: Champion Edition design support, Capcom USA

Now there's a very smart, humble guy. He was so talented and he was so quiet. [...] He was a planner through and through. And that's the difference. Game designers in America are idea and story guys sometimes. You know, sometimes mechanical guys. There's a wide range of what designer means. But a planner is someone who figures out how the fucking shit's gonna work, and wields all that creative energy and figures out how to make it happen. And Nishitani was the first guy I met that resonated with me as, 'Hey this is how you do game design.'

[Ed. note] When asked to give an example of his kitchen sink approach in the 2014 *Polygon* article, Nishitani pointed to the character Dhalsim, and how his arms and legs initially stretched a short length – but after feedback from the team, Nishitani agreed to let them stretch across almost the entire screen. That's not to say that Nishitani incorporated every idea. Tezuka tells a story about asking Nishitani why he wasn't using *SFI*'s pneumatic buttons for *SFII* – saying, 'Isn't that a better idea?' – and Nishitani laughing at the request. (Though Nishitani said in a 2018 interview for Capcom's website that the team considered using pneumatic buttons for *SFII* early in the process.) Also, in the 2014 *Polygon* article, Okamoto said he proposed giving the game's only female character, Chun-Li, a shorter life bar because he felt women were weaker than men.

→   AKIRA YASUDA
      Street Fighter II planner, Capcom Japan

He did say that. Nishitani was the one who turned that request down. I was together with Nishitani on that decision. Yeah, I remember being with Nishitani when we made that decision.

I had no idea [Okamoto suggested that]. I think that since women live longer maybe their life bars should be longer. [*laughs*]

[Ed. note]

In the 1980s and 1990s, Capcom's office culture cultivated behaviour that often crossed the line of what many would consider appropriate. Okamoto, who managed the *SFII* team, earned a reputation as someone who constantly tried to get a rise out of coworkers, making sexual jokes and playing pranks by, for example, sending out tapes that that were supposedly work-related but contained pornography. Around the office, managers offered harsh criticism and employees worked long hours, sometimes sleeping at the office and washing at a nearby bath house.

In a 2020 YouTube video, Okamoto discussed some of this behaviour, saying he would get mad at Yasuda if Yasuda didn't come into the office on Sundays, calling himself 'very strict' and saying he would 'crack the whip a lot' to get employees to work long hours. 'I thought the company was going to fail unless everyone fought as if their lives depended on it,' he said.

In that same video, Okamoto told a story about *Mahjong Academy*, an erotic mahjong game that he assigned Nishitani and Yasuda to work on after hours during the development of *Forgotten Worlds*. To make the game, Okamoto asked female employees to model swimsuits in erotic poses for reference material, saying his now ex-wife helped with the shoot, and recorded female employees moaning and breathing heavily, while he served as the male voice actor. 'Basically, total sexual harassment by way of power harassment,' he said.

Okamoto frames this discussion as praise for Capcom founder Kenzo Tsujimoto, saying that when Tsujimoto found out about this project, he refused to release it. Capcom ended up selling the game under another company's brand, in order to protect their reputation, and the game ended up being a hit. Okamoto, who also called himself a 'slavedriver' due to the amount of time he asked employees to work, justified the project by saying, 'I felt if we didn't do all this, Capcom was going to go bankrupt. I did feel vindicated in that many people told me afterwards, if we hadn't made this, Capcom would have gone bankrupt.' In YouTube videos, Okamoto has publicly apologized to his former staff for asking them to work excessive hours in that era.

Funamizu refers to Capcom at the time as a 'black company' – a term used in Japan to refer to a business that doesn't follow proper labour laws, and commonly used to describe game companies of that era. He says it while laughing, pointing out that he doesn't mean it as a harsh criticism. Other former staffers we interviewed are split over whether they think the term applies to Capcom, with some pointing to it being a different time and Capcom being a family business that had yet to go public.

THE ACCIDENTAL COMBO

As it turned out, the team's willingness to pull in unexpected ideas led to one of *Street Fighter II*'s most popular features. To reduce the reliance on luck, the team made it easier for players to perform certain moves, which opened up the game in a way the designers hadn't intended, allowing players to link together multiple hits before their opponents could react. In short, they invented the combo. Some called it a bug.

→   SHINICHI UEYAMA
       Street Fighter II lead programmer, Capcom Japan

We had recently made *Ghosts 'n Goblins*. You know how in that game, your character flies backwards when he gets hit? His armour goes flying off, but during that period of time while he's in the air, he's invincible. So for Capcom's games back then, a system where you took damage and then took damage again immediately, without any kind of invincibility frames, that was pretty rare. The first game we implemented that in, where you could damage an enemy right after they'd already taken damage, was *Final Fight*.

→   NORITAKA FUNAMIZU
       Street Fighter II series producer, Capcom Japan

Smack, smack, smack, smack, smack, smack. You could really rack up the hits. If you got the input timing right, you could just keep going on and on.

→   SHINICHI UEYAMA
       Street Fighter II lead programmer, Capcom Japan

Exactly. It was from that game that we got the idea for consecutive hit moves [in *Street Fighter II*]. After that, special moves got thrown into the mix, and more complex ways to do combos came about.

→ MOTOHIDE ESHIRO
Street Fighter II programmer, Capcom Japan

Early on in development [on *Street Fighter II*] it became clear that we were being a little too strict and a little too severe with the input methods. So when you did the down, down-forward, forward punch [input to perform a fireball], you had to hit punch at exactly the moment you were hitting right on the joystick or it wouldn't work. And it was just really hard for people to get their heads around that – it really felt like you were doing it right and it wasn't working. So we decided to open up that timing a little bit, just by a few frames, so that if you hit that punch button within those few frames you'd be OK and your fireball would work.

And as a side-effect of that – so I guess if you wanted to call it a bug, you could, but really it was a side-effect of giving people more time to enter the button – players could perform combos. So if you were doing a crouching kick by holding down, and then pressed right and punch when your character was doing that animation, you could connect those together. It wasn't intentional to let players combine moves into combos, but it wasn't a bug in that it was planned to make it easier to do your special moves.

→ NORITAKA FUNAMIZU
Street Fighter II series producer, Capcom Japan

We wanted to make the moves easier to do, so basically we made it so you could cancel a regular attack in the middle and do a special move. But it turned out that during this time, if you pressed the buttons very fast, it could theoretically register two hits instead of one.

→ SHINICHI UEYAMA
Street Fighter II lead programmer, Capcom Japan

It was a mistake.

→   SEIJI OKADA
      Street Fighter II programmer, Capcom Japan

If I had to say, yeah, it was.

→   NORITAKA FUNAMIZU
      Street Fighter II series producer, Capcom Japan

But it was interesting, so Nishitani said to leave it in.

→   SHINICHI UEYAMA
      Street Fighter II lead programmer, Capcom Japan

It's hard to say whether it was some brilliant invention or actually a failure. But it was interesting, so we left it in.

→   NORITAKA FUNAMIZU
      Street Fighter II series producer, Capcom Japan

It was a product of chance. Nishitani decided to leave it in on the mere word of two or three people, and I thought, *Wow, this guy. He's a genius or something.* [laughs] [...] Normally, you wouldn't leave something like that in your game, not in that state. A normal person would think, *Oh, it's off. We have to fix it.*

→   SHINICHI UEYAMA
      Street Fighter II lead programmer, Capcom Japan

What a normal person saw as something broken, Nishitani saw as something interesting.

ART SHOW

As Capcom sorted out plans for *Street Fighter II*'s gameplay, they also put together a team of artists to design characters and backgrounds under the guidance of planner Yasuda. After the success of *Final Fight*, Yasuda had built a reputation not only for his illustration work, but for his ability to translate character designs into intricate pixel art – and on *Street Fighter II*, he continued that work while overseeing the creation of a new group of characters.

Given the rudimentary tools available at the time, this accounted for Capcom's biggest expense on the project. But many say the expense paid off.

→   SCOTT SMITH
       Street Fighter II marketing manager, Capcom USA

It was probably the most beautiful game for its time – the background animations, the character animations ...

When Bill Cravens brought the first *Street Fighter* [*II*] board back from Japan, nobody knew what it was. [...] They installed it in the break room, right? So we had a break room with like, three soda machines, two other machines and then a bunch of arcade games. *Final Fight*, [puzzle game] *Super Buster Bros.*, [shooter] *UN Squadron* and I think [action game] *Strider*. And I think they pulled open the *Strider* cabinet, drilled some more holes, put up the buttons, and said, 'This is kind of amazing.' And people took a look at it, and then all of a sudden people were pounding on the buttons and Chun-Li did her lightning kick and the place was just like, awed. We had never seen animation like that before. It was better than the *Final Fight* stuff. And then Blanka did his electricity effect and we knew at that point that this was something special.

→ CHRIS TANG
Street Fighter II tournament player

What I really liked was – and in retrospect, it's still true today – that [the characters' key frames were iconic]. The poses that they do when they do a Hadouken or Sonic Boom – those are all top of their class. [No game has done better key framing or had more] memorable poses since then. And the way [your attacks flow] when you hit something, it feels very impactful. There's something very masterful about that first *Street Fighter II*, especially when it was a little slow, in retrospect.

→ TOM SHIRAIWA
Street Fighter II translator, Capcom Japan

[Yasuda] is such a talented artist. [...] When he designed characters, he [planned out their moves up front] in a way that the animation looked best. [...] No other artist could do that. He was a pioneer.

→ JAMES GODDARD
Street Fighter II: Champion Edition design support, Capcom USA

If you look at some of the fighting games out there that are so-so, they don't have good colour-form break-up. So when [characters] throw a kick or a punch, it all kind of bleeds together so you don't track the limbs that well. And this guy was way ahead of his time on all of that.

→ AKIRA YASUDA
Street Fighter II planner, Capcom Japan

I was extremely satisfied with the animation, because at that time, I was familiar with every last detail of the character art, down to the individual 16×16 sprites. Also, back then at Capcom, more than illustrators or planners, it was pixel artists who were critical. They did animation work too, you see, and it was Capcom's character animation that really sold the games. So on Street Fighter, I was able to get into the nitty-gritty of every

little character detail and that made it the most satisfying work
I did at Capcom.

[Ed. note]   Former colleagues describe Yasuda as one of the
most talented and dedicated employees at Capcom,
and also one of the most atypical, noting that he
often slept on the floor at the office and spoke
bluntly to co-workers. Publicly, he became known
as the designer of Street Fighter's first female
character: Chun-Li.

Of course, while I was designing her, I did think she would
be well received. But after 30 years, for people to still be
so fond of her ... well, naturally that's going to mean she's
important to me. In regard to how I felt at the time of the
development, I think the vibe of the entire game, of all
the characters, would have been significantly different if
Chun-Li had not been included. You see, in *Street Fighter I*,
the fact that there were only male characters, it makes it
this kind of cool, realistic, manly world, you know? But
adding a woman increases the 'entertainment factor' of the
game. So there was a question of which direction the game
should go in. Should we continue in the tough-guy aesthetic
of the first game without any women? Or should we add a
woman, and if so, what kind of moves should she have? I
remember being a little worried about all that.

→   YOKO SHIMOMURA
       Street Fighter II composer, Capcom Japan

Chun-Li has big thighs, right? So back in the day, I asked Yasuda,
'Why does she have such big thighs?' And he started shouting and
went off and was like, 'I can't believe you don't understand the
appeal.' And he started explaining the attraction. And you know,
I'm a woman and I asked the question but it kind of got awkward

when he started explaining his fetishes. I mean, he has really strong feelings toward his creations. There's a reason for everything being the way that it is. When I heard that, I thought maybe that's something that everybody thinks, but everybody doesn't go out telling everybody. But he just told me.

→   DAVE WINSTEAD
        Technical associate editor, GamePro magazine

I think [Chun-Li is both a strong female icon and a sexualized figure]. [...] She's badass and all of her moves are really cool. But then at the same time, she does have a lot of key shots that if you were to freeze on them, you're like, *Oh, they spent a little extra time on that frame.*

[Ed. note]   In the years following *Street Fighter II*'s release, the series developed a reputation for portraying female characters in an overtly sexual manner – a direction initially led by Yasuda, whose work over the years has attracted critics for its erotic elements.

→   AKIRA YASUDA
        Street Fighter II planner, Capcom Japan

I don't necessarily see nudity as something scandalous or sexual. I think it's natural. I do like drawing nude bodies, but it's always done for a reason. For example, with classical painting, God was depicted as nude, so humans like Mary Magdalene were drawn that way too. Even the paintings in the Sistine Chapel by Michelango feature nudes, right? Manet's *Olympia*, too. So to me, it's just natural ... to me, art and the erotic are something inseparable, I guess. If people feel the need to come up with excuses or explanations for the public, that's all well and good, but personally it's not something I feel the need to do.

THEME SONGS

Once the team locked in *Street Fighter II*'s concept and art style, the audio fell to Yoko Shimomura, a composer who joined Capcom in 1988 and had contributed to a variety of projects, including *Final Fight*, but had yet to make a name for herself. Years later, Shimomura would go on to become one of the most highly regarded composers in the game industry, working on some of its biggest franchises including role-player juggernauts Final Fantasy and Kingdom Hearts. But in her early days at Capcom, she went through a crash course in learning how to compose music for games.

→   HARUMI FUJITA
    Composer, Capcom Japan

Shimomura ended up joining Capcom quite some time after I started there. She had studied piano in school, but when she joined, she had no composition ability whatsoever. I remember her coming up to me and asking for some advice on how to compose, and I initially told her, 'Go try make a song and see how you do.' So she did, and then she had everyone on the team listen to it. They were all quite speechless. The room went kind of silent. The song was terrible, right? And I remember having to say, just to break the silence in that room, 'Yeah, this isn't going to work.' I mean, obviously now she's a wonderful composer.

→   YOKO SHIMOMURA
    Street Fighter II composer, Capcom Japan

Yeah, I had no idea how to make music when I joined Capcom. I had studied classical music before then, but to be in a company like that, obviously you had to know how to make music that sounded very catchy – using bass and guitar, how to make rock tracks and jazz tracks, etc. Because I had studied classical music, I didn't know much about that. So, yeah. I felt like I joined the company without having the right set of skills needed to do the job.

→   HARUMI FUJITA
       Composer, Capcom Japan

It was my job to train employees in how to do their job, so I did that, for sure, but I didn't teach her how to compose. I think she learned that on her own. Shimomura was very lucky, because all the games that she worked on happened to be hits. And slowly but surely, she was able to build up her skills.

→   YOKO SHIMOMURA
       Street Fighter II composer, Capcom Japan

I think in this job, you constantly have to strive to keep growing, and in those days I think I was able to build up my skills pretty quickly. Of course, back then, I don't think I really thought about it in that way.

[Ed. note]   A couple of years after joining Capcom, Shimomura landed on the game that would define her time there, *Street Fighter II*, heading up the game's composition and sound effects.

When a project came around, Capcom usually looked for people in the sound department who were free at the moment, and I was free. [...] There were two or three projects that needed sound composers at that time, and I just happened to pick *Street Fighter II*.
Sometimes you do have to wonder how things could have turned out, if circumstances were just a little bit different. If we had done *this*, maybe *this* project would have turned out *that* way instead.

→ HARUMI FUJITA
Composer, Capcom Japan

When was *Street Fighter II* made? 1991? And I quit in 1990. [...] I did feel [a bit jealous]. Sometimes I feel like if I had stayed at the company, maybe I could have worked on it. [...] My son always asks me, he even asks me today like, 'Why did you quit? You shouldn't have quit.'

[Ed. note]   Fujita clarifies that her son's comments don't specifically relate to *Street Fighter II*, but to working at Capcom in general.

→ YOKO SHIMOMURA
Street Fighter II composer, Capcom Japan

At first, I was worried if I'd be able to pull the job off right, because it was a fighting game and I wasn't sure if that would match my style.

Before *Street Fighter II* came along, the sound composition across all Capcom titles had a heavier tone, a cooler tone. But for *Street Fighter II*, I made it more catchy, and in a certain sense, lighter. I had more fun with the tracks, especially with E. Honda's theme song. It's a fun song, not a heavy or serious track. There were people within the company saying, 'OK, this seems a little off from Capcom's style,' but Nishitani said, 'No, this is fun. This is just what we're looking for. We should do this.' So it turned out that the music I wrote for *Street Fighter II* ended up challenging the previous convention of cool and masculine music that Capcom had – not that I intended that, but that's how it turned out.

I feel like I was aiming for a kind of pop sound. Maybe Japan has a very different definition of pop than other countries might, but I was aiming for something with a pop or casual feel to the music.

Shimomura worked closely with Nishitani to come up with an approach that would match the game's theme of a trip around the world.

Nishitani would come up to me and show me designs of the characters and explain the personalities of the characters and ask me to make theme songs for each character. And then I would look at the backgrounds and the character descriptions and all that, and I noticed that each character had a unique background. And because of that, I suggested making each theme song based on their background country and culture. It was like a brainstorming session – he would have his orders and I would come up with ideas.

Other team members participated in that brainstorming as well.

I think the wild personalities on the team carried over to how the game was made. Usually on a game, the programmers don't have a say about the music. But with *Street Fighter II*, I composed a track that I was thinking, 'Oh maybe this could be good for Guile's theme song or Ken's theme song,' but I didn't say anything. I just composed the song and let everybody hear it. And then the programmer who was working on Guile, [Motohide Eshiro], was like, 'OK I love this song. I like this track a lot, so I'm taking this track for my stage.' Usually programmers won't say things like that, so I was surprised. But it turned out that was sort of what I was intending it for in the first place. [...] I think I realized I was on the right track when I made Guile's theme.

→ KAZUNORI YAMADA
    Super Street Fighter II console sound designer, Capcom Japan

Shimomura left Capcom before I started there, so I just knew her music as a player. But when I first heard her tracks, they blew my mind. The great thing about her work is not that it's particularly complex, but the way she creates a very catchy tone, kind of like Michael Jackson. In a short segment she's able to describe a lot. Once you hear a bit of Ken's theme or Chun-Li's theme, you instantly feel like you're in this special place. A lot of people know her for her work on games after she joined Square Enix, but I feel like my favourite work of hers is what she did on *Street Fighter II*.

→   CHRIS TANG
             Street Fighter II tournament player

That CPS-1 flat-top cabinet that *Street Fighter II* first came in [in the US] – it had a really nice subwoofer so you could really hear all of the kicks and punches. What I did was I brought my boombox to 7-Eleven and I recorded all the music. I called my friends who were in other parts of the country; I still had friends in Hawaii [where I grew up]. I'd say, 'Dude, you have to hear this. This is *Street Fighter II*.' [...] I'd play it over the phone. I was just so proud of how good *Street Fighter II* sounded. And I still think that the CPS-1 version of it really hits home for me.

TRANSLATION STRUGGLES

For the most part, Capcom Japan developed *Street Fighter II*'s features, characters and mechanics without much influence from Capcom USA. When it came to character names, however, the US office played a bit of a role. When they saw the characters, some in the US office were concerned that the African American boxer was named M. Bison, because the name sounded a lot like 'Mike Tyson'. The character also looked like Tyson, as it was common practice for the team at Capcom Japan to take inspiration from pop culture when designing characters. So for the Western version of the game, Capcom changed the name, which had a ripple effect and led to three name changes for the game's boss characters. 'M. Bison' became 'Balrog', 'Vega' became 'M. Bison' and 'Balrog' became 'Vega'.

→   TOM SHIRAIWA
       Street Fighter II translator, Capcom Japan

At that time, there was no localization department. Actually, there was no such word as 'localization'. It was just 'translation'. And I was the only one in [the Japan sales] office itself that actually liked arcade games, so I had to take charge in that translation job.

→   SCOTT SMITH
       Street Fighter II marketing manager, Capcom USA

There's always something [that gets lost in translation]. [...] But usually we had a reason.

→   IAN ROSE
       General counsel, Capcom USA

There was the concern that M. Bison was way too close to Mike Tyson.

→   SCOTT SMITH
Street Fighter II marketing manager, Capcom USA

The concern was Mike Tyson was still big at that time and Nintendo had *Punch-Out!!,* and so they just didn't want to get into it.

→   TOM SHIRAIWA
Street Fighter II translator, Capcom Japan

[Capcom USA executives] believed they could get sued. But at that time, all the name graphics had already been done, so there was no way to create another graphic just to replace it. [...] So whatever fit with the character graphics was OK. I mean, it was not the best choice. There was a lot of argument that 'Vega' – that doesn't fit with the character, with the clothes. But there was no other choice. It was a reluctant decision, but getting sued is a much bigger problem.

→   KATSUYA AKITOMO
Street Fighter II: Champion Edition background artist, Capcom Japan

Also, you know the mid-boss, the third-in-command, called Vega in the United States? Well, Vega is the name of the main boss in Japan, but it's also the name of a star in the constellation of Cygnus, so it was considered a little too feminine for English speakers. That's why the guy with the claws is called Balrog in Japan, but they changed it to Vega outside of Japan.

→   CHRIS TANG
Street Fighter II tournament player

They had to do what they had to do to not get sued, so I'm OK with that. [...] I guess it's just history now and it's trivia, right?

[Ed. note]   In addition to swapping the three boss names, Capcom made other small localization changes to the game, such as altering the name of Guile's friend Nash in the backstory. He became Charlie for the Western release.

[With Nash changing to Charlie], it once again came from the US. I always did a literal translation of the original Japanese, and of course I translated it as Nash. Then they gave it to someone at Capcom US, and they came back and changed the name. I asked them why, but they said, 'Nash is not an English name, basically. So we've got to change it to something else, otherwise people will not recognize it as a name or maybe they may not have some attachment to this character, and he's supposed to be a US soldier.' And they suggested, 'How about Charlie?'

Back then, the developers were not so familiar with overseas projects, so whatever the US [staff] said, the developers felt like they had to do; otherwise the game wouldn't be accepted overseas. And I kind of believed in that too. But after a few years we started to realize, 'Hey, this is just their ego.' [...] They wanted to change everything they could [so they could say they played a role in the development]. Even the titles, right? Like [how Capcom changed horror game *Biohazard* to *Resident Evil* in the West. After] we learned that, developers actually often refused to listen to their suggestions, or tried to get a second opinion from someone else. But back then on *Street Fighter II*, whatever Americans said was the absolute truth we had to follow.

ARCADE SUCCESS

In early 1991, Capcom distributors began to ship *Street Fighter II* to arcades around the world. Capcom had put more money into it than any other arcade game to date, and many at the company were hopeful that the approach would pay off, continuing *Final Fight*'s success. Though things started slower in Japan because players weren't accustomed to competing with one another, it didn't take long for the game to gain a following.

→   CHRIS JELINEK
    G&G Software general manager, Capcom USA

I remember very distinctly when the *Street Fighter II* cabinet first arrived [at Capcom USA]. Capcom, at that time, had a lunch room that they used for their game machines, just to have them set up for the employees. They also had sort of a darkened, oversized closet that probably held about ten machines. Maybe eight to ten. [...] At the same time Capcom had *Final Fight* and it also had [action game] *Mercs* and a few other shoot-'em-up type games or [side-scrolling brawlers], but *Street Fighter II* was just something totally different, you know? It felt different.

→   BRIAN DUKE
    Street Fighter II Western regional sales manager, Capcom USA

It was freaking amazing. I mean, when I saw the test one that came into our office, I literally played and played and played that thing all week long. I think I probably spent more time than I did working playing the game.

I remember when we tested it and I went up to the location where we were testing, which was up in Foster City. And if I remember correctly, I think it was a Nickels and Dimes location and we had it there and everybody was standing around watching these people play, and then they found out that we were part of Capcom. Kid goes, 'Oh, can I play one of your people?' And [Capcom USA vice-president of sales Bill Cravens] points at me and says, 'Hey, he's one of the best.' And he goes, 'Oh, great. Can I play you?' And I went, 'Oh yeah, sure.' So I took Chun-Li and he took E. Honda and I remember I got my ass whooped. I could not believe this guy. I mean, every time that I would play against the computer, I'd beat E. Honda. Playing against him – he was one of the kids that had spent hours and hours on it – I didn't even win one match. And I'm serious, that was the last time I ever played against anybody on any test game, at least in public. I did it all the time [before that]. To be the king of the players at Capcom and then get my ass whooped by some kid at an arcade, I went, you know, 'I'm getting too old for this stuff.' But it was huge.

[Before *Street Fighter II* was released, Cravens] was always talking to me about it. 'Just wait until that comes. Just wait until we have this one out.' And I was banking on that and hoping on that, and literally, I think it was a year or a year and a half after I joined, that's when I saw [*Street Fighter II*] come to life.

[Ed. note]   Cravens left Capcom just as *Street Fighter II* was going on sale. Capcom vice-president of sales and marketing Jeff Walker took over his role, overseeing US sales.

→   JEFF WALKER
      Street Fighter II vice-president of sales and marketing, Capcom USA

I got [an early version of *Street Fighter II* in the US office] and normally [...] we would test the game for ideally four weeks before I would go to market with it and pitch it to my distribution network. Well, I only had six days the way it turned out, because of course the board came in late and we had already planned distributor meetings.

So I remember being down in Fort Lauderdale, Florida, and we're launching the game down there. And I didn't even have the earnings back yet. I mean, they were coming in – we had one unit in Sunnyvale Golfland; the other one was in Milpitas [both in California]. So I had my testers go out there and I said, 'Hey man, I've gotta have some kind of idea what's in there.' So they said, 'Well we opened the cash box up [on one of them]. We haven't even hit the weekend yet, just been cruising through the week.' And … I think it was like $650 that was in there. I go, 'That's not bad. That's not bad.' So I said, 'Well, let me just do a little surmising. Eh, it'll probably end up doing about 800. That's a really good report.' So I'm down in Florida basically telling my distribution network, 'I think it's gonna be about an $800 a week game, based on testing in Milpitas.' And then seven days came up after my distributor meeting, and the thing made $1,300.

So one of the things that we quickly found was, Golfland says, 'We're having problems with the players, because everybody's backed up on the unit. Can we get another one?' 'Yes, you can get another one.' We bring another one out. Now I'm afraid if I put a second one in there I'm gonna cannibalize it. I'm gonna have two doing $600. Not the case at all. They both do 14. So now we know we've got a juggernaut on our hands. Sunnyvale Golfland and Milpitas, I believe at the peak, were probably operating up to 15 units inside there. And you know, the game went through the ceiling.

→   BRIAN DUKE
        Street Fighter II Western regional sales manager, Capcom USA

The only way that you ever got to a thousand dollars a week earnings in any sort of game that I had been associated with was when you had three- or four-player multiplayer-type games, or ones where [you had a big machine and operators charged] a dollar per game or a dollar fifty per game. [...] I remember when we first started shipping, I had to send people about 10 percent of their order because we just flat out did not have enough to meet the demand.

→   ZENJI ISHII
Editor-in-chief, Gamest magazine

I think for the first year after *Street Fighter II* came out, we only had one issue [of *Gamest* magazine] without much Street Fighter coverage in it, and it turned out that that issue saw a dramatic drop in sales. After that, we realized we had to keep up our Street Fighter coverage to help maintain sales. [...] *Gamest* was monthly so every year, we'd have 12 issues. And when Street Fighter was at its peak, I think two-thirds of those issues had Street Fighter covers. At least two-thirds.

→   BRIAN DUKE
Street Fighter II Western regional sales manager, Capcom USA

We sold, if I remember correctly, it was around 20,000 [units of the original *Street Fighter II*]. [...] I remember having orders every month of a thousand standing orders [on the West Coast] and we would only get in 1,200 for the entire US at a time.

→   JEFF WALKER
Street Fighter II vice-president of sales and marketing, Capcom USA

We did – between dedicated and kits – we did about 20–25,000, both with *Street Fighter II* and [later with the follow-up, *Champion Edition*].

[Ed. note]   The comments below refer to the success of both *Street Fighter II* and *Champion Edition*.

The game just took off. [...] Even the LA riots worked out for me because when they were looting the street, they were running down the streets from the 7-Eleven stores with Street Fighter games in their hands. [We got lots of] press because there were the cameras going up on these guys running down the street with Street Fighter games.

→ ZENJI ISHII
   Editor-in-chief, Gamest magazine

When *Street Fighter II* came out, there weren't any other fighting games that could cut into its sales. It had the market to itself for a while, so arcades would have several *Street Fighter II* machines, if not dozens of them. And then eventually SNK, and Sega with [3D fighting game] *Virtua Fighter*, entered the market and that sort of created this market where most arcades made the vast majority of their profits on fighting games. Comparatively, other genres did not bring in nearly as much money, and I think that lasted for maybe about ten years after the release of *Street Fighter II*. This was a point where everybody who visited arcades played fighting games, pretty much.

→ JEFF WALKER
   Street Fighter II vice-president of sales and marketing, Capcom USA

[When *Street Fighter II* got big,] I did a couple of semi-controversial things. One of the things was I made all my distributors pay me everything they owed me before I started shipping the game, so we could collect all our money. I thought it was gonna be stupid any other way. [...] Normally, you know, they're supposed to pay in 30 days, but then they pay the hot hand. Whoever's got the product, they pay them quicker. So I just sat back and said, 'We're gonna collect the money.' So it was really good for Capcom. I also told the distributors, 'Go collect from your operators. Let's get some money in for this game.' So it was one of the first times of really using the product like that to control everybody's cash and exposure on the deal. [...] We ended up doing $78 million dollars-worth of Street Fighter that year, so it was a good thing we did it.

→ BRIAN DUKE
Street Fighter II Western regional sales manager, Capcom USA

I remember one of our distributors even got super, super healthy and super, super big by requiring that any of their customers had to pay cash, had to be current on their account and had to pay up front. So it was just unbelievable that customers would be paying up a $10,000 or $20,000 account to be able to buy a dedicated machine for $2,500. And the price went up after a while.

→ IAN ROSE
General counsel, Capcom USA

The American sales force, of course, they were kind of freewheeling guys. They were well compensated, but they kind of played by their own rules or by the rules of the industry as they understood it. And you know, [as time went on] there was a tension there [between Capcom USA and Capcom Japan].

→ SCOTT SMITH
Street Fighter II marketing manager, Capcom USA

I mean coin-op, how do you put this? They were kind of the Wild West. The people they worked with – you know, it's a cash-only business and I'll just kind of leave it at that.

→ JEFF WALKER
Street Fighter II vice-president of sales and marketing, Capcom USA

It was a total Wild, Wild West show. Like nine people ran the whole industry, which at the time was bigger than the consumer [game industry], the record industry and the movie industry combined.

[Ed. note]   As with many comparisons of this sort, you can slice the numbers in different ways. Walker points to the Street Fighter II series making more than a billion dollars across different parts of the industry.

→ MATT ATWOOD
Street Fighter Alpha 3 public relations manager, Capcom USA

It was much more of a cavalier time. The trucking industry was the one shipping all these arcade units, and you had lots of speculation – I don't know if it was speculation – that of course the mob was tied into distribution just like magazines back in the day.

There were rumours that, because the mob was involved in the arcade business, it wasn't just arcade units that were going along with the units – there was a way to slide up the screen and hide some other shit in there. There was, of course, talk of drugs and [...] some of the parties they would talk about [...] they were pretty raucous. A lot of alcohol; a lot of other stuff. It was much more kind of a remnant of the that 1980s party scene where everything was good times and you walked in and, you know, [there was] coke on the coffee table. [...] I think it was sort of part of the language back then. It was much more of a schmoozy [industry]. Relationships mattered a lot more back then.

→ JEFF WALKER
Street Fighter II vice-president of sales and marketing, Capcom USA

It was definitely polar opposite cultures [between Capcom USA and Capcom Japan]. You know, I had a nice big office in Santa Clara, and I got paid a ton, and all my sales guys drove Porsches and Mercedes, and we had unlimited expense accounts; we golfed Pebble Beach every month. It was crazy. I go over to Japan, and my same counterpart is making a fraction of what I'm making and he's sitting in a cubicle.

→ BRIAN DUKE
Street Fighter II Western regional sales manager, Capcom USA

It just was phenomenal. It was the best thing that I've ever been associated with. [...] I made more money that year than I ever have made in my life. [...] I remember one year, I made more than they said the president of the company, George Nakayama [was making]. [...] We were on a 2 percent commission [in the US sales department], and very shortly after that year they switched to 1 percent commission, and I continued selling that game for two or three years. It was beautiful. And after the 1 percent they cut out the commission completely.

→   CHRIS KRAMER
      Street Fighter II series game counsellor, Capcom USA

Capcom in Japan was called the house that 100 yen coins built, right? Because the company's fortune was started by *Street Fighter II*.

SOFTWARE GLITCHES

By any metric, *Street Fighter II* was a success in arcades. And while glitches were common in many games at the time, success meant players discovered more of those glitches – the more people playing, the more they found. The most infamous of these centred on the character Guile. While using him, players could freeze the game, stun their opponent (in a move nicknamed 'Handcuffs') and grab their opponent from across the screen (nicknamed the 'Air Throw' or 'Magic Throw'), among other things.

For some players, these glitches made for fun Easter Eggs. Many at Capcom saw them differently.

→   JOE GANIS
         Street Fighter II software tester, Capcom USA

Guile had a particular move where he would start a throw animation, and then you would be stuck – your sprites would be basically conjoined for the rest of the match. [...] And likewise, he had something called the Air Throw where he would make a throwing motion, and it didn't matter where you were on the particular playfield – you would just immediately take throw damage and fall directly to the ground. And that was kind of disconcerting.

Then there was an even better one where a Guile player, if they knew what they were doing, was able to reset the machine right there on the spot with a particular command setup there between the joysticks and a couple of buttons.

→   ZENJI ISHII
         Editor-in-chief, Gamest magazine

I remember a bug with the Sonic Boom where it basically stopped Guile from attacking. At the time, only players from one arcade knew specifically how to pull it off, and it's funny because one of the writers for *Gamest* actually went to a part of Japan where a tournament was being held locally, and he was there to report on the tournament. But then when he participated himself, he ended up losing because he encountered that bug and he was unable to fight back.

→   `TOMOTAKA SUZUKI`
        `Street Fighter II series combo video creator`

I remember hearing about the Magic Throw bug. [...] I thought it was remarkable.

→   `ZENJI ISHII`
        `Editor-in-chief, Gamest magazine`

[A video tape from Korea called 'The Horror of Guile' showing various glitches] made it over to the editorial department. [...] I remember people were trying to figure out what technical aspects were behind a lot of these bugs, but I remember the editorial department – they got the tape and they put it on the TV and everyone was laughing.

→   `MOTOHIDE ESHIRO`
        `Street Fighter II programmer, Capcom Japan`

That was actually my first programming job at Capcom when I joined the company. So the hardest thing was basically everything – getting used to the difference between what I learned in school as a programmer and the way you really do things on the ground.

I'll tell you the story of when I heard about [Guile's glitches]. We were having an event where we had invited players and journalists to come play *Street Fighter II*. It was one of the first times it was even out there – it was just starting to get big – and the higher-ups picked me to play an exhibition match against some users. We were having the staff play against other people. And a journalist – a game journalist, a Japanese guy – approached me and said,

'Hey, check this out. I found this crazy Magic Throw with Guile.' And he showed it to me. When I saw that, the first thing I thought was, *I have to quit. I can't do this any more. I think I'm gonna quit my job*. And luckily, Nishitani said, 'Hey, if you're gonna let something like that bother you then you can't make games any more, period. You can't go to another company and do it either. This is part of the business.' So he stopped me from making any drastic moves. But yeah, I felt terrible.

→   TAKESHI TEZUKA
          Street Fighter II tester, Capcom Japan

The thing is, back then at Capcom we still didn't really have an 'official' bug checking process for our arcade games, so before we submitted the final ROM to the factory for production, my co-worker and I spent all night playing it and checking it over, just the two of us. And that was actually the very first time we did a proper bug check. [...] I mean, before that point, everyone thought it was a really fun game so they played it a lot, so in that sense it had received a lot of play testing. But we were the only two people to check the final ROM, and only for that one long all-nighter.

      We had no idea the Guile bugs existed until after the game came out.

→   SEIJI OKADA
          Street Fighter II programmer, Capcom Japan

Those were some wicked bugs. That was 30 years ago, but yeah, I still remember.

→   CHRIS TANG
          Street Fighter II tournament player

I would always – if it was at the end of the day, I would go to the Street Fighter machine and I would lock the game up. Just because it's funny to do that. But I wouldn't cheat in a fighting game. [...]

Having bugs in fighting games is just par for the course, and if you have enough people playing a game that intensely, then it's going to happen.

→ KEN WILLIAMS
Assistant editor, Electronic Gaming Monthly magazine

There was like an unspoken code when you were playing *Street Fighter II* games. If you wanted to show off a little bit, 'OK great, that's fine. That's nice. You used a glitch. Congratulations.' It's like, 'Oh, you threw me three times. Oh, congrats. Real skilful there.' Especially when some of them were almost unblockable. There's not a lot of skill in it. Anybody can learn to do that. But trying to chain a bunch of combos together – that takes some skill.

→ SCOTT SMITH
Street Fighter II marketing manager, Capcom USA

In a game of this complexity, things were bound to crop up. [...] Obviously you want a product to be perfect, but in the coin-op world there was no way to really do ROM upgrades. [...] It's not like you could have a Wi-Fi enabled arcade cabinet that you could dump a new ROM to very easily. It was just a product of the time. There's bugs everywhere. It's just damn hard to fix them when you've got a static board.

→ SHINICHI UEYAMA
Street Fighter II lead programmer, Capcom Japan

As creators, it's really rough for us, because those are really failures on our part.

→ JAMES GODDARD
Street Fighter II: Champion Edition design support, Capcom USA

It's more disappointment than anything else. I mean, glitches are gonna happen, but the fact that it was something so nasty that – depending on the rev of the board – that basically that'd

be it, quarter over. I mean, the fact that it was ruining players'
experiences and creating drama, that wasn't necessarily good for
Capcom's reputation with the operators, because that was starting
to impact money.

SHENG LONG

Around the world, press coverage of *Street Fighter II* dominated enthusiast magazines, and in the US the game frequently appeared on the covers of *GamePro, GameFan* and *Electronic Gaming Monthly,* among others. Generally, the coverage consisted of previews, reviews and strategy guides. But in the April 1992 issue of *Electronic Gaming Monthly,* the editors put together an April Fool's joke that went on to become a significant part of Street Fighter history.

→   KEN WILLIAMS
       Assistant editor, Electronic Gaming Monthly magazine

At a high level, there was always a bit of a tradition that we had started where we had these little fun things we would do around the office, and this had nothing to do with the April Fool's joke. A lot of the guys, we would experiment with Photoshop, and as new versions came out and you had new capabilities and things like that, we would try different things and just see how we could shnazz up our layouts and do cutouts and different techniques and stuff. Because there were no guides for this stuff. This was all brand-new, bleeding-edge technology. So we had no internet to look up how-to videos. We had to learn it all ourselves, which was kinda fun. I think [*EGM* assistant editor Martin Alessi had put together some Easter Eggs that way], and I think it was somewhere in January of that year we had gotten our hands on a JAMMA board for *Street Fighter II,* which was my favourite game of all time, at the time.

So I got to do the layout off the actual arcade boards, which was amazing to me. I was able to take screens of the actual game, not just some console version. I was just taking so many screenshots. I had different angles of different moves, and different animations of the moves and all that, and I got the bright idea. I'm like, *You know what? Let me make some fake screenshots*, just to have some fun with it. Because I had always laughed about the Sheng Long thing myself, because even I was taken in originally before I knew what 'Sheng Long' actually meant. So I was always like, *Oh, there's gotta be some hidden character*. I was always fascinated with hidden stuff in the game.

[Ed. note] For the English version of *Street Fighter II*, Capcom translated a Ryu win quote that was meant to say, 'You must defeat my Dragon Punch to stand a chance' as, 'You must defeat Sheng Long to stand a chance.' Many players interpreted this as Sheng Long being a secret character in the game, when the term actually referred to a move in the game. Capcom later added to this confusion when they referred to Ryu and Ken as students of 'Master Sheng Long' in the Super NES *Street Fighter II* instruction manual.

Williams says that part of the reason he was interested in Street Fighter secrets went back to the original *Street Fighter*, which didn't spell out its special move commands and came with cabinet artwork showing a flaming jump kick – a move that didn't exist in the game.

It was all secretive at the time. Not like it is today – everything's pretty much out in the open. There's not a whole lot of good secrets out there. There's some, but back then it was … I just remember when *Street Fighter II* came out and people had finally figured out all the moves, and they were just wondering, *Who's this Sheng Long they keep talking about?*

So back to the JAMMA board. I have all these screenshots in front of me, of all the different types of match-ups that you could possibly have in the game that I could choose from. I'm like, *Well, what if I made a Sheng Long? What if I made a character? How would he be?* He'd obviously have to be a Shotokan character, right?

[Ed. note]   A Shotokan character being someone who uses Ryu and Ken's fighting style.

Because it's Ryu's catchphrase, right? It's gotta be his master or something. Or somebody that it makes sense. When you read it out loud, it sounds like, oh yeah, 'you have to beat him', you know, 'to even stand a chance'. Because you'd think, *He's my master.* That was the lore, the mystery. And so I just cobbled some screenshots, cut out a couple of characters in different poses, and slapped 'em on the screen. And I just had one screenshot, and it started to come together. And then I'm like, 'Hey guys, come over here. Look at this.' Because we're all in this big room with these little half-cube things where we had our computers, so it was really easy to pull someone over and say, 'Hey, come over and look at this.' This had nothing to do with April Fool's at the time. It was just having fun with Photoshop and having all these screenshots.

So people would start to input their little ideas. Like, 'Oh, we could add this; maybe we could add this.' And like, 'Yeah, yeah, let's try this.' And so I would work it up. And then we got the final screenshot, the one with the flaming Dragon Punch, right? That was the one where we were finally like, 'Yeah, we like this.'

And we're all like, 'Hey!' [*EGM* editor Ed Semrad] was in this one little office to the side. And then he came out and he's like, 'Hey guys, we need to come up with something for our April Fool's issue.' And we were just like, 'Look at this!' It was really fun, because it was very organic the way that it ended up in the magazine. So we got approval from Ed and [publisher Steve Harris] to work that up a little more.

So I made a couple more screenshots to put into the gag. And then we all kind of put together little tidbits for, how do you get to him, and what happens when he gets on the screen, and all that fun stuff. Then you got the Fuldigen, HA – that was a *Martin* special.

[Ed. note]   A city and state in the article that translated to: 'Fooled you again, ha.'

I liked that one. It was just a lot of fun. That was probably one of my highlights of my time with Sendai Publishing.

→   DAVE WINSTEAD
      Technical associate editor, GamePro magazine

I actually believed it a little bit until I talked to James Goddard, because I wasn't [working at Capcom] yet. He was like, 'No, that's bullcrap. There's no Sheng Long.' But he goes, 'It's funny, though, isn't it?'

→   CHRIS TANG
      Street Fighter II tournament player

I knew it was a joke. I guess I knew it was BS. I guess it's funny. [...] My circles? Definitely too obvious.

→   SCOTT SMITH
      Street Fighter II marketing manager, Capcom USA

It caused me and [Capcom USA marketing manager] Joel Pambid untold pain. [...] There were four people in marketing. That's it. And we would answer the phone calls, right? And kids would call up and say, 'We read this in *EGM*.' And it was just a flood of calls. [...] It's the same kind of thing we would get when [fans thought] Guile could put handcuffs on people. You know, 'I've seen that. My friend saw it.' And it just was a pain in our neck. It was a great joke, but it would have been better if it had happened to somebody else.

CHAPTER 03

FATAL FURY

For a brief moment after Capcom released *Street Fighter II*, they had the fighting game market to themselves. The game caught players and the industry off-guard, so while other studios were eager to hop on the bandwagon, most didn't have a head-start or existing knowledge of the genre.

Except, of course, for SNK.

As Takashi Nishiyama, Hiroshi Matsumoto and the bulk of the *Street Fighter I* team had settled in at SNK, they too had been planning a *Street Fighter* follow-up – in their case, a spiritual successor called *Fatal Fury*. The game starred three original characters – Terry, Joe and Andy – and introduced gameplay features like the ability for players to jump between stage foregrounds and backgrounds. According to Nishiyama, *Fatal Fury* turned out much like a *Street Fighter* sequel would have in his hands, had he stayed at Capcom.

'I think if I hadn't left Capcom, I probably would have made a Street Fighter II,' he says. 'The first *Street Fighter* was a successful project overall for Capcom and I don't think there would have been a scenario where we didn't make a Street Fighter II. [...] If we'd stuck around, I think we would have ended up making a game that resembled what we ended up making at SNK, which was *Fatal Fury*.'

THE RIVALRY

Between *Street Fighter II* and *Fatal Fury*, Capcom and SNK played the first two cards of the fighting game era. Neither was the first of its kind, but the two games broke through to players with bright visuals, flashy special moves and precise gameplay. And they both happened to come from development studios in Osaka.

→   ZENJI ISHII
       Editor-in-chief, Gamest magazine

Did they have a special relationship or a rivalry? I think you can even go back to the creators at the top. When they were together, I observed that Nishiyama and Okamoto had a sort of rivalry between themselves, going back even before *Street Fighter*. So I think a lot of that did manifest in *Street Fighter II* and *Fatal Fury*. And they were both able to create games that became hits, so I think the dynamic that was going on between the two was quite remarkable, actually. Not just the companies and not just the games, but among the two creators as well.

→   TOYOHISA TANABE
       Art of Fighting pixel artist, SNK Japan

It felt like whenever one company would release one game, the other company would release something in response to that. So when Capcom released *Final Fight*, we came up with [side-scrolling brawler] *Burning Fight* at SNK. When *Street Fighter II* came out, we came up with *Fatal Fury*. So it really felt like there was a sense of a back and forth rivalry between the two companies.

[Ed. note]   *Fatal Fury* shipped to arcades in late 1991, and
                    was one of the first fighting games to catch on
                    in the wake of Capcom's success. As a result,

some fans called it a *Street Fighter II* clone, not knowing that the development team had a history with the genre.

→ TAKASHI NISHIYAMA
Head of R&D, SNK Japan

Rather than be mad about it, I just think it was inevitable that people might think that. We were making *Fatal Fury* at the same time they were making *Street Fighter II*, and *Street Fighter II* came out two or three months before us. But, of course, you can't copy a game in two or three months, right? Plus, we're the ones who made the first *Street Fighter*, you know? So even though people were saying that SNK copied *Street Fighter*, to us it was a meaningless criticism.

And, of course, Capcom knew we were the ones making *Fatal Fury*, so they knew that we weren't copying them. As for whether player comments had bothered us, though? Not really. I guess it was just background noise for us.

[Ed. note] While Nishiyama remembers *Fatal Fury* shipping a few months after *Street Fighter II*, records put the gap at closer to nine months.

A DIFFERENT APPROACH

When *Fatal Fury* showed up in arcades, players criticized it for being similar to *Street Fighter II*, but loved its stylish art and character design – qualities that SNK ended up relying on for much of their lineup. As the fighting game genre took off, SNK put the majority of their development resources into a roster of competitive franchises, which included Art of Fighting, Samurai Shodown and The King of Fighters. SNK's games quickly developed a reputation for a sense of style that set them apart.

→   TAKASHI NISHIYAMA
          Head of R&D, SNK Japan

When making *Fatal Fury*, we focused a lot on the character and story elements – basically what I enjoyed about making *Street Fighter*.

→   HIROSHI MATSUMOTO
          Producer, SNK Japan

One of the things I was happiest about with *Fatal Fury* was that it had a more anime-like look to the characters. Usually, if you practise a specific fighting style, you have to wear clothing that kind of fits that. But I think with *Fatal Fury*, we were able to make it more anime-like in the sense that they could be wearing anything. So I think that was something we were quite happy with.

       I also liked that we were able to put in fighting styles that were very unusual in Japan at the time, styles that only hardcore martial arts fans would know about. One of them was Brazilian capoeira; another was Taekwondo.

→   TAKASHI NISHIYAMA
          Head of R&D, SNK Japan

One the things I enjoyed the most about *Fatal Fury* was the special moves. The animations and effects that appeared on screen when you were doing them were quite flashy and very anime-like, and I think a lot of anime fans – both in Japan and overseas – really liked that about *Fatal Fury*, whereas I feel like *Street Fighter* was a lot more conservative in that regard.

→   ZENJI ISHII
                Editor-in-chief, Gamest magazine

Our *Street Fighter II* coverage in *Gamest* at the time was oriented around the fact that it was a competitive game and a lot of people were really into it – and the scene itself was quite interesting, which is why we often covered it from that perspective. On the other hand, our SNK coverage was more focused on the characters themselves, because people were into SNK's games because of the character designs. I think we realized there were two very different types of fans out there that were reading our content.

→   TOYOHISA TANABE
                Art of Fighting pixel artist, SNK Japan

At the time, I felt that Capcom's games placed a great deal of importance on the gameplay – things like the balance and how good they felt to play. Those seemed like Capcom's main focuses. Gameplay was also important to SNK, of course, but SNK's big thing was making something entertaining. You saw that in the character designs, the visuals … SNK really focused on those, and on an overall presentation that declared to players, *You're gonna have a good time!* For example, in *Art of Fighting*, the characters were almost comically huge for the time. Then there's a game like *Samurai Shodown*, which introduced the world to a fighting game with swords and had this bold, fun Japanese aesthetic to it. I think SNK was especially good at making games like that.

       If I were to compare it to martial arts, in my mind Capcom was like a boxer and SNK was more like a flashy pro wrestler. Boxing has more severe rules – it's serious and you're really trying to knock the other guy out. Pro wrestling is serious too, but a huge part of it is trying to entertain the crowd.

→   ZENJI ISHII
        Editor-in-chief, Gamest magazine

I think the biggest difference I can observe between SNK and Capcom is that Capcom – the competitive gameplay was part of their focus, but they also designed characters to have more of a worldwide appeal. They didn't just appeal to Japan but to people overseas as well, whereas I felt like SNK, at the time of *Fatal Fury*, designed characters that would be well received within Japan, but not necessarily everywhere else. And I think a lot of those differences continue even today. In the case of Capcom, I think they're one of the rare publishers here in Japan who make characters that target everybody instead of just Japan.

COMPETING WITH STREET FIGHTER II

Fatal Fury was a hit for SNK, leading to numerous sequels and – years later – two of the most critically acclaimed fighting games of all time: *Fatal Fury Special* and *Garou: Mark of the Wolves*. Yet for many fans and developers, the biggest challenge the original *Fatal Fury* faced was trying to compete with a game as ahead of its time as *Street Fighter II*.

→ TAKASHI NISHIYAMA
Head of R&D, SNK Japan

The most difficult aspect of making *Fatal Fury* was the fact that *Street Fighter II* came out two to three months before us, and when we saw it for the first time, we were astounded. Seeing the way they'd managed to solve a lot of the issues from the first game, and the visual improvements, we felt very pressured knowing we had to compete with it. In that sense, we knew we had to do something different, something to distinguish our game. Because of the timing, *Fatal Fury* was going to end up being released in the same window as *Street Fighter II*, you see. So we figured people would probably say we copied them. We had to find our own niche, and do something that would make us stand out. That was probably the hardest thing.

→ STEPHEN FROST
Street Fighter 30th Anniversary Collection producer, Digital Eclipse

Street Fighter II made this giant leap in the responsiveness of the controls and how the characters felt, and it felt more like your movements were in flow with what the characters were doing. It made sense as far as doing a quarter-circle for a fireball and it flowed with the character and things like that. [...] Especially early on, the responsiveness of the controls and the fluidity of the animations [in SNK's games] weren't quite up to where *Street Fighter II* felt and looked.

I think *Fatal Fury*, in some ways, is almost like this 1.5, right? It's somewhere between *Street Fighter I* and *Street Fighter II* in a lot of ways, and had some improvements and different variations, but you can certainly see the evolution of the team and the controls and how it feels along that path.

→   TAKASHI NISHIYAMA
              Head of R&D, SNK Japan

In terms of the more detailed aspects of their game design, in that sense I think *Street Fighter II* was a superior game to *Fatal Fury*. Our game was more casual, with simpler controls, which meant it didn't have as much depth. That lent the game a certain shallowness, and I think *Street Fighter II* definitely outperformed us there. To put it another way, *Street Fighter II* was geared more towards hardcore, serious fighting game players, and *Fatal Fury* was for casual players. That wasn't necessarily our intention when making it but that's how it ended up, and it was an area where we saw room for improvement.

→   HIROSHI MATSUMOTO
              Producer, SNK Japan

What I wasn't satisfied with were the game's competitive fighting aspects.

→   DAVE WINSTEAD
              Technical associate editor, GamePro

I did enjoy [*Fatal Fury*] a little bit, but I remember selecting Andy and just going, *zip, zip, zip, zip* in the corner to people, and it was kind of mean. But yeah, I thought the game looked really cool and sounded really cool. I wasn't a super fan of the gameplay, with popping back and forth in the background, but that changed later. *Fatal Fury 2, Special* and all [those games] came out and I started enjoying it a little more. It felt like it was a little more refined, plus you had more than three characters to choose from. And then when it got into *Real Bout*, it seemed like it just kept getting better and better, right? And sooner or later it turned into *Mark of the Wolves*, which was one of my all-time favourite Neo Geo games. And the King of Fighters series. I love those, too.

→   JAMES GODDARD
             Street Fighter II: Champion Edition design support, Capcom USA

I love those games. I love *Fatal Fury*. I love *Art of Fighting*. I love *King of Fighters*. I love all those games, and back in those days when they came out, they were amazing. They were the quality competitors to Street Fighter. Obviously, *Mortal Kombat* [from Midway] – clearly quality, right? And then there was *Fighter's History* [from Data East], which was, you know, interesting [...] it was a legitimate fighting game, but it just didn't really have the depth. And then *Fatal Fury* was a real fighting game in that it had the depth and there was a lot of nuance. For me though, as a player, I always struggled with the SNK controls back in those days.

> [*Fatal Fury*] had a lot of swag, right? It was just different than Street Fighter. Instead of being like these tropes from different locations around the world, it was like, dude with his hat backwards. So it is a trope but it's a trucker guy who happens to be really handsome with abs and blond hair.
> I just thought the game had a lot of swag, I guess is the way to say it. It's not the way I thought of it then, but if I reflect on it now, yeah. It just had attitude.

→   ZENJI ISHII
             Editor-in-chief, Gamest magazine

From my perspective, while *Street Fighter* started the series and *Street Fighter II* is technically its sequel, it felt very much like *Street Fighter II* was its own separate game. *Street Fighter* created the basic form, but to players at the time and hardcore arcade enthusiasts, they really felt like Nishitani and Capcom had created something unique with *Street Fighter II*. Nishitani created one of the first versus fighting games that really felt complete, so *Street Fighter II* had a very special presence that few other games had.

But, of course, if it weren't for Nishiyama and his contributions to *Street Fighter I*, *Street Fighter II* probably would not have existed. And because he made a hit game with *Street Fighter I*, Nishiyama was able to go to SNK and he ended up making fighting games that people adored. *Street Fighter II* was a great game, not just overall but even if you get down to the nitty-gritty details of how the game was made, everything just came together so well and it was really difficult for any other game to match what *Street Fighter II* had done. But in terms of the companies out there at the time who were trying to make their own competitive fighting games, I think SNK definitely held its own. Sega and Konami tried to develop their own fighting games in order to get into the market, but they were not successful. So I think SNK did really well for itself back then.

CHAPTER 04

STREET FIGHTER II: CHAMPION EDITION

Following *Street Fighter II*'s success, Capcom didn't wait another four years to keep the series going. Instead, they took an incremental approach, building on the game's popularity with a simple follow-up just over a year later.

    Champion Edition didn't overhaul any gameplay systems or add much content, but it introduced two often-requested changes – it let players select the four boss characters, and it let them use the same character as their opponent. For fans at the time, those two changes felt monumental. Players were so hungry for more that they were thrilled with whatever they could get. And the game ended up outperforming *Street Fighter II*.

THE GAME THAT DESIGNED ITSELF

A basic concept on the surface, *Champion Edition* was, essentially, a response to player criticisms. Adding mirror matches and playable bosses was the sort of idea that would pop up in arcades, on school playgrounds and in game magazine reader mail sections.

Tracking down how it happened internally gets a bit more complicated.

As is a bit of a trend through this book, the stories told by Capcom USA staff don't always match the stories told by Capcom Japan staff. In the case of *Champion Edition*, we've also come across multiple stories of how people on the US side remember it happening. The first of these comes from James Goddard and Jeff Walker, who worked closely together and generally tell the same version of what happened.

→   JAMES GODDARD
     Street Fighter II: Champion Edition design support, Capcom USA

We were shot down the first time we pitched *Champ Edition*. [The team in Japan] said, 'Why would anyone want to play the same character, and why would anyone want to play the bosses? We don't think that will be popular here.' And that was because they weren't playing head-to-head hardcore. Oh sure, they had tournaments, but it was not their culture. It was not like our culture where it was like, 'Man, I'm so tired of your Guile.'

Whenever I'd travel, instead of going out to strip clubs with the sales guys, I would actually go find a local arcade where Street Fighter was happening and I would talk to people. Because there was no internet back then. And I specifically got the same kind of thing from players, which was they wanted to play the bosses.

→ JEFF WALKER
SFII: CE vice-president of sales and marketing, Capcom USA

I was never a gamer gamer. I was just a marketing and sales guy, so James was basically the guy who was giving me the feedback and information for me to go back to Japan and tell them what was going on.

→ JAMES GODDARD
Street Fighter II: Champion Edition design support, Capcom USA

I came in and said, 'Look, they've shut this down. They think this is a stupid idea. I know it will make money.'

→ JEFF WALKER
SFII: CE vice-president of sales and marketing, Capcom USA

Well, it came Halloween time, and [I went to Golfland with James Goddard and] I see this phenomenon going on, and that is all the players are dressed up like the characters. And I'm going, 'Holy shit.' And all these really young Asian girls dressed up like Chun-Li, and I'm going, 'Wow.' And then I see this other thing that really racked my brain. They were getting mad because one player was Chun-Li on a game, while the other player wanted to be Chun-Li and had to go to another game.

So I called [Capcom founder Kenzo] Tsujimoto up and I said, 'I know this is a long shot, but I believe we can run this thing again.' And he goes, 'What are you talking about?' I said, 'Well, there's a real easy formula. We need to allow two players to be the same character. Let's come up with a game.' I came up with the name Championship Edition [sic]. 'Let's add a few new players, and let's let them play against each other.' And Tsujimoto said, 'Are you sure?' [...] And I said to Tsujimoto, 'It's way too soon to get off this game.'

So he flew in and he said, 'I want to see your distributors guarantee me that they'll buy at least a thousand of them to get me to cover the development costs.' This was back in the day. I can't believe that he would be talking that way [these days]. So he flew out there and I brought my six biggest distributors in, and Peter Betti from Betson Enterprises was the biggest distributor. [Tsujimoto] said, 'We want to see how many of you guys will take it. So first we want to see if we can get a thousand games out of this unit to pay for it up front.' So he goes around the room. [...] He goes to Peter Betti, 'All right, Peter, how many do you want?' [Betti] goes, 'A thousand. I'll pay you cash now. Let's get going.' [*laughs*] So anyway, just in that meeting alone those guys had committed to another 5,000 units.

→   PETER BETTI
        President, Betson Pacific

They asked us, 'If we did a Street Fighter II: Champion Edition, would [you] be willing to buy any of them?' I was there with my sales manager John Lotz, and we looked at each other and we went, 'Yeah, we'll take all of them.'

[Ed. note]   Walker doesn't recall pitching the game twice, but gives Goddard credit for the idea, adding that Goddard would often talk to [Capcom department head Yoshiki] Okamoto and the development group. 'Of course, I don't have to talk to or deal with any of those guys,' he says. 'I have a direct line right to Tsujimoto.'
Bert Kitade, a vice-president of Capcom USA who ran their arcade operations business as *Street Fighter II* took off, remembers the situation differently. After reading the above comments from Walker in the 2014 *Polygon* story that served as the basis for this book, Kitade reached out to give his version of the story.

Oh my god. That's the one I'm mad at. Because that's the one – Jeff Walker and I don't know who else went there, and that was around [the] November timeframe, we went to Japan and we're sitting there with Okamoto, and Jeff goes, 'We need another Street Fighter,' and on and on. He goes on and on about having another Street Fighter. But I have a computer background in addition to an accounting background [so I knew how much work that would take] … and Okamoto kept saying, 'No. No. No.' He kept shaking his head.

> I mean, Jeff was saying he wanted to do all these new things with it. I said, 'Jeff, he's not going to finish it.' I said, 'It'd take too long to develop something like that. You're talking two years.' I said, 'We need something now.'

And I told Okamoto, 'You know what? Why don't you bring the boss men down so [players] could play [as those characters]. That's all you've got to do, and it picks off all these other problems you have.' And I had a list because I had the arcades, so I'd go to arcades all the time. Maybe once a month, I'd fly down to San Diego and spend time in the arcades. I wouldn't even tell the general manager I'd be down there. I'd go there and just spend time in the arcades by myself, and people started noticing. The kids started to know who I was [and tell me what they wanted in the game]. 'Hey, fix this. Go to do that, and do this.' So I wrote all this stuff down and I gave Okamoto all the things – and he probably knew most of them anyway, the problems that they had. But the big thing was I told him, 'Just get something quick. It doesn't have to be a big change because you've got all the programming already for the [bosses]. How much more work would it be just to pull [them] down in [and let players use them]?'

> And that was in November and then we just left. That was it. And game companies in Japan, they don't like suggestions sometimes. But what ended up happening was, probably [around] February [... Capcom USA president

George Nakayama] called me and Jeff into the meeting room. He said, 'You know what? We got a new game.' I said, 'What the hell?' He goes, 'It's Street Fighter. We don't have quite the name. We think it's Champion Street Fighter.' I go, 'Oh, gosh.' He kind of explained it to me. I go, 'God damn, that's the same thing I told Okamoto I wanted done.' And he goes, 'That's probably the only thing you can do in such a short period of time, right?' He only had like, three months. That was the [quickest thing he could do].

And then George said Japan wanted us to take 5,000 games at the time, before year-end, because our year-end was March 31st. They were thinking of giving us 5,000 so that they could make their number. And he said 5,000. I said, 'OK.' George looked at Jeff. 'How many can you sell?' And I said, 'I'll take them all.'

[Our route business was] in charge of several thousand games. So I said, 'We'll take them all.' Whatever it was, we'll take, you know. Jeff goes, 'I've got to have some. You can have half.' 2,500 [to him]; 2,500 to me. I said that was fine. So Jeff went back. That's when Jeff had the meeting with the distributors and asked Betson and all those guys how many they wanted. And that's when Betson came back and said [they'd] take all of them.

[Then] March came around and George says, they're not going to send us that many. They are going to give 2,000. So we did it. I said, 'Well, OK, I'll take them all.' And then Jeff goes, 'Oh, no, no. We agreed with half and half.' So he took 1,000 and I took 1,000.

And that's when we went out and put the game out into the market.

[Ed. note]   Walker disputes Kitade's account, saying, 'He wasn't even part of the process. He came in very late in the game as the financial guy, to bring some social order to my sales guys, and he was [running the route business with operations manager Satinder Bhutani].'

Elsewhere on the Capcom USA side, coin-op regional sales manager Brian Duke remembers Walker playing a big role in getting *Champion Edition* off the ground, while console vice-president Joe Morici remembers Goddard pushing hard to make the game happen – and says he thinks the idea was an easy sell, since the team in Japan was already considering making the game.

On the Japan side, Noritaka Funamizu and Akira Yasuda both remember the idea coming about from *Gamest* magazine, Japan's biggest arcade game publication at the time.

→ NORITAKA FUNAMIZU
   Street Fighter II series producer, Capcom Japan

It was created as a response to user demand, as well as something *Gamest* recommended we do.

→ AKIRA YASUDA
   Street Fighter II: Champion Edition planner, Capcom Japan

From what I remember, Okamoto came up with the idea by talking to *Gamest* about it. But I mean, I would imagine it's possible that somebody from Capcom USA told him to make it as well. [...] I don't have any evidence proving it one way or another. I mean, I think with *Street Fighter II: Champion Edition*, there were probably 10,000 or more people, tons of people, that wanted to have the characters that weren't playable in the original version, so it was a common idea. This was a time when, you know, each game that came out after would have more and more characters. I mean, *Street Fighter I* had one or two characters. *Final Fight* had three characters. So *Street Fighter II* was just kind of a natural progression of that.

Honestly, I don't really remember [if we had a direct influence on Capcom making *Champion Edition*], but it wouldn't have been unusual for us to run a feature suggesting something like that in *Gamest*. We did, also, sometimes give direct feedback to developers on what we thought a game needed. This was before the era of PCs and email, so we wrote our suggestions down on paper and sent those over. I don't know to what extent they considered our feedback, or whether any of our ideas were actually implemented, but one example would be Ryu's Shoryuken ... and actually, his Hurricane Kick too. For both of those, we suggested that the invincibility time should be longer, otherwise Ryu would end up feeling too weak.

> *Gamest* did sell extremely well. Also, in the summer of 1991 when *Street Fighter II* came out, we held a national tournament, at a time when most game centres weren't doing that. Several hundred people participated. Partly due to the success of that tournament, we realized as magazine editors that regular coverage of fighting game tournament events would encourage players to become more invested in *Street Fighter II*. Up to then, you see, there hadn't been a fighting game tournament 'culture' in Japan.

[Ed. note]   Asked about Goddard, Walker and Kitade's involvement in the ideas for *Champion Edition* and *Street Fighter II Turbo: Hyper Fighting*, Okamoto posted on Twitter in 2021 that his memories of the situation are 'a little vague' and that Capcom Japan highly valued the feedback they got from Capcom USA as they didn't have a strong understanding of the American market. 'However, as to their claims that "I made that" or "It was my idea" ... well, I don't think they were that closely connected [to the development process]. A hit game has many developers; a game that flops has only a few.'

In a follow-up message, Okamoto wrote that many people pitched ideas to Capcom Japan's research and development group, so he's open to the possibility that much of what Goddard, Walker, and Kitade say is true, but he believes Nishitani should get the credit for the project because he took those ideas and distilled them into the final game.

Asked about the possibility that multiple people could have suggested the idea for *Champion Edition*, or that each of the above stories could have happened but might not have been the trigger to put the game in development, Goddard, Funamizu and Walker stick to their stories.

→   JEFF WALKER
            SFII: CE vice-president of sales and marketing, Capcom USA

Well, I'll say this. If I didn't sign off on it, it was never even going to Japan. [...] And there was also a certain level of animosity, first of all. When I was there, the Japanese guys didn't have the balls to complain about me or anybody else like that. They just shut their mouth and did what they did. But as the younger guys came in, they were starting to feel like the US was getting too much credit for stuff. [...] Everyone wants to take claim of it, and again, it was very simple. If it wasn't for Peter Betti, James Goddard and me, there was no game. Period.

→   NORITAKA FUNAMIZU
            Street Fighter II series producer, Capcom Japan

Well, it's true that we had all sorts of meetings with distributors for every region. Japan, America, Europe, Asia and so forth. And in these meetings, we would decide together with the distributor for that region how much they wanted to order and whatnot. But I don't think that's how *Champion Edition* ended up getting made.

I've been working really hard to be humble over the years and, especially the last two decades, really just changed how I approach things. And to a fault, I've been a little quiet on some of the Street Fighter stuff, but looking back at it, on this one, no. *Champ Edition* was the players' idea. I was the conduit for that and I pitched it. I was told, 'No, it was dumb' – because this is how we talked back then. 'No one wants to play the same characters. And sure, play the bosses, but it's not that important and we're doing really well with *Street Fighter II*.' Jeff made it happen from there and I'm sure a bunch of executives, they all got together. [...] It gets a little fuzzier as I try to be generous, but it's not as simple as it's just my idea. It was the players' idea. If I hadn't passed that on, the voices were loud enough that eventually it would have been heard anyway, but I was definitely the starting point for it. Jeff made it happen from there.

> I understand a lot of people probably had the same kind of idea there, if they were listening to the players. It was obvious, but obviously Jeff backs up my part of the story, and I don't know all that was happening in Japan, other than the initial response was 'no'.

BIGGER THAN SFII

Champion Edition shipped in March 1992, just over a year after *Street Fighter II*, and marked the peak of the series' early 1990s popularity. In interviews, sources have given different numbers, though everyone we asked recalls *Champion Edition* outselling the original *SFII* – especially in Japan, as competitive play started to catch on.

Akira Yasuda puts *SFII* at 50–55,000 units and *CE* at 75,000, but doesn't specify whether those are domestic or worldwide numbers. Jeff Walker estimates that Capcom USA sold 20–25,000 of both games, which matches an April 1993 *RePlay* magazine report that put *SFII* at 21,000 and *CE* at 24,000. And in an interview for the March 2002 issue of *Edge* magazine, Funamizu put *CE* at 140,000 worldwide, though speaking for this book, he says he doesn't recall those specific numbers at this point.

→   JAMES GODDARD
       Street Fighter II: Champion Edition design support, Capcom USA

Street Fighter II was really a unique thing, and the view of it was, in Japan, more of an action game because of the way it was set up. It was one credit [and then people stopped]. In America, and a lot of the other countries, it was like total kung-fu schools. Everybody was going around and playing each other head-to-head. It was all about that. That's why we had four, five, six machines on locations, earning a thousand dollars each a week or more.

And so when *Champ* came out, it solved that problem because not only could you play as the same character now – so now there was no barrier of, *I'm going to wait to play because you've got Guile and you're on a 20-game winning streak, and forget that shit* – there were no barriers to who you could play, and you could play the bosses. The game was way better balanced, except for Bison.

Then here's the key thing. In Japan, there was a story, because I played Zenji Ishii, who was the editor of *Gamest* magazine, and one of the strongest players in Japan. I think he'd won a tournament. And he played me at an arcade show and I just kept changing characters, and he was Guile and Ryu, and I went 50/50 with him. I'll say him being on American sticks and buttons probably added to that. And then he was like, 'How is this even possible?' You know, through the translator. And he wanted to know if I was one of the best players in America, and I said, 'I don't even make the top 10 in local tournaments,' and he was blown away. And we talked about the fact that we played head-to-head [in the US].

So fast-forward, he writes an article about it, and then during *Champ Edition*, he talked specifically about [the cultural difference]. I think there's a quote with me saying, 'You'll never beat us if you don't start playing head-to-head.' We did one thing in development that was key. On the Japanese board, we made it so that if you pressed the second player [start] button, it flashed a message that said, 'I welcome any player' in Japanese. And *Gamest* started selling that stronger, talking about, 'Hey, we've got to just play each other.' And then they figured out the back-to-back cabinet thing [where players could play against one another without having to see each other], and so I think that had a big impact for their market.

→   ZENJI ISHII
        Editor-in-chief, Gamest magazine

If you look at it through today's lens, I would say it's a little bit different and that's because of the way Japanese society was at the time. Before *Street Fighter II*, there was no competitive gaming culture, right? The game made competitive play more and more popular, but the problem was, it was often still hard to find people to play with. I remember one time when one of the stores that *Gamest* was operating decided to host a *Street Fighter II* tournament. I think it was intended for maybe 8 to 16 participants, but then we ended up getting 100 people to come and participate. So we realized that *Street Fighter II* tournaments had to take place fairly often in order to maximize their potential, so that's how tournaments were held nationally.

> We realized through that experience that writing articles about the competitive landscape was what generated the most interest – both in terms of selling the magazine, and also in the game itself. So there was kind of a dynamic two-way relationship there, where if you don't figure out how to make the game exciting for people, then you won't sell enough magazines. But in order to make the game exciting, you have to make sure that your magazines have the appropriate content that will get people excited for that game. So our thought process was always, *How can we make Street Fighter interesting for people?* That's something we always thought about. It just turned out that the competitive gaming scene had a lot to do with why people were interested in it.

→   NORITAKA FUNAMIZU
    Street Fighter II series producer, Capcom Japan

I think *Champion Edition* was more successful because the player-versus-player competitive aspect of the original *Street Fighter II* was somewhat limited. Both players couldn't choose the same character, for example. That became possible in *Champion Edition*. Also, there was this new cabinet design – which I think was created by someone who worked at a game centre, actually – where the two players were facing each other, but you couldn't see the other player directly, and that setup was very popular in Japan at the time. The other reason was just timing. We had very fortuitous timing, which really allowed for *Champion Edition* to be extremely successful.

→   JAMES GODDARD
        Street Fighter II: Champion Edition design support, Capcom USA

When *Champ Edition* showed up on test, I got in a lot of trouble for that. We had advertised that it was coming, and so it threw the test off in [certain people's minds]. But what it actually did was we had to have a sign-up sheet. We actually had a monitor up on top with a […] breakout box that a guy had made, so people could see. And there were 80 people stacked in Sunnyvale Golfland and the sign-up list was hours long. You had to wait for your turn to rotate in and so they were pissed because that just ruined the natural test that it would have been. But it also spread a huge word of mouth from that. I mean, it was crazy how many people were there, and it just clogged the whole arcade and we only had one machine, so that was a big thing.

> I got in trouble for that. This is why they accuse me of stuff, you know? But I was all about getting people to be there. Word would have spread within a day anyway, but man, that was something else. That whole weekend that was there, it was a non-stop line, open to close, of a hundred people waiting to play.

→   JEFF WALKER
        SFII: CE vice-president of sales and marketing, Capcom USA

One of the things I tried to do, which was controversial … When *Championship Edition* [sic] came out, I said, 'We've gotta stop having the operators getting 25 cent starts and 25 cents to continue. This is a game that they should be getting 50 cents to start and 25 to continue.' So I did something – I locked the operators out of being able to lower the start play to 25 cents, so everyone had to be at 50. And took a ton of shit from that in the marketplace, and had to eventually go back in and do a chip change to allow everybody to do that.

> My thing was, I just knew at that stage that it was a juggernaut that was not gonna happen that often, that

everybody – everybody from the arcade to the operator to the distributor to Capcom – needed to really monetize that game. So I tried to do everything in my power.

→   JAMES GODDARD
Street Fighter II: Champion Edition design support, Capcom USA

By the time it came out, we had so much momentum. [...] I'm getting phone calls all day long from kids calling in, and operators calling in trying to find out more about it, and we're sending them the tournament rules and we're encouraging them to stack up machines and do tournaments. And I don't know. If it was easy to capture the magic of what was happening in a bottle, then anybody could make that shit, you know? But I mean, truly everything worked out just right for it and that's why it surpassed [the original *SFII* in sales]. It was a great game. I mean, it really catered to what the players wanted.

> You hear the stories about how pushy I was. It wasn't just because I was a hardcore player. It was about what the players wanted. I travelled the country and I knew what the players wanted over here. They knew what the players hopefully wanted over there. They wanted to see the multiplayer finally succeed, and *Champ Edition* just hands down was exactly what the players wanted.

That was very important, and I think that's why this thing really took off. It was like a hurricane of perfect stuff. That's the dumbest quote ever right there.

DEFENDING AGAINST COUNTERFEITERS

One side-effect of Street Fighter's early 1990s success was it led to a sea of unofficial arcade boards. Counterfeiters poked a hole in the financial model of the coin-op industry, where games sell with high margins to offset low sales numbers, and sold games for less than their official prices – and in greater quantities than Capcom was able to manufacture. At the time, Capcom ran ads in trade magazines calling the copies 'illegal to make, illegal to sell, illegal to operate'.

→   IAN ROSE
        General counsel, Capcom USA

I joined Capcom in 1992. [...] They'd come to the conclusion that they were at the point now where they could save some money by bringing the legal function in-house.

One of my big challenges in that period was to try to [...] make it harder for the pirates, the copycats, to succeed. And it was an interesting thing, because it's not piracy as we think of it these days with mostly pure digital assets. Instead, these were people who were coming up with pirated versions of the game on a piece of hardware – you know, a printed circuit board that had to be in some ways designed from scratch. So it was kind of a worldwide phenomenon that, as the game became as successful as it was in the arcades in the first instance, it became something that developed on an international level as we understood it, by folks in different countries playing a role in the design and manufacturing and distribution of these counterfeit *Street Fighter II* boards.

In a year, let's say, or in a several-month period in the early days of the *Street Fighter II* arcade game release, we might have sold 25,000 units, for example. And we had reports and estimates of maybe several times that number of counterfeit versions out there in the marketplace.

→   NORITAKA FUNAMIZU
      Street Fighter II series producer, Capcom Japan

There was the legal aspect to it, but I think the problem was more that the bootlegs proliferated in certain areas before we had good distribution agreements in place.

One thing I heard was that there was a company based in Nagoya that was involved in making pirated versions of *Street Fighter II*. They would supposedly reward their employees with stacks of 10,000-yen bills if they met certain production targets. I heard they had three people there doing that, and that every hour they'd be getting 10,000-yen bills for each board they copied. So they were really incentivized to violate the copyright protection and produce these bootlegs.

→   BERT KITADE
      Head of operations, Capcom USA

[George Nakayama and I] went down to Mexico City and took a look at [various counterfeit copies]. We talked to a lawyer down there about what we could do with the counterfeits, and we went to a couple of the arcades down there. [...] It's kind of funny because [for a few years before *Street Fighter II* hit] nobody would even think of wanting to copy arcade videogames, because they really didn't make that much money.

→   SATINDER BHUTANI
      Operations manager, Capcom USA

I had a friend who was a very good technician [...] and he took me to Tijuana, in Mexico. Would you believe there was a small shed [filled with fake Street Fighter arcade marquees]? We had to walk down [narrow streets to find it because you couldn't drive there] and he showed me Street Fighter marquees. There must have been a hundred different versions of marquees. Some with half-naked women on the sides [or however] people would like to have it designed. They were all being made for spurious Street Fighter games. As for the knowledge I was given, if I remember correctly, there were five copies to every one Street Fighter sold by Capcom.

→   IAN ROSE
              General counsel, Capcom USA

The rumours were – the kind of the gossip in the industry – that at a given time at the height of the popularity of the coin-op game, it might have been something like a ten-to-one ratio, counterfeit to real, or maybe higher. It was at least five or ten to one, and it may have been significantly higher than that.

→   BERT KITADE
              Head of operations, Capcom USA

There were rumours about how people got software and all that stuff to copy it, and some of it had to be kind of true, but that was never proven. […] The coin-op games industry itself is a very back-alley type industry because it's made up of – it's all coins, right? [With an all-cash business], things go any which way. When videogames got into the home entertainment, it became more of a legitimate industry, but until that time, George and all these guys, Tsujimoto, would always tell me how to watch out for operators.

→   BRIAN DUKE
              Street Fighter II: CE Western regional sales manager, Capcom USA

There were rumours left and right about a lot of different companies in our industry at that time. The Yakuza being involved; the Mafia being involved here. We heard some companies that wanted to get into the gaming thing with slot machines were prohibited with the ownership that they currently had. So I mean, it was never the cleanest industry, but I'll tell you, it was one hell of a lot of fun.

In addition to dealing with counterfeit copies, the US coin-op industry of the early 1990s went through extensive debates over the legality of 'parallel boards', imported arcade games from Japan that US distributors could sell at lower prices than local versions. Around the same time, Capcom ran into issues with hackers adding chips to legitimate boards to alter games in different ways. For Rose on the legal side, most of his work targeted direct copies, which drew a clearer line over what was legal.

→   IAN ROSE
           General counsel, Capcom USA

We tried to get law enforcement involved [in tracking down counterfeit copies] where we could, both here and internationally. We hired law firms that could help us file lawsuits against those that we, through investigation, found to be distributing the games.

We had some successes. [...] I remember that we had, for example, in [Southeast Asia] – which was probably where a lot of the hardware was originating – we had a law firm help us with [local] police to go after a group over there that [was] at least a source on some level of the pirated boards. And obviously we were on the US side. We had our parent company in Japan. But I came into Capcom as legal counsel on the US side before they had much of a legal department in Japan, at least with real lawyers. So we ended up running a lot of this anti-piracy programme from the US, and even in [Southeast Asia] we were the ones working with our lawyers and the police over there. We sent one of our technical people over. There was a raid and a litigation and so on that, at least temporarily, put those folks out of business.

And we did similar raids on the US side. We had everybody from the local police to the FBI to customs people involved at different times in doing raids or interceding shipments of games coming in through the border. There was kind of a high-class problem, but a real problem, of limited supply. The demand was such that we couldn't keep up. And so that of course drove the counterfeit sales, and it meant that we had issues with how many we could sell.

→ BRIAN DUKE
Street Fighter II: CE Western regional sales manager, Capcom USA

I was turning away orders because we just couldn't place them. We couldn't get enough product.

[Ed. note]   Capcom initiated a handful of lawsuits against companies manufacturing and selling counterfeit Street Fighter games. In August 1993, for instance, Capcom won a lawsuit against a Korean company called Cointek, which a New Jersey court ordered to pay $90,613 to Capcom and $55,000 to the government, according to *RePlay*.

→ IAN ROSE
General counsel, Capcom USA

[At one point when dealing with a law firm and the police in Southeast Asia, Capcom USA sent technician Y. Ming Chiu overseas to] verify what was counterfeit and what wasn't. And he described one occasion where he'd gone to court to testify, and then that evening, everybody had gone out to dinner or was hanging around a bar – and this is not unusual even in the US – and the defence attorneys and the prosecutors were kind of talking together. But he says that on one of those occasions, he was approached by somebody who said, 'Hey, if you back off your testimony and just make it muddy, we'll pay you some money.' It was some tens of thousands of dollars or whatever that they were willing to pay him. [...] Clearly, there was a lot at stake for those guys who were manufacturing those boards.

[Ultimately, I'm not sure whether our effort] was productive or not. [...] It was like *Whac-A-Mole*. You felt like it had to be done, but you knew you had no chance of being completely successful, or even significantly successful. There was such a profit incentive in doing the counterfeit stuff, and [it was] so hard to catch any big chunk of it. And you know, I remember having that discussion internally of [whether it was worth the effort]. [...] We probably one year spent upward of a couple million dollars in legal fees – and maybe that included some of the Data East litigation; that was also very expensive. [...] But it was a high-class problem, because the company was doing very well despite those problems.

CHAPTER 05

STREET FIGHTER II TURBO: HYPER FIGHTING

As Capcom dealt with counterfeit copies, they also stumbled onto a related problem: third-party upgrade kits.

Often referred to as 'speed-up kits', 'jump kits' or 'enhancement kits', these chips weren't sanctioned by Capcom yet turned official Street Fighter boards into variants such as Accelerator Pt. II and Rainbow Edition, offering mid-air fireballs, the ability to change characters on the fly, and perhaps most notably, a faster overall speed.

As a concept, this was nothing new – upgrade kits were common in the 1980s and even led to one of the industry's biggest hits: *Ms. Pac-Man*. But for a company that had just set a precedent with a limited follow-up of its own in *Champion Edition*, this posed a problem. Not only was Capcom not making money on these kits, but some players liked them better than the real thing.

Capcom had little choice but to keep up.

THIRD-PARTY UPGRADE KITS

Once the third-party kits showed up, it didn't take long for them to spread to arcades around the world. Thanks to the amusement industry's loosely regulated distribution network, the kits moved far and fast, offering a new twist on the industry's most popular game.

> 'For a while there, I felt like everybody and their mother was selling some sort of different Street Fighter kit,' says Todd Cravens – whose father Bill sold these kits, among other things, after leaving Capcom.

When news of the kits hit those who worked on and played Street Fighter, reactions varied.

→   ZENJI ISHII
           Editor-in-chief, Gamest magazine

Well, I laughed at first. I thought it was interesting in the context of how far people could go and what strange things people were capable of when they went and hacked into the game. Of course, there was no way this version of the game was ever going to make it onto the competitive scene, so in that sense there was very little for us to talk about in the magazine. It was definitely an illegal or an unauthorized version of the game.

→   JAMES GODDARD
           Street Fighter II: Champion Edition design support, Capcom USA

It all happened pretty fast. I know that my bosses definitely got calls from operators saying, 'Hey, how do I get one of these things?' And it's like, 'What are you talking about?' So there was initially that. I vaguely remember there being some kind of a discussion about it. Like, 'Hey, have you heard anything about this?' 'No.' And then within days, [I found one].

→   NORITAKA FUNAMIZU
Street Fighter II series producer, Capcom Japan

I remember seeing [one of the third-party kits] and wondering, *Wow, they really like the game enough to do this?* I was just wondering, *How did they do that? How did they reverse engineer the game and figure out how it worked?* You should probably ask Ueyama about this as well.

→   TAKESHI TEZUKA
X-Men: Children of the Atom planner, Capcom Japan

You should probably ask Ueyama about that. I remember him being quite upset about that game.

→   SHINICHI UEYAMA
Street Fighter II: Champion Edition lead programmer, Capcom Japan

Well, I didn't feel sad or angry, in particular, at the beginning. I was like, *Oh, they seem to have worked hard and oh, you can do this? Interesting.* But then the problem was when it started becoming bigger and bigger, then that's when I started to feel like, *OK, well this is probably not good.*

→   JAMES GODDARD
Street Fighter II: Champion Edition design support, Capcom USA

What I remember about it is the fact that there was so much buzz then among the players. 'Oh, is there a special version? What is this? How can you do fireballs in the air?' [...] That shit was like, 25 to 30 percent faster [than *Champion Edition*]. It was almost unplayable. But boy, people were having a blast.

[Ed. note]   While operators bought anything Street Fighter-related they could get their hands on, and lots of players loved the third-party kits, the upgrades quickly revealed one of the key lessons of game design: if the game's not balanced, the appeal doesn't last.

→ TOMOTAKA SUZUKI
Street Fighter II series combo video creator

I mean, I wasn't really interested in [Rainbow Edition] because it wasn't an authentic original *Street Fighter II*. I think they went too far with all the modifications they made. I think there's more meaning and significance in playing the original arcade board than there is in playing anything else.

→ CHRIS TANG
Street Fighter II tournament player

It's not legitimate. You have a couple of guys that want to throw down at Street Fighter, they should be able to throw down with consistent, proper rules.

→ TOMOTAKA SUZUKI
Street Fighter II series combo video creator

Even if we say 'Rainbow Edition', I believe there are like 30 or 40 different variants of it. Plus, it's not an authentic version. It's an illegal version of the game, and I don't think that's a good thing. If I were to record Rainbow Edition videos myself, I feel like it would hurt the value of the videos that I'd made before that.

→ JAMES GODDARD
Street Fighter II: Champion Edition design support, Capcom USA

At the time, [I] had my head all around balance and the importance of [being] fair and making sure the game was awesome and fun. [So] I was more annoyed by what I was seeing, but at the same time, I was little geeked out by some of the dumb shit with Guile's Sonic Boom being a boomerang and doing a Spinning Piledriver from the air. Hell yeah. Let's go.

→ STEPHEN FROST
Street Fighter 30th Anniversary Collection producer, Digital Eclipse

For some reason, when Rainbow Edition came out, [Accelerator Pt. II] came out, and *Fighter's History* and those games came out – those are all very, very cheap games, and for some reason, we all found fun in that. Like, who could out-cheat or who could out-do things better.

→ JAMES CHEN
  Street Fighter series commentator

I played Rainbow Edition when it was popular [...] because *Champion Edition* was so busted and not even competitive at the time. I mean, it was just all Bison, right? So when Rainbow Edition came out, I know a lot of people played it because it was novel. It was goofy, but at least it was something new.

→ JAMES GODDARD
  Street Fighter II: Champion Edition design support, Capcom USA

[The big problem was] the fallout with the operators, the operators just going, 'Hey, we don't want [*Champion Edition*] anymore.' They were buying these $200, or whatever they were, Taiwanese aftermarket ROM upgrades, and the amount of chaos that was causing just took a while to really sink in. We knew it was trouble, [but it took time to see] how scary that threat was.

AN OFFICIAL RESPONSE

Due to the popularity of the various upgrade kits, it was only a matter of time before Capcom came up with one of their own. The game they ended up developing, *Street Fighter II Turbo: Hyper Fighting*, featured a faster speed, a handful of new special moves and character balance changes.

As for how *Hyper Fighting* came about, again, different versions of the story exist.

→   JAMES GODDARD
         Street Fighter II Turbo: Hyper Fighting design support, Capcom USA

Rainbow Edition came out, the Taiwanese ROM upgrade with all the crazy fireballs in the air and the helicopter kicks working in the air – just everything broken. Super fast, super broken. We start hearing how these things are getting installed and operators are earning money off of them, but we're not getting any of the action. So I go down to – I don't know, Galaxy Arcade? I think it was in San Jose. I go and I take a look at this Rainbow Edition and I spend a good four hours playing it, looking at it and going, 'Man, this is just garbage.' On one hand, it's kind of like, 'Woo – look at these crazy-ass fireballs in the air.' And on the other hand, it's just like, 'But it's so unbalanced.'

I come back, and I spend the next few hours writing [a letter] to Japan saying Rainbow Edition is utter shit, utter garbage, there is no threat here, it is completely unbalanced and it's a fad. Because as a player, emotionally, that's how I felt. However, before I sent that fax off, I went into the cafeteria to play *Champ Edition*.
I sit down to play [against my co-worker Joel Pambid], and the weirdest thing happens. He picks Guile; I pick Zangief. I go to play, and oh my god, the game felt like it was underwater. [...] I had

just spent the last four to six hours playing Rainbow Edition at 25 percent speed increase, so *Champ Edition* felt like shit. It was so slow. For the next two hours, I could not shake that. And it threw my timing off. [...] It was just kind of this oh-my-god moment where I went, 'The real threat of Rainbow Edition is not all the fireballs in the air and the craziness. The threat is the speed is addicting, and it changes everything.'

> So I scrapped my report. I was there until three in the morning writing what my initial takeaway was, and then how much my motor skills were affected in just four to six hours of playing. [...] I got the fax out saying, 'Look, we need to do our own ROM upgrade to compete against these guys. We can kill them if it's balanced – it's spectacular but it's balanced. We can absolutely kill these illegals, but it has to be competitively priced, and it has to be just balanced to the next level. We have tons of feedback of what's wrong with *Champ Edition* on a tournament level. We could put in a bunch of stuff. It'd be awesome.'

And I send that over. They were really worried about it, so they said, 'OK, fine.' [...] Everybody agreed, 'OK, we'll give it a shot.'

[Ed. note]   Similar to the situation with *Champion Edition*, Funamizu – who oversaw *Hyper Fighting*'s development as Akira Nishitani moved on to other projects – doesn't recall it starting with a proposal from Goddard. In this case, he points to a general feeling around the office that Capcom had to do something to hold off the third-party kits, and a specific request from Capcom founder Kenzo Tsujimoto. And as it turned out, Funamizu says, this happened after Capcom had started development on a different Street Fighter sequel.

→ NORITAKA FUNAMIZU
Street Fighter II Turbo: Hyper Fighting producer, Capcom Japan

Champion Edition sold very well, so naturally that meant we were going to have to make a sequel.

At that time, what we had really wanted to make was a fighting game that was perfectly balanced. We also wanted to add new characters, though at that point, nothing else had been firmly decided. Those ideas eventually went on to become *Super Street Fighter II*, but while we were working on it, the [upgrade kits] showed up. In most countries, there are copyright laws where if you release your new product first, it gains copyright protection there. So Capcom was worried that if they didn't create something right away, they wouldn't be able to stop these copies from being produced. We were then asked to create something right away, as quickly as possible. And unfortunately that meant working through Christmas and New Year's.

We ended up making that game in like, three months. We fast-tracked it to get it done very quickly.

→ SHINICHI UEYAMA
Street Fighter II Turbo: Hyper Fighting lead programmer, Capcom Japan

This is all just what I've heard, and I have to stress that I don't know if it's true or not. It might not be. But apparently, at that time, Capcom learned that pirated versions of its games were proliferating in countries outside of Japan, and the president, Kenzo Tsujimoto, learned the severity of the situation when he met with operators in America. There were fears that if this persisted, the market itself would collapse – that if bootleggers started profiting from these games, it would end up harming the quality of the gameplay and the entire industry. What I heard is that Capcom decided to release its own 'copy' of Rainbow Edition to stop that.

→   NORITAKA FUNAMIZU
Street Fighter II Turbo: Hyper Fighting producer, Capcom Japan

Right. [...] That's what we've heard, that it was Kenzo's decision.

→   SHINICHI UEYAMA
Street Fighter II Turbo: Hyper Fighting lead programmer, Capcom Japan

Word came down to my boss, [Capcom executive Takashi] Aoki. He brought a bootleg version over to my desk and [asked me to make something similar to it]. Later he told me to write 'TURBO' in big red letters there in the centre. I said, 'OK, you got it.' So Chun-Li got a new move, we changed the background colors, we put the 'TURBO' text on the title screen, and James provided some ideas too, like Dhalsim's teleporting.

[Ed. note]   Funamizu says that department head Yoshiki Okamoto made the final call on whether to move forward with the game. Okamoto, as part of the same Twitter reply mentioned in chapter four, said his memories are foggy and Capcom Japan took the feedback it got from Capcom USA seriously, but he doesn't think that Capcom USA team members were close enough to the development process to take credit for the ideas behind *Champion Edition* and *Hyper Fighting*. We were unable to reach Aoki for this book.

DEVELOPMENT DEBATES

While Goddard and Funamizu have different recollections of *Hyper Fighting*'s origins, they both recall Goddard working with the team to help balance the game – and running into disagreements over the game's speed in the process. The third-party kits had shown the appeal of characters flying across the screen, but they hadn't convinced everyone at Capcom that the game could be balanced and competitive at that pace.

→   JAMES GODDARD
            Street Fighter II Turbo: Hyper Fighting design support, Capcom USA

The Japanese were like, 'This is crap. We don't want to speed it up. We do not want to speed this up.' And so anyway, because the business guys were all involved, they agreed to bring it to the – I think it was the AMOA [Amusement & Music Operators Association] show. Because it was all about the same timing.

So they took a version of the game to the AMOA show with Chun-Li throwing a fireball and at 5 percent faster, and we got hammered at the show. Hammered by the operators basically saying, 'Fuck you guys. We'll buy the illegal one for $150 or $200 rather than this piece of crap here.' And so Mr Tsujimoto, who was the head of all of Capcom, had heard about this and that the numbers were not looking good coming out of the show, so they came to me and said – he's like, 'You will design this ... and you have until tomorrow.'

So I spent all night with my apprentice, Joe. We sat together, designed the whole thing out, a whole bunch of changes [such as making it 15 percent faster instead of 5 percent], and then we pitched them. And there was a lot of resistance. They flew me over to Japan a week later for two and a half weeks to do the development and sit with the Japanese to make it happen.

→ JOE GANIS
Street Fighter II Turbo: Hyper Fighting software tester, Capcom USA

Basically, James came up to me one day and said, 'Joe, Japan think they're gonna do some more stuff on Street Fighter. What's on your mind?' So I took a yellow pad and I wrote down everything I thought of, and thought of a bunch of counter-play elements [to give players more options against projectile attacks like fireballs], and gave that to James. And he said he'd take it to Japan and he did.

→ TOM SHIRAIWA
Street Fighter II series translator, Capcom Japan

We had a lot – a lot – of arguments. Whenever James came over to Japan and had a meeting with the team, it was always a very exciting meeting. People would get so excited that they'd yell at each other.

→ ALEX JIMENEZ
Super Street Fighter II design support, Capcom USA

James is so over the top, it's ridiculous. [...] He's one of these *Big Lebowski*-type guys – loud, crazy, really enthusiastic, energetic. [...] They used to call him E. Honda because he was so pushy.

→ TOM SHIRAIWA
Street Fighter II series translator, Capcom Japan

James was somewhat pushy at that time, and when he saw some issue with the game he'd always request to fix that as soon as possible. But sometimes the team had [other] issues to deal with. They couldn't think about the US market only. They'd sometimes get contradictory feedback from other markets, like the Asian and European markets. So there were many reasons why they couldn't make changes, but still James was saying, 'This change has to be made.'

→   JAMES GODDARD
       Street Fighter II Turbo: Hyper Fighting design support, Capcom USA

Tom was there for all the crazy shit. Dude was like, 'Just let it go.' He had to deal with a very riled-up version of me. [...] I was way over the top once upon a time.

→   ALEX JIMENEZ
       Super Street Fighter II design support, Capcom USA

[Tom] was awesome. He went to bat for us many times. We had all these crazy ideas, and he always had this kind of resolve: 'Oh, why do you do this to me?' He was a good guy and stood up for us.

→   TOM SHIRAIWA
       Street Fighter II series translator, Capcom Japan

The most challenging part was, you know, whatever James said, the team said, 'Isn't it just your personal opinion? Is this what all American people [think], like an average opinion from the American players? How can you prove that?' That was always the most challenging thing to prove to them. And then because James was a very hardcore Street Fighter II player himself, there were some characters he particularly liked. So he was more into Zangief balancing, sometimes [trying to make him stronger]. When the team sees that, then James' report doesn't sound credible anymore. So I always tried to make sure that his reports sounded fair to everybody.

→   JAMES GODDARD
       Street Fighter II Turbo: Hyper Fighting design support, Capcom USA

A big nightmare fight happened over there, over the fact that basically no one wanted to make it faster, and unfortunately the market spoke. My mentor Akira Nishitani was very disappointed with the fact that I wanted to make it faster. He no longer was my mentor after that. Because he had down, to the milliseconds, how people could respond to seeing a fireball [by jumping over it, and then how the other player could counter with an] uppercut. And this was breaking all of that research he did. And I just showed him, at the end of the day, you speed it up 15 percent, people will adapt and they'll be able to see it. So that created a bit of a falling out. [...] On *Hyper Fighting*, [Nishitani] washed his hands of it.

[Ed. note]   In the 2014 *Polygon* article, Nishitani said he didn't move on because of differences of opinion over *Hyper Fighting*, but because Capcom's beat-'em-up *Aliens vs. Predator* needed help. He added that he felt *Hyper Fighting* was 'a bit fast' for his tastes, but he wasn't opposed to that decision – instead, he thought the speed made the game more about predicting attacks rather than responding to them, which required tuning it differently.

→   JOE GANIS
    Street Fighter II Turbo: Hyper Fighting software tester, Capcom USA

I think Japan was feeling that it was moving too quickly, and I was definitely [Goddard's] back-up on that; I was like, 'This *Turbo* stuff is so much improved over the standard version. The gameplay is faster; the movement is just as precise as it was before but you have to be able to process things so much quicker.' And of course you'd also spend more money because *Turbo* fights [ended] a little bit quicker.

→   TOM SHIRAIWA
    Street Fighter II series translator, Capcom Japan

The team [in Japan] never believed making it twice as fast would make for reasonable gameplay. 'It will end up losing all the strategies.' But actually trying [the third-party] versions told them it could be fun. That helped them to be convinced there was a need for this. And of course, we did not want some pirates to take away our potential profits.

→   NORITAKA FUNAMIZU
Street Fighter II Turbo: Hyper Fighting producer, Capcom Japan

We ran into a lot of challenges on *Hyper Fighting*. The animation skipping frames ...

→   SHINICHI UEYAMA
Street Fighter II Turbo: Hyper Fighting lead programmer, Capcom Japan

Yeah, the animation was an issue. [...] Because we sped up the game, sometimes, say you had a three-frame animation, the first and third frames would show, but the second would drop out.

→   NORITAKA FUNAMIZU
Street Fighter II Turbo: Hyper Fighting producer, Capcom Japan

Finding just the right speed at which that problem wouldn't occur was a real pain. Honestly, there were a lot of things that didn't fit right, or would get de-synced, when we raised the speed of the game. That was something James didn't understand. He wanted us to make it go even faster, and we had to keep telling him that would break the game.

→   SHINICHI UEYAMA
Street Fighter II Turbo: Hyper Fighting lead programmer, Capcom Japan

One time, I actually showed James how the game would look if we programmed it at the speed he wanted. I said, 'No one's going to be able to play this!' James might have been able to enjoy it that way, but we didn't think anyone else would, especially newcomers to the game. I explained it to him as plainly as I could, but I remember he didn't like hearing that. [*laughs*]

[Ed. note]   Goddard says the speed debates came to a head after Capcom agreed to put two versions of the game on test to see which players liked better – one with the changes he wanted, and one with the changes Funamizu wanted.

Funamizu liked to let people know they were wrong and remind them of their place. [We spent] two hours going to this arcade that was way outside of the main test sites in Osaka to ensure the changes I had designed would be safely tested without word getting out, and he's riding me off and on about how I should be prepared to be embarrassed and how it's going to be a failure and, you know, 'Don't take it too hard.' We get there and there's just fifty kids around this machine, freaking the fuck out. So that was the moment that my career went *woo* in the business and went sideways at Capcom, because it was a big thing to go from knowing what USA players wanted after the *Rainbow* bootleg hit, to 'Oh shit. Wait, what's happening? Even in Japan, people like this shit.'

> [I remember] literally walking up the steps – still getting prodded to be ready for disappointment and even better: design humiliation – when some guy that was part of the staff came running down the steps and met us, and said some shit really excitedly to the translator. Funamizu's face dropped and the translator looked at me and said, 'Well, you're going to be happy but this is not good.'

It's a success. And because I was called out and challenged on the design changes for this test, the guy started losing face and that was really something not intended or even something I could understand was going to happen.

> Unfortunately, it did not stop there. We go to America with my version of *Street Fighter II: Hyper Fighting*, and he brings his version. We tested an A/B test, side-by-side. Mine out-earned his, three to one, because mine was what the players wanted. The other version was much slower, had different balance tweaks and commands like press down and three buttons to do a teleport with Dhalsim; press this way and three buttons to teleport, and other

changes that just did not resonate with the hardcore players at that location. Believe me, I know the guy's super talented and he was way bigger than I was in Capcom, but putting it side-by-side like that [...] made it a direct challenge and he lost again – and so did I, career-wise, from that.

In clear hindsight, [we didn't intend to make him to look bad. Capcom USA] wanted the version. We had Rainbow Editions running wild and [Funamizu] got stuck with me as the co-lead when Tsujimoto authorized the creation of *Hyper* and they sent me – with my ass on the line for it – to go make it happen. That put us on a collision course and his disadvantage was he was not deeply connected to *Street Fighter II* and *Champion Edition*'s player base, and I was, so it became a thing. *Here's this pushy kid from America, you know? He's not even a designer. He's like, an apprentice. He's barely learning. He's influencing all of our games.* [...] You know, *Who is this guy?* So he wanted to put me in my place, and this was famously told to me by [a different translator]: 'At some point, you've just got to let it go.' It was wise advice, but I couldn't let it go. It was about our players. It was about the game. So this might be why Funamizu doesn't want to give me any credit, and that's fine. I've always danced around some of the stuff I've shared today, however it is important to share the kinds of hurdles we as designers may face and [how we] sometimes end up in a tough choice between choosing career path or passion. None of us wanted to change *Champion Edition* this way, but Rainbow Edition bootlegs forced our hands, and in the chaos some of us clashed hard.

Ultimately, after that A/B test, everyone realized this was really going to be a good upgrade to the game. We worked together and really polished it, put more time into it than originally planned – less than one month became six-to-eight weeks – to give the players worldwide an amazing game.

It's very possible that there were two versions of the game tested.
I do not remember that particular point very clearly, but it's possible.
If I'm understanding correctly, James says that the version that he
wanted to do was the one that got better received and therefore,
Capcom went with it. I don't think that's true because I was the
one who made those decisions back in the day. I really don't
remember, sorry.

> If we're talking about *Hyper Fighting*, I think the biggest
> difference ended up being the game speed. James thought
> the game should be even faster, but we had received a lot
> of feedback from Japanese players that it shouldn't be that
> fast. So I think that's probably why we ended up doing
> tests, to gather more feedback on that point.

The way I remember him then, was that he was this non-Japanese
person, this foreigner who came into the company, and in Japan
many people don't look well on those who are outspoken and
freely give their own opinions. I fully intended to have a good
working relationship with him, though.

> In terms of trying to verify what he actually did, from
> my viewpoint, he worked with the Japanese staff in order
> to develop the game. I also felt like, at the time, having a
> person like James on the team was kind of a status symbol
> for us. At the end of the day, I think he probably remembers
> the things he did himself, whereas I can't remember
> specifically what he did.

I did feel like perspectives were just naturally going to be a little
different between the Japan side and the US side, and that's actually
why I took a lot of the US side's opinions very seriously. Capcom
tried as much as possible to listen to what James and others said.
Nowadays you can just talk to anybody on the team directly, right?
But back in the day there were more go-betweens, specific people
who communicated with the overseas departments, and that was

how information got to me, which probably had an influence on the level of communication we were able to have.

[Ed. note]   Multiple people speaking for this book have pointed to limited communication between Capcom USA and Capcom Japan at the time, saying that misunderstandings didn't just happen, but were common.

HYPER FIGHTING'S SUCCESS

Hyper Fighting hit arcades in December 1992, marking the third of Capcom's Street Fighter CPS-1 games. It was immediately popular, being cheap enough (around $200) that many arcade operators bought in, though the low price of an upgrade kit meant Capcom didn't see the same sort of financial upsides as they had with *Champion Edition* – at least, until they released a console version the following year.

> In fact, in a 2021 YouTube video, Okamoto said that Capcom didn't factor shipping costs into their *Hyper Fighting* kit sales in America, which he said led to Capcom taking a loss on the project. Okamoto blames this on a Capcom USA president he refers to as "N-san," which may refer to George Nakayama, who Okamoto says was opposed to the release of *Hyper Fighting* from the beginning. Okamoto says the shipping mistake frustrated staff at Capcom Japan, who felt like their effort had been wasted.

Still, many on both sides consider the game a success, and the game's faster speed appealed to a large number of players. In their April 1993 issue, *RePlay* magazine reported that, a few months in, Capcom USA had sold 11,000 arcade upgrade kits, and 2,000 additional *Champion Edition* boards with *Hyper Fighting* pre-installed.

→   JAMES GODDARD
      Street Fighter II Turbo: Hyper Fighting design support, Capcom USA

Hyper Fighting ended up being so strong that, not only do we sell tens of thousands of the ROM upgrades, we sold well over 5,000 [more *Champion Edition* boards]. We just sold more, and then that thing took off like crazy. Sold how many? Four or five million Super Nintendo [cartridges] worldwide? I mean, the player demand just kind of made [the unofficial kit] problem go away.

> I know there's versions [of the unofficial kits] out there. Some arcades probably held onto them as a cool thing, but when your customers are coming in and going, 'I don't want that. I want this', then they go buy the real thing.

We got really lucky. We were really lucky that worked.

→ NORITAKA FUNAMIZU
Street Fighter II Turbo: Hyper Fighting producer, Capcom Japan

As for what I think went well, basically just increasing the game speed … and as you know, there was that pesky illegal version going around, so I was happy we were able to release our own proper, official sped-up version.

→ JAMES GODDARD
Street Fighter II Turbo: Hyper Fighting design support, Capcom USA

To this day, I can't go back and play original *Street Fighter II* or *Champion Edition* worth a shit because I'm just used to the faster stuff, right? And I'm sure some people reading that [who I used to play] would go, 'You never could play it worth a shit anyway.'

→ NORITAKA FUNAMIZU
Street Fighter II Turbo: Hyper Fighting producer, Capcom Japan

I would say with *Hyper Fighting*, we were very successful in suppressing or reducing the impact of the pirated version. We were able to convey the message that this is our game, right? This is the real thing. And I think the game was very successful for that reason.

→ CHRIS TANG
Street Fighter II Turbo: Hyper Fighting tournament player

In a sense, I'm thankful to Rainbow Edition existing to facilitate the need for *Turbo: Hyper Fighting*, and then James and Dave [Winstead, who also worked on *Hyper Fighting* at Capcom USA] got to do their thing and we had what I feel is the most balanced version of the game.

→   JAMES CHEN
       Street Fighter series commentator

When they made *Hyper Fighting* and *Hyper Fighting* was so good, that just made everybody stop [playing unofficial versions] instantly. So, in making *Hyper Fighting*, they did a good job. They did exactly what they needed to do, right? Which was to counteract the Rainbow Edition.

→   CHRIS TANG
       Street Fighter II Turbo: Hyper Fighting tournament player

Turbo: Hyper Fighting is kind of like my high point for all fighting games. That was the game that everybody in the world played the most when there were only a few fighting games around. And I don't know if it's ever going to get as good as that again.

CHAPTER 06

BRINGING THE GAMES HOME

As with most popular arcade games of the 1990s, it was only a matter of time before *Street Fighter II* made its way to home consoles.

While Capcom had released the original *Street Fighter* on consoles years earlier, most notably in the form of a TurboGrafx-CD release under the name *Fighting Street*, at that point the series didn't have the sort of clout to make a major impact on the market. But after *Street Fighter II* took off in arcades, suddenly Street Fighter wasn't just another brand to sell on consoles, but a brand that could sell consoles.

THE SUPER NES DEBUT

Given Capcom's publishing history and existing relationship with Nintendo, few were surprised when Capcom announced *Street Fighter II*'s first console destination: the Super Nintendo Entertainment System (known as the Super Famicom in Japan).

Like most Nintendo consoles, the system built its reputation on Nintendo's in-house software, with critically acclaimed games like *Super Mario World* and *The Legend of Zelda: A Link to the Past* leading the way. Yet for a short period of time in mid-1992 – just a few months after *Champion Edition* hit arcades – *Street Fighter II* disrupted that balance and became the system's breakout hit.

→   JOHN GILLIN
        Street Fighter II SNES director of marketing, Capcom USA

In the summer of 1992, the Super Nintendo system had come out, but they had a very, very thin library. As has always been Nintendo's case, they'll come out with a very good starting library that they develop internally, but very, very little of anything from third parties at that point. And Nintendo was getting beaten by the Sega Genesis.

→   SCOTT SMITH
        Street Fighter II SNES marketing manager, Capcom USA

The SNES sold well initially, but in the US the Genesis had really found a foothold with *Sonic* and the whole 'blast processing' [marketing], and so it was not a slam dunk for Nintendo anymore. [...] When we came out with *Street Fighter* [*II*], suddenly that evaporated. It was, 'If you want Street Fighter, you have to have Super Nintendo.' It was the only game in town.

→   JOHN GILLIN
      Street Fighter II SNES director of marketing, Capcom USA

[Nintendo] really put some pressure on Capcom and said, 'We want to have *Street Fighter II* come out on the console as quickly as possible.'

→   SCOTT SMITH
      Street Fighter II SNES marketing manager, Capcom USA

Things happened very quickly. [...] I mean, I think when we did the Super Nintendo version of *Street Fighter II*, basically Nintendo stopped manufacturing [other games] in Japan and held everything up so they could make *Street Fighter II*.

→   TATSUYA MINAMI
      Street Fighter II series console planner, Capcom Japan

The thing that really sticks out in my mind is how crazy the schedules were. [...] I wasn't involved directly in the first Super NES port, but then I came in afterwards and led the *Turbo*, Genesis and PC Engine ports. [...] All of those were super tight schedules. I remember just having tons of people, comparatively, on these projects.

→   KAZUNORI YAMADA
      Super Street Fighter II SNES sound designer, Capcom Japan

The biggest challenge was trying to cram the games into the limited hardware capacity. [...] The Super NES had limited capacity. So if there was a sound like 'aaahhh' – a long sound – we couldn't fit the full voice in, so instead we made a small 'ah' sound and repeated it as 'ah', 'ah', 'ah', 'ah'. That made it sound like the full voice, but saved on space. We had to come up with tricks like that to be able to fit all the audio in. [...] I was involved in some of the later ports, but [sound designer Tatsuya] Nishimura, who was there before me, implemented that to save space on the Super NES.

→   YOKO SHIMOMURA
        Street Fighter II arcade composer, Capcom Japan

Basically, it came down to reducing the number of elements in each song so they would fit the new hardware requirements. And the sounds that were available on the console were different as well, so I had to talk to a specialist at Capcom who was in charge of the Super NES sound in order to find out how we could take the original arcade tracks and scale them down a bit so they would work on the new hardware. I didn't actually compose the console version tracks myself, but I remember having discussions about them and trying to figure out a way to maintain the original feel of the arcade tracks for the console ports.

→   TATSUYA MINAMI
        Street Fighter II series console planner, Capcom Japan

I also remember all the programmers working super hard during the day, and then telling them that they had to go to sleep. One of the things that I remember very distinctly is the [quality assurance] teams would come in in the morning. And so when the programmers would go to sleep, we'd have to take all of the data that we'd been working on, burn it to EPROMs, take those, do checksums on them, and then manually push them into the circuit boards and make tons of sets of these so the QA teams could check the game starting in the morning.

That work would go on all night, and there would often be times when we'd be working until four or five in the morning, just making the actual prototype ROMs for these guys to be able to start the checks. Right now if I tried to do it, I'd probably double myself over and pass out, but back then, once we'd finished that, we'd go out, have a couple of beers, and then go to bed and come back in the morning.

→ SEIJI OKADA
Street Fighter II SNES programmer, Capcom Japan

I remember just going in to work every morning and working until the wee hours of the night. There was no 'tagging in' – you had to work morning through night! [...] We couldn't just take the arcade data over and move it over. All of that had to be reprogrammed to run on the Super NES.

→ SCOTT SMITH
Street Fighter II SNES marketing manager, Capcom USA

I personally think that *Street Fighter II* had a lot to do with the success of the Super Nintendo in the United States. I think without it, without that key game, [Nintendo] would have had a much harder time selling units up against the Genesis and *Sonic* at that point in time.

THE GENESIS/MEGA DRIVE PORT

While *Street Fighter II* gave Nintendo an edge against Sega, Sega executives continually pursued Capcom, wanting the game on their system as well. Given Nintendo's long-standing relationship with Capcom, that wasn't an easy sell – Capcom was one of the first third-party companies licensed to produce games for Nintendo hardware, and the two companies had close ties. But for some at Capcom, the game's sales potential on the Genesis was worth rocking the boat.

→   IAN ROSE
    General counsel, Capcom USA

There was a very close relationship, or a reasonably close relationship, between Capcom and Nintendo. [...] I remember [Capcom founder Kenzo] Tsujimoto came over with his entourage, and on our way to CES [in 1992] a few of us went up to Seattle and paid a visit to Nintendo, and spent a couple of days with Nintendo. [...] We spent time at [Nintendo of America president Minoru Arakawa's] house; we went out to dinner with him and the whole thing. And it was those relationships and how important they were, I think, that drove a lot of the business connections and decisions.

→   LAURIE THORNTON
    Street Fighter II series public relations manager, Capcom USA

Everyone knew that Capcom was Nintendo's darling. The relationships back in Japan were very tight. I recall needing to withhold info about our specific launch plans and platform details while lots of negotiating was taking place behind closed doors.

→ SCOTT SMITH
Street Fighter II series marketing manager, Capcom USA

What I remember is people from Sega coming down to meet with Joe [Morici], and I remember our trip. I went with Joe up to the Redwood Shores Marine World Parkway offices of Sega there and met with the vice-president of Sega. [...] They obviously wanted the game. Pretty darn badly, because they owned the US market until *Street Fighter* [*II*] appeared.

→ JOE MORICI
Street Fighter II series senior vice-president, Capcom USA

I would like to believe I was pretty instrumental in getting [Capcom Japan] to start to support the Genesis system. I kept pushing that. I would go to Japan every month. [...] Capcom had a company house. We'd meet all the time and go down there and discuss what was going on.

→ NORITAKA FUNAMIZU
Street Fighter II series producer, Capcom Japan

I think [Capcom Japan console division head Tokuro] Fujiwara spoke with Sega, and he found out that they were making a six-button control pad for the system. I think that's how that version ended up getting made.

→ JOHN GILLIN
Street Fighter II series director of marketing, Capcom USA

Over in Japan, the Sega executives were courting the Capcom executives [...] there was some drama that went on over there [...] it was difficult. But in the end, Capcom agreed to create a Street Fighter version for the Sega Genesis. And I heard that made the folks at Nintendo none too happy.

→   SCOTT SMITH
Street Fighter II series marketing manager, Capcom USA

Finally we got the OK from Japan like, 'Yes, they will devote resources to the Genesis.' And we did a press conference after much back and forth, with Sega at the Sofitel [hotel in Redwood City, CA]. We had a breakfast for the press and whatnot and announced the partnership between Capcom and Sega. Although I think the art had [Capcom action star] Mega Man shaking Sonic's hand, obviously the first game was going to be *Street Fighter II: Champion Edition*.

→   TATSUYA MINAMI
Street Fighter II series console planner, Capcom Japan

I remember it being like early multiplatform development [with contracts and negotiations that were uncommon at the time], because there were agreements with the hardware manufacturers. So if you put it out on Nintendo here, then you had to get it out on the Genesis and PC Engine by this time period or we'd be breaking contracts, etc.

→   JOE MORICI
Street Fighter II series senior vice-president, Capcom USA

[Capcom Japan was] having an outside house program [the Genesis version]. They weren't doing it in-house. It was probably in the spring of that year they had a version of *Street Fighter: Champion Edition* that they wanted me to look at. And they weren't happy with the quality of the game in Japan. [...]

I played it. I thought, *It's strong enough to release.* And I said, 'If we don't release it, and we release it against *Mortal Kombat* in the fall, [we're going to be in trouble]. You guys don't understand what the power of *Mortal Kombat* is. They're out-spending us, out-marketing us with a much different game than Street Fighter. It's not really cartoon characters like Street Fighter; it's more realistic. We should release the game now. We'll have four months ahead of *Mortal Kombat*. We'll get to market first. We'll kill them.' Well, they chose to wait, to go directly against *Mortal Kombat*. I think we released [the games] within a week of each other.

A lot of the orders I had were pending [...] I think I had orders for two million units, a huge amount of product that was coming on the boat. And once it gets made, you can't cancel the order. It's on its way; it's coming. So at that point, I said, 'Well, I think we're making the wrong decision.' They disagreed with me. I said, 'I still think we're making the wrong decision.'

[Ed. note]   When Capcom delayed the game, they brought its development in-house at Capcom Japan, increasing the cartridge's memory in the process. The result was a smoother-playing game, and a game that arrived not only two weeks after *Mortal Kombat*, but two months after the Super NES follow-up, *Street Fighter II Turbo*.

The game sold well. It didn't sell as well as we anticipated because we released it head-to-head against *Mortal Kombat*. They had Mortal Monday. They were really, really a good marketing firm; I've got to give them credit for that. The gameplay itself wasn't, I don't think, as good as Street Fighter, but it had great marketing.

[Ed. note]   When discussing Acclaim's marketing for the console versions of *Mortal Kombat*, Morici recalls a story of friendly rivalry.

A good friend of mine, Rob Holmes, was the president of Acclaim at the time – friendly competitors; it was really a different marketplace than it is today.

I don't remember if you ever saw that TV spot with *Mortal Kombat* and Street Fighter. I did a TV spot which typically you don't do – you don't really name your competitor point blank. But if you remember that spot, one of the security guards was going into a toy store. [...] So what happens is, you see a wall of videogames and it starts to morph, and then Blanka's hand comes out and reaches over and grabs the *Mortal Kombat* game on the shelf and then takes it and crumples it and throws it on the ground.

So I get a call from Rob Holmes at Acclaim. He goes, 'You're such an asshole.' Jokingly. So I think, 'OK, fine, yeah, whatever.' I said, 'Look, it was obvious that [*Mortal Kombat* was our] competition for Street Fighter. We might as well just address this and see what we can do.'

So what happens is we had a Street Fighter comic book. And I never saw it. There [was] a very limited number of them. But have you looked at all the advertising in the Street Fighter comic book? It was all *Mortal Kombat*. I still have it somewhere here, somewhere buried. I have a framed [Street Fighter] comic book with a letter from Rob Holmes saying, 'Serves you right. I took all the advertising out in your comic book with *Mortal Kombat*.'

THE WESTERN CONSOLE BOX ART

For Street Fighter II's console releases, Capcom USA's marketing department followed the trend of the time by creating their own box art rather than using the art done in Japan – so instead of getting Capcom Japan illustrator Akira Yasuda's *Street Fighter II* key art, for instance, Western fans got art from US-based illustrator Mick McGinty. The results led to strong opinions on both sides.

→ JOE MORICI
   Street Fighter II series senior vice-president, Capcom USA

[It was always difficult] to get assets [from Japan] to be able to market [games] properly. We did a lot of our own artwork here, because at a certain point the Japanese had enough trust in me specifically to let me do what I thought was appropriate for artwork and for graphics and things like that. So we just went ahead and did our own thing over here, and a lot of times Japan adopted our style.

→ JOHN GILLIN
   Street Fighter II series director of marketing, Capcom USA

When I arrived, here I am coming into a new industry, and there had already been some relationships that had been built between Capcom and its vendors and all that. And I was introduced to this really easygoing, laid-back guy named Denny [Moore], who had been doing work on other packaging for them – things like Mega Man, stuff like that. [...] When he [saw] Street Fighter, he had a couple of artists that he worked with that he really felt could capture the spirit of the franchise. So he went and talked to the artist who in fact did know about Street Fighter, played himself. And I remember whenever he would come back with the pencil sketches of what they were thinking about, I would say, 'God that looks great.' I mean, I loved their work. I thought they did such a great job.

→   CHRIS TANG
          Street Fighter II series tournament player

I just remember my first reaction to it was – you know, I was used to being disgusted seeing US versions of games. [...] I just had a really low opinion of all of the US box art at the time. And, yeah. *Street Fighter II* was just par for the course.

→   MICK MCGINTY
          Street Fighter II series package illustrator, US and EU versions

Well, it was totally by chance. I was freelancing starting around 1983 ... and one of my first and best clients was a guy named Denny Moore.

> [The first Super NES cover] was a real simple project where Denny said, 'Hey I've got this game.' And at this time, I mean, I don't think Denny knew how big of an impact Street Fighter was gonna have. He just said, 'Hey I've got this company, Capcom ... and they've got this game called Street Fighter. Here's some screen grabs.' And all I got from Denny and from the company was someone took Polaroids of some screens.

I wasn't a real realistic painter, but I could do this exaggerated realism. I could kind of give an American slant to the characters and the things they were trying to accomplish with that game. Because I think the first thing they realized was that they weren't going to be able to sell these games very well if they had the original Japanese art – which at the time, I didn't like. Anything I saw, it was just too foreign to me at the time. But now, 20 or 30 years later, I really love their work. It's just nice, edgy, colourful, action-filled – it's just cool stuff. And I think the American buying public, they don't have a problem with it now.

→   AKIRA YASUDA
    Street Fighter II package illustrator, Japanese version

When we were making *Final Fight*, I was told that my art wouldn't
be well received in America, so around that point I gave up trying
to get my art released in the US. I remember [Capcom Japan
department head Yoshiki] Okamoto complaining about the fact
that they wouldn't use my art in the overseas versions, but nothing
really changed.

→   JOHN GILLIN
    Street Fighter II series director of marketing, Capcom USA

[There] was a very long and ongoing debate about positioning
and product. There's a lot to be said obviously with the Japanese
heritage to the games and the fact that they were created in Japan.
And my personal feeling is that there is a dedicated die-hard group
of gamers who appreciate that heritage and certainly like to see that
reflected in any marketing materials that they see or are directed
towards them, and I appreciate that. But at the same time, the cold
reality of business is that we have to sell as many units as we can,
and therefore we want to make the product appeal to as wide an
audience as possible. And I think by really making it look more
Japanese in its look and feel, we might have alienated some of our
more mainstream American consumers.

> We really didn't have time to do a lot of exploratory
> packaging alternatives. And so we ran to market. We got
> that in. And then, you know, once you get that then you've
> got kind of a look and feel, and you want to try to reinforce
> that look and feel. [...] So I was happy with the artwork.
> That did well. I know that we did take some flack – you
> know, this was long before Twitter and Facebook and these
> kinds of forums where people could voice their opinions.
> But we thought we did a really good job with it, given what
> our challenges were.

JAMES GODDARD
Street Fighter II series design support, Capcom USA

Not one of my best shining moments, but I remember walking into Joe Morici's office. [...] I came in, and remember I'm a young guy but shit, I'm doing well at Capcom and heavily involved in the Street Fighter community and the success of things like *Hyper Fighting*. So I go in, and the *Hyper Fighting* [Super NES box] art was the last straw for me. I came in and I said, 'Joe, is there any way we can consider using some of the Japanese art because it's just more popular with the players and these guys don't even look like the characters?' You know, I had to have this nice conversation with him because he was a bigwig and I was still young. And eventually he gave me the whole, 'This is what we're doing', right? 'This is what we're doing and there's a reason why.' Marketing really believed that they were right.

> That said, you know, the art was horrible. It didn't look like the characters, and there was really no reason not to use the Japanese artwork. It wouldn't have made a difference either way, really, on the sales. You know, the game was popular. It would have just been better fan service to use more appropriate artwork. [...] As I've grown up, I've always felt bad about [it] – I could have handled that better. But it's one of those things where, at the same time, I was passionate about it. I actually told him, 'This art looks terrible.' He stopped talking to me after that.

JOE MORICI
Street Fighter II series senior vice-president, Capcom USA

He had a lot to say to me, but a lot of the stuff I didn't agree with so I just didn't go forward with it. [...] I was the head of the department at the time and running sales and marketing and I chose to go with what I thought was a better route.

[Ed. note]   In the years since *Street Fighter II*'s release, Yasuda's key art has taken on something of an iconic status, establishing a style copied by other fighting game developers and frequently being used as inspiration for Street Fighter-related projects – in Japan and the US.

→   SCOTT SMITH
      Street Fighter II series marketing manager, Capcom USA

It's easy to look back on these things with hindsight. You know, anime did not have anywhere near the acceptance [it's earned as time has gone on]. So we were always creating box art – whether it was Mega Man or Street Fighter – we were always creating art that would sell the game in the US.

CONSOLE SUCCESS

Despite challenges posed by console manufacturers, competitors like *Mortal Kombat* and packaging debates, Capcom's initial run of *Street Fighter II* home ports proved phenomenally successful.

According to worldwide Capcom investor relations data, the Super NES port of *Street Fighter II* sold 6.3 million copies, the Super NES port of *Street Fighter II Turbo* sold 4.1 million and the Genesis port, *Street Fighter II: Special Champion Edition*, sold 1.65 million. While those numbers have since been eclipsed by games in the Resident Evil and Monster Hunter series, when the Super NES version of *Street Fighter II* hit, it was far and away the most successful console game Capcom had released.

→   JOE MORICI
         Street Fighter II series senior vice-president, Capcom USA

[It was] definitely hundreds of millions of dollars we were doing. We were doing two or three hundred million dollars in sales, something like that.

→   PAUL WIEDERAENDERS
         SFII series coin-op Midwest regional sales manager, Capcom USA

It became a cult type of a game. It did well in the arcades, and then the home sales just skyrocketed.

→   SEIJI OKADA
         Street Fighter II series programmer, Capcom Japan

I mean, I wasn't particularly proud of [the original Super NES port]. But it was heartwarming to know that something I made sold that well.

→   JOHN GILLIN
       Street Fighter II series director of marketing, Capcom USA

It's funny, nowadays it's nothing – you look at what *Grand Theft Auto V* [sold 20-plus years later] and that's a drop in the pan – but back then it [...] really helped revolutionize the industry.

→   SCOTT SMITH
       Street Fighter II series marketing manager, Capcom USA

[For the first game] we didn't do any print advertising at all. We didn't need to because we were on the cover of every magazine.

→   LAURIE THORNTON
       Street Fighter II series public relations manager, Capcom USA

Street Fighter II was one of the biggest drivers of console sales. Capcom was the tail wagging the dog.

→   SCOTT SMITH
       Street Fighter II series marketing manager, Capcom USA

Remember those ads where they'd throw the television – you know, 'On Sunday, hey, pick up this TV for $500 at Best Buy' or whatnot, and they would plaster a screenshot on there of a TV show so it's not a blank screen? We had them put Street Fighter on there. It would appear in the weirdest places. [...] And then it took off from there, and then it just never ended, because suddenly people wanted to do licensing. You know, 'Oh, we want to do a cartoon series.' 'Oh, people want to license the characters, and we don't have a licensing division. How do we do this?'

→   LAURIE THORNTON
       Street Fighter II series public relations manager, Capcom USA

Our president in Japan, a very wealthy man, had a penchant for car racing, so on a personal whim in 1992, he sponsored a driver from Japan who made it to the Indy 500 time trials with a tricked-out Capcom *Street Fighter II* car. I was assigned to this 'special project', handling the PR and promo support, while trying to tie Indy car racing to fighting games, with little opportunity to conduct interviews since neither our president nor the driver spoke English.

Even though our involvement was not the brand brainchild of our head of marketing, the car and our presence garnered some tremendous buzz. Fortunately, this happened without our having to discuss the backstory on how and why we participated, which was anything but strategic. However, it was an early signal of a game property beginning to cross over into very broad consumer consciousness as millions of Indy viewers connected the dots and knew that Street Fighter was a videogame with presence at a marquee sporting event.

CHAPTER 07

EBB AND FLOW

With *Street Fighter II* out on consoles, Capcom was on top of the world. *Champion Edition* and *Hyper Fighting* were still earning well in arcades, and Capcom was pulling in record-breaking numbers in almost every division – from sales to licensing to operations. Still, that success brought certain challenges in its wake.

CONTENT CONTROVERSY

As one side-effect of the series being popular, millions of fans took time to study it and analyse what they were seeing. As with the discovery (and popularity) of glitches in the original arcade *SFII* release, more eyeballs meant more criticism, and sometimes players – and their parents and reporters – came across scenes they deemed inappropriate.

→   LAURIE THORNTON
     Street Fighter II series public relations manager, Capcom USA

Late one Friday, I got a voicemail message from a TV station in some obscure small town I'd never even heard of at the time. The reporter wanted to know if I could confirm or deny the following: a Street Fighter fan had claimed that in a nanosecond frame of gameplay, popular sumo wrestler E. Honda's mawashi [loincloth] flew open, thus 'exposing him', if only briefly. As proof, she also mentioned that the consumer had a videotape of the footage in question. Among her other questions: did Capcom condone the integration of illicit content in its games?

I'd have dismissed this immediately except, like a bad urban myth, I'd heard that for their own amusement, developers in Japan had actually done similar things in other games – snuck in 'questionable content' as their own inside joke. *Could my developers have done such a thing and gotten away with it? Could I confirm or deny this?* At first, I wasn't so sure. I asked the reporter to get the videotape to me for our own review, which ended up never materializing, and immediately asked my testing team and some of my marketing pals to help me investigate further over that weekend. We never found any evidence of an E. Honda flashing, but those who helped me 'research' it were never 100 percent positive either.

→   JUSTIN BERENBAUM
    Street Fighter II series customer service manager, Capcom USA

Every once in a while, we'd get a crazy call about somebody complaining about something. I remember one vividly because I ended up getting a call from the archdiocese of ... I forget what city. So one of the reps gets a call and he's talking to this person for a couple of minutes and he looks over – because most of us were in the same gigantic office – and he shakes his head. He just mouths 'help'. He just didn't know what to do. So I told him to put the person on hold. I always talked to my reps first to get the story from them, because I'd never believe what customers had to say initially, because they would make stuff up.

> He gave me [an explanation]: 'I've got somebody who claims to be from the archdiocese and somebody's mom complaining about something in a Street Fighter game. Can you help me out?' So I took the call and it seemed legit. It was some bishop from the archdiocese – I wish I remembered what town it was, or what city – on the phone with a mother who was pretty upset and irate that evidently her son had slow-motion video recorded himself playing one of the Street Fighter games, and evidently, when Chun-Li did one of her flips [...] an artist missed a pixel or two and so it made it look like Chun-Li was naked and didn't have any underwear on. And so the mom was irate. The [bishop] was threatening to talk to the congresspeople and all this stuff.

I literally kept them on the phone while we got a build of the game, and I had one of the other guys drop all the calls and start playing through it, and then I actually gave them my direct line number. I'm like, 'Look, we need to investigate this. I'm not going to comment until I know, but I can't imagine us doing anything like that on purpose,' blah, blah, blah. But of course, they were not happy about it. I'm like, 'Let me do this. Can I please go try to find this?' And I called them back an hour later. [...] You know, we played it.

We recorded it. We did it in slow motion. And it was one of those things we were actually able to replicate, but it really was somebody just missed colouring in a sprite or two.

> The funniest thing is then we had this conversation internally about, 'Why is this kid purposely recording and slow-motioning Chun-Li flipping upside down?' So we were thinking that, but we had to get back – I had to get back [to them] and actually had to write out kind of what I was going to say. I had to involve PR because we didn't want it to just turn into a disaster. And I had to explain it all, but imagine explaining to some 60- or 70-year-old bishop and an irate mom how games are made and how pixels are done and how it's done in Japan and all of that, and explaining how you see during 99.8 percent of this move, she actually is covered up where you can't see anything.

So it took a while, and I ended up having to [smooth things over. But then] how do I say this? They weren't happy, but then I think the mother started getting really pissed off at little Johnny. Because she started realizing that, OK, this may or may not be true, but the fact that her son was doing this kind of thing meant like ... what else is he doing?

> It was just one of those really funny stories that you [mostly] forget about when you run customer support because you get so many crazy calls, but that's one of those ones that, even 20 some years later, just sticks with me and I still tell people about.

[Ed. note]   Some of the criticism directed at the game came from scenes that more clearly depicted what customers were complaining about.

→   JOHN GILLIN
     Street Fighter II series director of marketing, Capcom USA

I got a letter from a father who was very, very upset with the game. And it turns out that one of those cutscenes at the beginning depicts two guys that are fighting. They're fist fighting; they're facing off against each other. There's a white guy and a black guy. They're the two that are fighting. And you look at the crowd surrounding them – the crowd is all cheering and, you know, the bloodlust is running thick. And you realize that the entire crowd surrounding these two is white. So you have all these white people, and there's this white guy facing off against this sole black guy and the white guy takes a swing and catches the black guy right on the chin, and the black guy goes down and everybody's cheering.

> And the letter I received was from an African American gentleman who was distressed at the racial overtones of that. And it was funny, because I had never really noticed that, but upon looking at it, it was like, 'Wow.' And the Japanese culture is a little bit different than ours as far as our history and all that, and the sensitivity to those kinds of issues. And so I immediately wrote him back and told him I was very sorry about that, that that was something I would raise with our headquarters. And I did. And you know, by that point in time, the game had already been out in the market for a while and there was no way to change it. [...] Whether it was intentional or not, I don't know. But it was interesting.

→   SCOTT SMITH
     Street Fighter II series marketing manager, Capcom USA

There were a number of little changes on the Super NES side that we had to go through [prior to the game's release], where you had frames of animation that were taken out [like with] the guy in the background [of Blanka's stage] that Nintendo thought was masturbating. ... There's a guy kind of cheering and moving his arm up and down, and it was a little jerky, you know? You have to remember how squeaky-clean Nintendo was in those days. [...] I'm sure Japan kind of rolled their eyes at that one, but they did what they had to do to clip some of these frames out.

→   JUSTIN BERENBAUM
           Street Fighter II series customer service manager, Capcom USA

We actually got in trouble on something [around the same time on Capcom's role-playing game] *Breath of Fire 2*. There was a scene when you were a female character when you went in to talk to this priest and he has you kneel before him and bow your head. It really looks like the character's giving him a blowjob, to the point where you're pretty sure the person intended it. Although it was plausible deniability.

→   NORITAKA FUNAMIZU
           Street Fighter II series producer, Capcom Japan

Anything in the backgrounds of games that was inappropriate probably came down to the fact that the company didn't check those things carefully back then, I think. Our scheduling back then made it very difficult to perform proper checks as well. Back in the day, in order to create the mask ROMs for games so they could be mass produced, you needed to submit the data as early as a year in advance, given the way the schedules worked back then. There were many times when we checked the data after we'd already released the game.

→   SCOTT SMITH
           Street Fighter II series marketing manager, Capcom USA

It wasn't too long after Street Fighter and Mortal Kombat and this growth of the fighting game genre that the [Entertainment Software Rating Board] came into being. Obviously it stems more from Mortal Kombat – my guess – than Street Fighter. But because Street Fighter was the first and it was head-to-head fighting and people

[were] punching and children [were playing], the pressure and the controversy [...] started to rear its head.

[Ed. note]   The ESRB formed in 1994 to create standardized ratings for games, such as 'M for Mature', following a US Senate hearing calling out titles like *Mortal Kombat* by name.

CAPCOM USA VS DATA EAST CORP.

In addition to concerns over content, Capcom ran into challenges with competitors encroaching on their territory with similar-looking fighting games. To a degree, Capcom couldn't control the situation, as clones were an established part of the business. Yet in one case, they decided to take action.

> At the same time Capcom was gearing up to release *Street Fighter II: Special Champion Edition* on Genesis, they were also putting together a lawsuit to take on one of their competitors. As games like *Fatal Fury* and *Mortal Kombat* had taken off, the industry had flooded the market with Street Fighter clones, most of which borrowed heavily from Capcom's playbook. With *Fighter's History* from Data East, though, some at Capcom claimed it hit too close to home.

In September 1993, Capcom filed suit alleging copyright infringement.

→ IAN ROSE
General counsel, Capcom USA

There were a number of games in the marketplace that were arguably copycat versions of *Street Fighter II*. And of course, I don't think *Street Fighter II* could have claimed to have completely originated the fighting game per se, but there were a couple of games, and *Fighter's History* was one of them, that had a lot of very close copying of the joystick movements that translated into character movements and so on. So I think the chairman, [Kenzo] Tsujimoto, was the one who ultimately decided that the company needed to go after somebody to kind of make an example and deter further copying.

→   CHRIS TANG
Game designer, Atari Games

People were afraid of getting sued by Capcom if you tried to make a fighting game especially. But, I mean, that one was more egregious. It was a lot closer than anything that I had worked on or had seen other companies do.

→   ALEX JIMENEZ
Street Fighter II series design support, Capcom USA

We were called to write expert testimony on it. We did our research for it and we were told to do a running comparison between the two games. [...] We looked at the games and said, 'Yeah, if imitation is the sincerest form of flattery, they are flattering us to death here.'

→   CHRIS TANG
Game designer, Atari Games

It was actually a competent rip-off. It was way better than the stuff that I was working on at Atari at the time. And I thought it had really funny voices. 'Piss, piss, piss off.'

→   JAMES GODDARD
Street Fighter II series design support, Capcom USA

I looked at it – we had the board. Played it. Dave and I sat down and we just really looked into it, really looked at the comparisons, and my opinion was that sure, they ripped off a bunch of stuff. But 'rip-off' is a strong word there. It's what a lot of people do.
     It was inspired by [Street Fighter] and knocked some stuff off from it. I mean, the fact that the same command inputs did similar-looking moves was the only thing, right? [...] Was the idea of a fireball patentable? The motion? A charge for a Sonic Boom? Or is this now just technique, like ducking or jumping? Can you really patent any of that stuff? And so I didn't like where it was going. I gave my opinion. It was like, 'This game is not going to steal money from us. *Mortal Kombat*

is a thing, you know? This game is not going to hurt us. I don't see what the big deal is. It's a cool game, but it's not a Street Fighter killer. Let's just keep making better [games]' – I mean, we were already making better shit – 'and continuing to make money.' [...] So I didn't really want anything to do with the trial. I made that clear.

I didn't want anything to do with it because I didn't fundamentally agree. So being the good boss that I was, I assigned Dave Winstead to it, which we joke about to this day. So he went in and tried to document everything, and he didn't agree either, but he documented everything. [...] He even got stuck testifying. What a nightmare.

→   DAVE WINSTEAD
       Street Fighter II series design support, Capcom USA

Nowadays, there are so many more Street Fighter-like games and no one would care. [...] But back then, they got really mad. Japan got really mad and they wanted us [to help with the case]. We didn't care. I'll be honest. In the US, we were like, 'Whatever. *Fighter's History*? Who's going to play that?'

→   JAMES GODDARD
       Street Fighter II series design support, Capcom USA

Data East sounded to me like more of a political thing, and I have to imagine that there was some kind of rivalry that was deep-rooted and long in Japan between people, and that was probably the main motivator. [...] When we wrote our recommendation that there wasn't anything there, they [still] wanted to pursue it. So it is what it is.

→   DAVE WINSTEAD
       Street Fighter II series design support, Capcom USA

It was an interesting experience [...] I had to sit there, cross-referencing their combos versus our combos, showing [the court] exactly what it looked like. We also had video that was shown above the bench there, and it was really weird. It was a really weird day.

→   SHINICHI UEYAMA
        Street Fighter II series lead programmer, Capcom Japan

Originally, I got a request from Capcom's legal department to analyse the similarities between the two games' coding.

→   NORITAKA FUNAMIZU
        Street Fighter II series producer, Capcom Japan

But [Ueyama] was so busy, I didn't really want him to do that. So I said, 'just don't do it', right?

→   SHINICHI UEYAMA
        Street Fighter II series lead programmer, Capcom Japa

But then, of my own volition, I ended up doing it anyway. [*laughs*] [...] I apologize that this is a little technical, but I did look at the code, and the hardware was completely different, so if you compared the specific programming it was entirely different – however, if you only looked at the algorithms and the flow of the programming, it looked extremely similar. [...] I was expecting Capcom to win if they analysed the code closely.

→   IAN ROSE
        General counsel, Capcom USA

This was during a legal era when there were a number of copyright so-called 'look and feel' cases. [...] And this was kind of a defining era in terms of what the courts were going to uphold as copyright infringement.

→   CLAUDE STERN
        Trial counsel representing Data East

The videogame industry was actually very, very young, and one of the questions was what represents protectable expression when you have a young industry.

If you look at *Fighter's History* compared to Street Fighter, there are certain obvious similarities. There's a colourful background and the fight takes place in a centre circle, the fighters square off, they're in an arcade game. [...] And so one of the questions was, 'Well gosh, is that really all unique to Capcom? Is that really something that they had created, and that they had all the copyrights to?'

The problem was that in a developing industry – we see this now today – if you start giving that sort of protection to the first entrant into a market, that entrant has got the opportunity to become a monopolist. [...] We very much saw the case as a case that ultimately put front and centre the question of could a person own a genre? [...] Could somebody come up with a new idea, a new way of doing something, and then ace everyone out from being able to compete in that field without coming up with a completely different look?

→   IAN ROSE
            General counsel, Capcom USA

There wasn't anything like it. There wasn't any other big lawsuit like that that Capcom filed during that period on that kind of basis.

→   CLAUDE STERN
            Trial counsel representing Data East

I think [Data East was] very nervous. There was some terrible evidence. I mean, the fact of the matter is the Data East artists were copying Street Fighter. The ultimate work wasn't a slavish copy – a pixel-by-pixel copy – but they had evidence that we were copying things. And our response was, well, what we were copying wasn't protectable. So for example, we might make a copy of one of their images, but then we'd change the image, change the background, change the fighter's stance, change the type of kick. But even then, there was a lot of similarity in the kicks and the moves. But of course our response was, 'Well wait a minute. Those are conventional moves within the martial arts field. You can't own that.'
Capcom was taking a position ... saying, 'Well look, the look and feel of Street Fighter and *Fighter's History*

are virtually identical, so therefore there should be infringement.' Our position was, 'Well no, actually … Capcom, look, two fighters, they're in a ring. That's a convention. [...] We need to be able to look at the work not as a unique artistic work, but rather as an embodiment of a variety of conventions that had been adopted over time.' Ultimately, that's what the court found. If you look at these works and you remove the conventional features, there's not a hell of a lot left.

→   IAN ROSE
               General counsel, Capcom USA

One of the big reasons that Capcom didn't get more traction was the courts had already given weak protection to these kinds of cases, or almost no protection [in other industries]. [...] The case settled, mostly because we weren't getting the traction we wanted with the courts, and we walked away.

→   JAMES GODDARD
               Street Fighter II series design support, Capcom USA

It's just as well they didn't win because look at all the wonderful stuff that's come since then. If they had won that precedent, would we be where we are with fighting games right now? I don't know.

CHAPTER 08

SUPER
STREET
FIGHTER II

Super Street Fighter II wasn't supposed to be the fourth Street Fighter II game.

After finishing *Champion Edition* in early 1992, Capcom started putting together plans for a follow-up. It would feature new characters. It would be the first game on the company's new CPS-2 arcade hardware. It would be Noritaka Funamizu's chance to lead a Street Fighter game, as Akira Nishitani moved on to other things.

When Capcom scrambled to develop *Hyper Fighting* in late 1992, though, it threw plans off schedule.

Capcom kept developing *Super Street Fighter II*, but ended up releasing it nine months after *Hyper Fighting*. And suddenly, their big follow-up was no longer the third Street Fighter II game, but the fourth – and it arrived to a different set of expectations.

It also didn't help that – from the outset – *Super SFII* was handicapped by Capcom's need to use up a surplus of ROM chips featuring old visual and audio data, limiting how far the development team could push new entries in the series forward.

'I don't want to say too much, but it was a miscalculation on the part of the sales team,' says Funamizu, noting that this was an ongoing problem following *Street Fighter II*'s early success. 'They saw how many boards we were selling and from that they overestimated how many ROM chips to order, resulting in a big excess stock. That's how *Super Street Fighter II* started, with them asking us to do something about this. [Capcom Japan department head Yoshiki] Okamoto got really angry, too, because if they continued to make their stock orders in this way, it would mean we'd never break free of this cycle, because with every new game we made they'd just order more.'

From the speed to the competition to the desire from players for something new, a lot can change in nine months.

A SLOWER GAME

Hitting arcades in late 1993, *Super Street Fighter II* released with some big additions. It was the first game since the original *Street Fighter II* to add new fighters, and the first to take a notable visual step forward. For many players, though, what stood out most was the speed. After spending nine months adjusting to the faster pace of *Hyper Fighting*, they found it hard to go back to something slow.

→   JAMES GODDARD
      Super Street Fighter II design support, Capcom USA

As *Super* [started development], it was great. They were making four new characters. [They were originally going to have two versions of Fei Long, and I suggested swapping one for a new character and pitched Dee Jay] based on Billy Blanks from [martial arts movie] *King of the Kickboxers*. And we were looking at balance stuff and it was kind of secret. Mostly, they wanted to work out the characters first … and then *Hyper Fighting* happened in the middle of that.

So we end up doing all this *Hyper Fighting* stuff, and development [on *Super Street Fighter II*] is still going on in the background. And at that point, because *Hyper Fighting* had changed the landscape during development of *Super Street Fighter,* of course the assumption would be we'd pull some of that over and build upon it.

I remember flying out there. In fact, it was Dave Winstead's first trip to Japan with me. We go sit down and look at *Super Street Fighter* and see all the stuff that we've been talking about for a long time. And *Super Street Fighter* was a bit of a nightmare, because there were so many things that happened on that game. One is they made it slow. I'm told, just before I sit down, 'Hey, you're going to be a bit shocked at this, so don't complain because there's a lot of changes that you are not going to be happy with.'

That's how it started. So we sit down and look at it. Of course, I'm excited to see all the characters. It's slow, and Dee Jay played more like Guile [than I had pitched him]. That was not really the idea at the time, but it made sense why it went that way. But *Super Street Fighter* just had a lot of problems, and it really didn't play right. It didn't play right because it was slow. It didn't play right because it was missing the spark that *Hyper* had caused, and so it wasn't acknowledging what was happening in the market on several levels.

→   DAVE WINSTEAD
        Super Street Fighter II design support, Capcom USA

Funamizu, who was the head of the project for *Super Street Fighter*, really liked it slower. I think he was more with the Japanese side that liked it slower, and [our Capcom Japan liaison Tom Shiraiwa] kept saying, 'It had to be that way; it had to be that way.' That's all he kept saying on the phone. And I think that that was him saying Funamizu was calling the shots. He had like, Nishitani clout, right? And Funamizu had done some cool games in the past, and went on to do some good games later, so I have nothing against Funamizu whatsoever. But at that time, I was a little angry. But at the same time, they'd look at us like, *Oh, here come some Americans. The game is made in Japan. These guys, what do they know?*

Funamizu actually told us that we ruined Street Fighter with *Hyper Fighting*, [saying] the fast speed made it unfair for people that didn't have better reflexes and all that kind of stuff. So they wanted to move it back down, and I kind of see their point. I see their point. [But] back then, I was furious. Like, 'What are you talking about? We've got to go faster and faster.' So they just basically told us that that's just the way it's going to be. 'It's going to be slow. Sorry, it has to be that way.'

There were other things, too, with *Super Street Fighter*, like they removed combos that worked in *Hyper Fighting*. I remember when we sat there, James was trying to do [one of Blanka's combos]. He was like, 'I can't seem to do that combo.' [...] He kept trying it over and over again. He's like, 'What the hell?' That was when James was starting to get tendonitis so it was hurting him to keep trying to do this move. I felt really bad and we were majorly jet-lagged, too, because we flew in and we went right to the office that evening and that's when we were hit with all this stuff, so there was a lot of friction, especially between James and Funamizu. I was usually the guy that just listened to them argue.

→   NORITAKA FUNAMIZU
        Super Street Fighter II planner, Capcom Japan

I wouldn't say something [like they 'ruined Street Fighter']. I mean, I felt like I had a good relationship with James back in the day and of all the people at Capcom I probably was the one who paid the most attention to what his opinions were.

> Back then, I think the company didn't do a great job of soliciting direct user feedback. Instead we relied too much on the higher-ups at Capcom, which is to say the sales team ... they had very strong opinions, but their information wasn't very accurate. They said they'd heard *Hyper Fighting* didn't do well because it was too fast. In reality, of course, players felt the exact opposite, that the speed was great. There were people like James who were saying the Americans liked it faster. But I guess that feedback was having a hard time reaching Capcom. Later, James was like, 'See, I told you!' I agreed then, and still do today. But the decision to make it slower, that was made by the company, not the development team, based on some bad information from the sales team.

→ JAMES CHEN
Street Fighter series commentator

Unfortunately for *Super Street Fighter II*, when that game came out, we had just played *Hyper Fighting*, and *Hyper Fighting* was so good. It was balanced and it was fast and it was just really cool. When *Super* came out, it was so slow. They went back to the original speed [...] it was super disappointing to go back that slow.

→ SETH KILLIAN
Street Fighter IV special combat advisor, Capcom USA

The slow speed of *SSFII* was definitely weird. After three installments of SFII, players expected changes to the characters, but overall the slow speed felt like a step backwards, and an appeal to an audience that didn't exist. Slower gameplay also had a big impact on the competitive side, where more reactive and space-controlling characters like Dhalsim and Guile became much stronger. The slow speed made it a lot harder to get in someone's face and rush them down, which had always been a big thrill in *Hyper Fighting*.

THE TOURNAMENT BATTLE

When Capcom introduced *Super Street Fighter II*, another element that caught people off-guard was a four-cabinet, eight-player 'Tournament Battle' version of the game, where players could hop on and play in small tournaments at any time, rather than waiting for Capcom or local arcades to set something up.

→   JAMES GODDARD
       Super Street Fighter II design support, Capcom USA

Here's where it gets really weird. [During the same trip to Japan], they show us into a room. They're like, 'Hey, look at this amazing thing we're doing. Since you love tournaments and you're promoting it, let's show you *Super Street Fighter: Tournament Edition*. This is what we're going to do.' And they lay out the whole thing with the four linked arcade cabinets, and it's like, 'Oh, this is amazing.'

'OK, it's single elimination. All right, that's fine.' And we're working through it and it sounds great. It's like, 'Awesome. OK, well, really big locations will probably be able to do this.'

And this is where it gets crazier. They're like, 'No. This is the only thing we're going to sell.' And I'm like, 'What do you mean? 7-Elevens can't fit this.' Eighty percent of our business was single-unit locations. 7-Eleven, you know? Lots of small arcades. Mom-and-pop arcades would not be able to have four.

'They already have four machines at a lot of these locations and this will unify them.'

'No, this is a problem.'

It's like, a $20,000 machine. You put in 50 cents. You play against eight people, or whoever – the empty chairs have AI. And only the winner stays and all the losers pay. So for a mathematical formula for making money, it looks great.

It's just not going to work for most locations. And frankly, as a novelty, sure. But this was the only way *Super Street Fighter* was going to be [set up] anywhere. There was no more you and I sit down and you and I just play. That was going to be gone.

So before I go into that meeting, I'm told, 'If you complain, you will be fired.' And Shiraiwa was saying, 'Please. Please, James-san. Please don't be pushy, like Honda, this time. Just, please. Just listen to what they have to say and just please.'

Get to the end of it and I looked at Okamoto and I go – because I'm already really concerned about the way the game is playing – 'Now we have a serious business infrastructure problem. Most of our locations aren't going to be able to get it, and again, we're not giving the players what they want, which is to be able to battle head-to-head. Winner stays, loser pays. We've taken that away from them.' I'm like, 'OK, well I guess it's time for you guys to fire me. I'm going to say what I have to say for the sake of the players and I'll understand if that's the end of my career, but here we go.' And I just laid it out for them why it was a business problem and also what I didn't like about how it was slow and that they took out changes that the players liked and that it was political.

Magically, I still had a job when I got back, and then I wrote up my manifesto on everything that needed to happen with Street Fighter and I decided it was time – over a couple of months of being shut out, I decided I was going to move on with my career. And so I packed up my ball and left.

It was really heartbreaking, because I walked away from multiple games in development. So *Super Street Fighter,* I like to call it the death of Street Fighter at the time. This was the first mortal wound to it. And it wasn't even Mortal Kombat that did it to us. We did it to ourselves. And everybody was in such denial about it.

[Eventually] the business did fix it so we didn't have to take the big tournament units. We had to sell a certain number of them, but [we] had to commit to 20,000 fully dedicated *Super Street Fighter II* cabinets. And as I'm exiting, I'm like, 'This game is not going to be the game you think it's going to be.' And I remember [Capcom USA president] George Nakayama telling me as I was leaving, 'I don't know why you're so down on it. It's going to be great.' And then it was just a disaster. Units sat in warehouses and players were like, 'What happened? Why is it slow?' They couldn't play. And I mean, *Super Street Fighter* is pretty famous for being a cool game but a black eye all at the same time because it just didn't do what the players wanted.

→   DAVE WINSTEAD
        Super Street Fighter II design support, Capcom USA

[Capcom Japan] really wanted to push the game as this big tournament scene with four cabinets, right? That was their big thing. Now, they didn't let us in on any of this stuff [early on]. We were just helping them. They were sending us video cassettes and stuff, showing us the newest stuff, and they would send us a board every now and then so we could kind of check it out and then we'd give them feedback.

> And then we flew over there and the first morning, they bring James and I into a room and we sit down and they're like, 'Hey, this is the deal. We're really excited to share this with you. The game is going to be connected – four cabinets, and they're all going to be linked up, and it's going to be round robin, and it's not best two out of three.'

And we're like, 'Wait, wait. There's going be a setting so you can set that, right?'

> 'No, no, no. It's going to be, you lose one round and you have to move to the next.'

We're like, 'That's not the way that tournaments work, at least not in the US.'

So right away, we had some problems, right? We're like, 'Players are not going to like playing against somebody they've never played against before.' And then, the damage in the game – it was pretty heavy. So a good combo will wipe you out, right? And then you didn't learn anything from that for your next round, because now you have to move on to the next person, and so that was kind of a problem. So we weren't super happy at that time. We're like, 'Wait, wait. If we're going to do the tournament thing, man, we've got to do it right.'

[Ed. note]   On the Japan side, Funamizu says the team pushed the Tournament Battle feature, in part, as a way to clear out their ROM chip supply.

→   NORITAKA FUNAMIZU
Super Street Fighter II planner, Capcom Japan

So we released *Hyper Fighting*, right? And one of our goals was to get rid of the excess stock we had. But somehow after *Hyper Fighting*, we once again ended up with more overstock. We wanted to release *Super Street Fighter II* with these new characters and that would be that, but we couldn't just release it as-is anymore; now we had to find a way to deal with this excess inventory. So one idea we came up with was a tournament mode.

→   TAKESHI TEZUKA
X-Men: Children of the Atom planner, Capcom Japan

I was the one who originally suggested the tournament mode. Unlike other companies' games, we didn't have a network or link mode for our games, and that was something we got a lot of requests for. Technically it wasn't possible, and so I remember joking one day, 'Maybe we should just have all the players switch seats.' They ended up using the idea. I remember one of the programmers was like, 'Stop coming up with all these weird ideas that I have to program!'

→ NORITAKA FUNAMIZU
   Super Street Fighter II planner, Capcom Japan

Around that time, Nishitani was saying he wanted to leave Capcom temporarily and take a trip around America. That was right after *Champion Edition*. Then he came back. Then Nishitani, Tezuka, and I were asked by Okamoto to do some research on the potential inclusion of a tournament mode, and we were asked to do simulated models of how to bring in revenue – looking at how many minutes and seconds players played per credit, how long we should let players play in order to maximize income – and the idea was that we'd use this data to craft a tournament mode.

→ DAVE WINSTEAD
   Super Street Fighter II design support, Capcom USA

When it first shipped, [Capcom's sales division was] going to force people to buy the tournament thing. The good news is they changed their mind after they put it on test for a while and it didn't do super well, and then all the sudden, it was like, 'Yeah, you can do what you want.' Because the first thing Sunnyvale Golfland did when they had their machine – because they bought it early to make sure they had it – I can't remember exactly how long it was, but it was probably a couple of weeks before they separated the machines.

→ NORITAKA FUNAMIZU
   Super Street Fighter II planner, Capcom Japan

The thing was, even though they were sold as a set of four, you could also use the cabinets individually for normal matches. What happened, then, was that as soon as we sold the sets, arcades split them up.

→   TAKESHI TEZUKA
X-Men: Children of the Atom planner, Capcom Japan

There were people complaining about changing seats after each round. They said it was annoying. For Capcom, they were happy that they were able to sell four arcade cabinets. [...] I heard that tournament mode wasn't really used very often. [Four arcade cabinets] obviously take up a lot of space, so there were times when they had to loan them out to other arcade centres.

→   DAVE WINSTEAD
Super Street Fighter II design support, Capcom USA

I only counted, I think, five [Tournament Battle setups in the San Francisco Bay Area].

→   JAMES CHEN
Street Fighter series commentator

I have never seen it in person. [...] I think the biggest problem, really, was just that *Super* was not popular.

→   STEPHEN FROST
Street Fighter 30th Anniversary Collection producer, Digital Eclipse

They actually had it set up in Oregon in a mall, Gateway Mall. I don't think they had it there for very long because I don't remember many people playing it. [...] The whole idea of playing one tournament and then it ending, I think, soured people a little bit. [...] Arcades were expensive. 75 cents, a dollar, and you could last longer in a normal game of *Super Street Fighter*.

→   DAVE WINSTEAD
Super Street Fighter II design support, Capcom USA

I think a lot of operators were like, 'Man, that's expensive. I've got to buy four of those?' And then when they don't earn, they're like, 'Man, that sucks.' In the US, they'd just break them up. I guess in Japan, they would [do the] same thing. Just use those Capcom

Impress cabinets or whatever, and just slide them around. [...] You could always kind of tell which ones were broken up [in the US], because they had the holes in the side where the cables would come through, and they all shared one marquee, so a lot of times, they wouldn't have a marquee on the top and [arcade operators would] have to buy that extra later.

[Ed. note]   In 2018, Capcom and developer Digital Eclipse included a special mode simulating the Tournament Battle experience in the Nintendo Switch version of *Street Fighter 30th Anniversary Collection*. Replicating the somewhat cumbersome arcade experience, players needed to round up four Switch consoles to set up local tournaments.

→   STEPHEN FROST
      Street Fighter 30th Anniversary Collection producer, Digital Eclipse

We didn't get any data [on how often people played it], not that I'm aware of, and to be quite frank, I don't feel that a lot of people would have played that mode, just from the standpoint of, *What are the odds of having that many Switches together?* We imagined it like, *Well, if you're at a fighting game competition?* I could imagine people bringing Switches and playing it that way, but it was more kind of a [fan service] thing, right? It was like, this is something that a lot of people haven't seen. It existed in the United States for a very limited amount of time. I would assume that a vast majority of Street Fighter fans have never seen it or dealt with it, and we have an opportunity to showcase it in some way, and so we jumped at that.

CUT CONTENT

Goddard and Winstead say another issue came up during the development of *Super Street Fighter II* when Capcom Japan built a stage inspired by the Los Angeles riots. They say the setting was uncomfortable, both because of its portrayal of a serious event in a lighthearted way, and because it was the backdrop for the second black character in the game, Jamaican kickboxer Dee Jay.

→   DAVE WINSTEAD
    Super Street Fighter II design support, Capcom USA

Dee Jay was being designed and originally, he was more of a thug. Kind of more like an M. Bison but on the streets of LA. It was right after America was in the news big time with the LA riots. And [Capcom] Japan decided to make that a stage. So there were windows broken into with TVs and stuff being stolen, and there was a cop car in the artwork, upside-down behind him. That was going to be a stage, and we saw that – Alex [Jimenez], James and I – and we're like, 'That is not going to fly here.' In their defence, they were very open and took our feedback.

→   JAMES GODDARD
    Super Street Fighter II design support, Capcom USA

It was very unfortunate. This is an example of culture and this is another moment where – I mean, now we're talking about *do the right thing* a lot. And it's important. This is one of those moments, back then, where I didn't even think twice about doing the right thing.

I show up and I'm looking [at the game] – I think it was on the same trip, man. What a nightmare. I'm pretty sure it was on the same nightmare trip. Yeah, because it was my last trip to Japan. And they show me the Dee Jay stage and it's *Time* magazine's LA riots scene with the cop car flipped upside down, shit burning, everybody standing on shit going, 'Yeah!' What a nightmare. That's Dee Jay's stage. And my stomach and heart just sank. I was just like, 'Oh.' And they had it really roughed out and it was pretty far along on the art. It's like, 'We can't do this. This is a tragedy. This is a terrible situation. This is oppression. This is just everything wrong. We're celebrating this in this game with Dee Jay, who's got nothing to do with this. He's Jamaican. He's on the beach. He's just a happy, positive guy. He's not a gang banger, you know? He's none of these things that the stage is talking about. He's not in LA.'

So I was like, 'Where the hell do the LA riots come in? Is he just visiting and he got caught up, and he's just trying to get through it?' And so they were like, 'Oh, well no. We just thought this was [something that happened] in culture, so we didn't think it was that bad.' They didn't realize what they were doing, and so they said, 'Well, it's too late to change it now.' But I absolutely was very passionately going, 'No, no, no. This is one of the worst things possible we could do.'

And I mean again, it wasn't meant to be racist. It wasn't intentional. This is just [that they had different] interpretations of different cultures, and so they picked this, and so I fought against it and we got it changed to the stage you saw. People were like, 'Oh, this beach thing is just kind of dumb and generic.' It's like, 'You should know what it almost was.'

→   NORITAKA FUNAMIZU
        Super Street Fighter II planner, Capcom Japan

I don't remember us designing that stage in the first place. It might have been an idea that somebody had, but I'm not sure if it was ever actually implemented. [...] I think that if something like that had happened, and we were told it wasn't a good idea and were asked not to include it, we probably would have agreed without any trouble.

[Ed. note] Over time, Capcom Japan continued to build their reputation for adding sexual and culturally inappropriate references to their games. Some made it into finished games; others were cut prior to release.

→ JAMES GODDARD
Super Street Fighter II design support, Capcom USA

There [are] innocent mistakes and then there's mischievous things. I'll tell you one. So Cammy – well, first of all, she was the camouflage girl and so my team pitched 'Cammy' for camouflage, and they liked it and they went with that.

But Cammy, when we looked at the pixels, somehow they had slipped in, on the pixels on her skintight suit – sorry, this is offensive – but camel toe. It's like, 'How the hell did they do this?' We're looking at the pictures and these are Polaroids they've sent to us. And it's like, 'Oh, hell no. We can't do this shit.' One of the marketing ladies saw it and she got pissed. Of course, right? And I had already written a thing saying, 'Hey, get rid of this. Please don't do this. This is unnecessary.' That would have just been dumb. No reason for that.

By the time *Super Street Fighter II* arrived in arcades, it was a victim of high expectations. Fans wanted something new to justify a fourth iteration, something different to compete with games like *Mortal Kombat II*, and something fast to keep up with the pace they'd learned in *Hyper Fighting*. And while Capcom was able to move things forward in a few ways, they weren't able to make everyone happy.

→   CHRIS KRAMER
         Street Fighter II series game counsellor, Capcom USA

I think *Super* was kind of the start of the downslide for the franchise, because there had been so many Street Fighter II titles in a row that I think *Super Street Fighter* [didn't stand out from the pack]. I know the game caught a lot of flak from people because there were only four new characters and there wasn't really that much introduced in terms of changes, even though the art was significantly improved and the game was rebalanced.

→   JAMES CHEN
         Street Fighter series commentator

I love the way the game looked. It was beautiful. Sound effects were kind of weird. I always remember being like, 'I miss the original CPS-1 hit sounds.' They were so good. But *Super* came out and honestly, it felt like a massive flop because whereas *Street Fighter II*, all the way up until *Hyper Fighting,* was just super popular everywhere you went and people played it and they loved the game and everything ...

When *Super* came out, I distinctly remember that barely anybody really played it. In fact, we had one of those mini golf places that had an arcade [inside]. There were two floors. [...] It was a place called Castle Park, and they always had a bottom floor and upper floor of the arcade, and the upper floor of the arcade is where they put some of the old games or the games that were lesser played, and the more popular games were downstairs. And I still remember Castle Park had *Hyper Fighting* on the first floor and *Super Street Fighter II* on the upper floor because nobody played it.

→ NORITAKA FUNAMIZU
    Super Street Fighter II planner, Capcom Japan

Super Street Fighter II did not sell very well, especially if you take into account that it was released on new hardware. I think I remember hearing that it sold only something like 12,000 copies. [...] Because the game speed was too slow, right?

→ JAMES GODDARD
    Super Street Fighter II design support, Capcom USA

[Capcom Japan] was just missing the mark on what the players wanted. And again, I think if you look at the history of Capcom with Street Fighter, when they are working with universal feedback from all the countries, and they have product champions at the different regions and they're able to talk, magic happens. Look at Seth Killian and his team and *Street Fighter IV*. It was history repeating itself where it's like, 'Oh, there's this great unification and everybody's working together and it's all about the player again.'

I feel like I'm taking this whole thing a little bit to the asshole land, and it's not my intention. It's just being more straight about it now, because I think it is easy for history to repeat itself and I hope that there's other young designers out there who maybe are going to struggle and they can see, sometimes you've just got to stick to your guns. There's a much better way to approach it than being called too pushy and too bullish. But if you really believe in things for the players, you've got to stick to your guns. And I think it's important for companies to remember you can't just cater to every single bit of feedback, but you sure as hell cannot do a 180 on players.

[Ed. note] In addition to many of the changes that Goddard and Winstead disliked, they say Capcom Japan also became more resistant to taking their feedback on new ideas. Winstead cites features like super moves with a colour backsplash that he says he wanted to include in *Super Street Fighter II*, but were declined by the team in Japan. Winstead stayed at Capcom through the end of *Super Street Fighter II*'s development, while Goddard took a job at Namco. After a short stint apart, Goddard convinced Winstead to join him at Namco, where the two worked on an original fighting game called *WeaponLord*.

→   DAVE WINSTEAD
         Super Street Fighter II design support, Capcom USA

[Capcom] didn't use any of the supers and all that fun stuff that we [had designed for *Super Street Fighter II*]. And I felt really defeated. So, I stayed there for a while. I kind of felt like they weren't listening to us at all anymore. We were kind of the stars, and then all of a sudden, we weren't the stars. At the same time, we had other things that were happening, and the US consumer division was getting stronger – and bless all those people, but they were forcing us to use the US art for the arcade machines as well, and I was a super anime fan, right? And I loved all Capcom [Japan] art. I loved all that stuff, and it was just killing me that we were using other people's artwork [...] so I felt a little defeated there, too. So as things progressed, I decided to leave.

CHAPTER 09

SUPER STREET FIGHTER II TURBO

Following a mixed reaction to *Super Street Fighter II*, Capcom almost immediately went about fixing their mistakes. It quickly put a team together to not only add the speed back, but include variable settings, super moves, a secret character and a layer of polish that made the game an ideal fit for tournaments, even though it didn't come in a Tournament Battle configuration.

Five months after *Super SFII*, *Super Street Fighter II Turbo* appeared in arcades.

While Capcom had gone down two diverging roads with *Hyper Fighting* and *Super SFII*, *Super Turbo* brought them back together.

BRINGING BACK THE SPEED

Behind the scenes at Capcom, *Super Turbo* came about for multiple reasons – Capcom wanted to give fans what they requested, but they also needed to use up excess ROM chips, and a fifth iteration could achieve both of those goals.

With a short timeline, Capcom didn't have the ability to overhaul anything major, so they focused on changes that didn't require large amounts of new art and animation. According to Winstead, many of the features in *Super Turbo* came from ideas he and the Capcom USA team had proposed during the development of *Super Street Fighter II*.

→   DAVE WINSTEAD
      Super Street Fighter II design support, Capcom USA

I would always call [Capcom Japan liaison Tom Shiraiwa] around 7, 7.30 at night and we'd just have a little pow-wow. So he called me a little earlier this time, and I was already at home, and he was like, 'We need to talk about the sequel.' I'm like, 'The sequel? To what?' He was like, 'to *Super Street Fighter*. We want to call it *Super Street Fighter Turbo* like you wanted to originally.' And I'm like, 'Well, that's great.' And I had already put in my notice that day, that I was going to leave and go to Namco because *WeaponLord* was starting, and I was so upset with Capcom. I was just like a hurt fanboy, you know? I worked for them, but I was a hurt fanboy at the same time. They were making all these wrong decisions.

Tom was like, 'Yeah, we're going to do the supers that you designed and we're going to do all this fun stuff.' And I'm like, 'That is great.' And then I was like, 'Tom, I hate to tell you this but I put in my two weeks' notice today.' And he said, 'Why?' He just kept saying, 'Why did you do that?'

And I told him the reason why. I was like, 'Well, it sounded like no one was listening.' He was like, 'It had to be that way.' He just kept saying – he wouldn't tell me why, but he was just like, 'There's a reason why we had to do what we did. We had to release it slow. It had to be that way.' That's all he kept saying. I'm like, 'Well, I don't understand why because everybody hated the game.' They didn't hate the game, but it was one of those things where people were starting to finally go, 'OK, Capcom's releasing the same game over and over again.'

So it was one of those things where they finally decided, *Yeah, we're going to do this* Super Turbo *version*, but I was on my way out, which was really difficult for me. But it was generally everything that we designed in there, which was nice. We got the supers. We got the super fireballs. We have the turbo speed. And there [were other moves and features] that we were trying to get in there.

→   NORITAKA FUNAMIZU
          Super Street Fighter II Turbo planner, Capcom Japan

With *Super Street Fighter II*, we ended up reverting the speed of that game back to the original and a lot of people didn't like that. They liked the game better when it was faster and didn't understand why we slowed it down. So we listened to their feedback. Then there was the fact that we again had excess inventory [of mask ROMs], so they asked us to make another sequel right away. I was like, *Not this again* ... I got really angry.

Back then, unlike today, game development was very secretive, even within the company. You couldn't really talk in great detail about what you were doing to people not involved in your project. The other issue was that we had no direct access to user feedback until after a game would come out. So all of our advice came from sales and marketing people, including some Americans. But eventually [Capcom Japan department head Yoshiki]

Okamoto and I realized that if we kept taking our cues from these salespeople, we'd never get rid of this excess inventory. We were both angry about it, and we didn't want to listen to them anymore. I knew we had excess PCBs. But personally, if I was going to make another Street Fighter game for Capcom after this, I said it's on one condition: that I don't have to reuse those mask ROMs again. 'The excess PCBs, that was our problem. But the excess mask ROMs, those were your guys' responsibility! You guys made the mistake, so you fix it somehow.'

The other condition I personally had for doing a sequel was that we'd get to add a new character ... and Akuma was the character who came out of that process.

A NEW CHALLENGER

Following the four new characters in *Super Street Fighter II*, Capcom included a single new fighter in *Super Turbo* – one hidden from the character select screen and only unlockable under specific circumstances, yet one that instantly became one of the series' most popular characters. Akuma played like a stronger, faster version of Ryu and Ken, utilizing the same fireball/Dragon Punch-heavy Shotokan fighting style.

→ DAVE WINSTEAD
WeaponLord associate producer, Namco Hometek

I thought [Akuma was] cool. But I also thought, *Oh my goodness, man. This guy is overpowered*. But yeah, I didn't have anything to do with Akuma. That was on their side. And I remember when I saw Akuma at the JAMMA show. [...] [He had] the little mid-air fireball and all kinds of fun stuff.

→ TOMOTAKA SUZUKI
Street Fighter II series combo video creator

I think Akuma is quite a cool character in terms of his design and his personality. I always found it interesting that even though he's very strong, he also takes a lot of damage. I thought his mid-air Hadouken was too strong, though. It made it very difficult to fight against him in competitive play. [...] At some point Akuma got banned for tournaments, and I don't think he's allowed today. [...] Just do mid-air fireballs all day. You'll be fine. Zangief will just lose, you know?

→ JAMES CHEN
Street Fighter series commentator

I still remember the first time I tried to input the code to get Akuma and I couldn't get it to work. I went to my local mall with my girlfriend at the time, and I was trying to input the code and it wouldn't work, and I was like, 'man' [...] I was trying to get it to work and I couldn't and then my girlfriend was like, 'Let me try.' And then she got it to work and a whole bunch of people were there. They were like, 'Oh my god. How did you do that?'

[Ed. note]   In Japan, Capcom refers to Akuma by the name 'Gouki'. For the West, Capcom USA's Scott Smith came up with 'Akuma'.

→   CHRIS KRAMER
         Street Fighter II series game counsellor, Capcom USA

Our contacts in Japan would send us stuff and they would – it's the *Mega Man*/*Rockman* thing, right? Someone in the US says, 'Well, you can't call this game *Rockman* because that means drug dealer in the US,' or something crazy like that. So we would always be asked to figure out what the American names for things were going to be, and there was too much confusion [over the name Gouki, so] Scott pulled 'Akuma' out of a story he had read in the news.

→   SCOTT SMITH
         Street Fighter II series marketing manager, Capcom USA

[Capcom Japan] wanted to send the [*Super Turbo*] board for test at Golfland. We normally tested at Golfland there in Sunnyvale. So they were sending the chips out and [they said], 'By the way, there's this new character and here's a picture of him' – which was the standard picture of Akuma, with I don't know if it's kanji on the back, which says 'demon' – 'and here's the backstory.' And we got like four sentences of 'Gouki, Gouken, Goutetsu'. And it was just very confusing to American ears. So they said, 'Do you want to change it?' Which, sure. As you know, we had no problem changing things.

So previous to this, in it must have been 1994, there had been a story about some Japanese parents who wanted to name their child Akuma, and it went up through the court system in Japan and they were barred from using the name because it [means] 'devil'. It's like naming a child Adolf Hitler. So it just stuck with me because I either read it in the newspaper or heard it on Sarah and Vinnie back in the early days of their [radio] show. And so when we were looking for a name and we saw the writing on the back, that was a cool, different name that was unlike anything else that had been done for the series. Some of the choices you make when you do your work, people like; some of them, they don't. That one, they don't seem to have too much of a problem with.

SHENG LONG REDUX

For many fans in the west, seeing Akuma in 1994 brought back memories of EGM's Sheng Long April Fool's joke from 1992. Not only was Akuma a super-powered Shotokan character, but he threw red fireballs, had a flaming Dragon Punch, and even jumped in and took out M. Bison before fighting the player if they met a difficult set of criteria – all things that EGM had written about Sheng Long. When EGM's Ken Williams first saw Akuma, he says he knew right away what he was looking at.

→ KEN WILLIAMS
Assistant editor, Electronic Gaming Monthly magazine

That was probably one – I don't even know how to describe the feeling at the time. It was kind of like that mind-blown meme where you just go, 'Whaaa.' [*laughs*] That was kind of my brain at the time. I just remember seeing that, getting the code to get him, and ... it's like having a déjà vu moment. Because when you're creating the original trick, and then you almost see it play out in front of you, [that's amazing]. It's a little different, right? But it's obviously inspired. And it was just a very heartwarming moment, I guess is probably the best way [to describe it]. I'm like, *Oh wow, they really liked it and they actually took it and made it real*. Because we had heard that they liked it. That they thought it was amusing. But for them to actually take that concept and make it their own just added to the lore, right? It just added to it. So it made it even more legitimate. As fake as it was, it legitimized it.

[Ed. note] While the Sheng Long joke gained significant traction in the US, we asked seven former Capcom Japan team members who worked on the series about it, and none of them said they were familiar with it or thought it inspired Akuma.

→   AKIRA YASUDA
           Super Street Fighter II Turbo character designer, Capcom Japan

Is that the case? This is the first time I've ever heard that.

→   TOMOTAKA SUZUKI
           Street Fighter II series combo video creator

I've never heard [of *EGM*'s Sheng Long joke].

→   NORITAKA FUNAMIZU
           Super Street Fighter II Turbo planner, Capcom Japan

I don't think that had anything to do with it.

→   ZENJI ISHII
           Editor-in-chief, Gamest magazine

I had no idea this joke was even a thing. I might have heard it back in the day. Back then, the attitude they had towards bugs – and I've heard this about Dhalsim's Yoga Teleport, for instance – was that if the bug was interesting, they'd deliberately try to include it in the game. So if they found a bug with a player disappearing, for example, they'd turn that into a teleportation move. So maybe that attitude of not seeing these things as 'weird' had something to do with it.

→   DAVE WINSTEAD
           WeaponLord associate producer, Namco Hometek

[When I first saw Akuma], I knew for sure that they were inspired by that. It was definitely Sheng Long, right?
       We did mention the whole Sheng Long thing [to Capcom Japan]. Me and James talked to them about that all the time, and we showed them that stuff. But it doesn't mean that it actually trickled down to the designers that were

working on that at the time. So, maybe. I mean, he is different. Sheng Long wasn't this demon guy, right? He was more like the sensei of all these guys. He's just more of the good guy, right? So it's different. But I definitely thought about it. I was like, 'That's Sheng Long.' But that could just be because we're in that Western environment where Sheng Long was what everybody talked about in the arcades.

→   CHRIS KRAMER
         Street Fighter II series game counsellor, Capcom USA

You've got to understand – there was little to no internet at that point in time [...] so there were a lot of misunderstandings about things in Street Fighter. People didn't know how to pronounce Guile's name. People would call us on our customer service line and they're like, 'Who is Sheng Long?' And there was a lot of stuff like that, because there was limited text, so people had to kind of invent a lot of the background for the characters in their heads, or try to pick out details from their backgrounds and things like that. So I don't know if the Akuma thing was directly from [*EGM*] because at that point in time, I don't know if the Japanese dev team would be too aware of what [*EGM*] was doing, quite honestly. We take for granted the fact that now, anytime anybody sneezes, you read about it on Reddit or NeoGAF or something like that, and there are 10,000 reaction videos on YouTube. Getting an issue of Famitsu in the US was like finding the lost ark at that point in time. We would have one or two shipped over from Japan every couple of weeks, and everybody would pore over them, trying to decipher what was going on.

→   KEN WILLIAMS
         Assistant editor, Electronic Gaming Monthly magazine

I didn't personally hear [from Capcom], so this is a bit of a telephone type thing. Because they don't call me or anything. Nobody calls me. Nobody knew who I was anyway. But we definitely heard, apparently, that they were amused by [the April Fool's joke], and they didn't want to say anything about it. In fact, if I remember correctly, they were really amused by the thought and the workup – because they knew it was fake right away, obviously – but they didn't [comment on it publicly]. Nobody wrote an article saying, 'Oh, by the way, this is fake.' In fact, it was the exact opposite. Because so many people took it as gospel. I don't know if it was because more people were going to the arcade and dumping quarters and they were getting good profit off of that. I have no idea. I don't know how that all works.

→   JAMES GODDARD
            WeaponLord producer, Namco Hometek

[I never heard anyone from Capcom Japan say the Sheng Long joke inspired Akuma], but for sure it did. In fact, when that Sheng Long thing happened, I was accused of making that happen, because I would pass on all the rumours that players wanted. [...] So then later when they decided to do Akuma, I have to imagine that it was partially [to copy *EGM*]. They just didn't call him Sheng Long because that was the damn name of the Dragon Punch, right?

When you really look at Akuma, it's dark. It's all about the dark hado and the dark version, and that's a Star Wars thing, right? And many other [things] – it's not just Star Wars that has that concept of the dark version of yourself. So I do believe that most of it was original, but at the same time, the Sheng Long thing was known, at least among some of the more original designers.

[Ed. note]   According to multiple team members, Capcom artist Takenori Kimoto came up with the idea for Akuma and how he was implemented in the game – Funamizu remembers Kimoto dropping off a single sheet of paper at 11 pm one night with ideas for a secret boss character. While Kimoto's employer, Level-5, declined an interview request on his behalf for this book, people he has spoken to over the years say he wasn't inspired by *EGM*'s joke, but by Dragon Ball's over-the-top Super Saiyan character transformations. Specifically, they say the Dragon Ball connection explains why the character is based on Ryu (who attacks somewhat like Dragon Ball's Goku), why he has a flaming Dragon Punch (similar to how the Super Saiyan form lights Goku on fire), and why he jumps in and takes out M. Bison (similar to how Goku obliterated multiple foes in a famous scene). Asked about the chance of the similarities between Sheng Long and Akuma being a coincidence, Williams says he doesn't think it's possible.

→   KEN WILLIAMS
    Assistant editor, Electronic Gaming Monthly magazine

No. Not even a chance. [*laughs*] [...] When I saw the flaming Dragon Punch for the first time, I'm like, 'Dude' ... It's like, 'What else is in here, if they took that?' And you see all the little pieces come together. And the first time I saw Akuma zip across the screen and beat the crap out of Bison, I lost it.

I would almost say they're legally bound to not say it because that would make them have to pay a licensing fee, because it becomes almost a copyright thing or something to that effect. Because hey, I'd love to get a little side cheque for that idea. But you know what? It's still cool. To have something that you had a direct role in creating actually come to life, I imagine it's a little bit like people who actually design games for a living, when they see their creation live on the screen, and then they see people's responses to it, that's probably very fulfilling. So that's kind of how I look at it.

[Ed. note]   In Street Fighter's canonical storyline, Capcom
established Akuma as an evil character, rather
than Ryu and Ken's teacher. According to the
backstory, Akuma and his brother Gouken
studied under a martial artist named Goutetsu,
and Gouken was the one who trained Ryu and
Ken. Because of that storyline connection, when
Capcom ended up including Gouken as a character
in *Street Fighter IV* more than a decade later,
producer Yoshinori Ono joked in interviews about
his connection to Sheng Long.

As the fifth version of Street Fighter II, *Super Turbo* refined, polished and sped up the series in a way that few players criticized, but that didn't attract the same sorts of crowds as games like *Champion Edition* had a couple of years earlier.

> Many point to increased competition and a sense of apathy towards a series that hadn't taken major steps forward to explain why. It also didn't help that *Super Turbo* initially only made it to consoles on 3DO – a system not known for fighting games, nor 2D games for that matter – and that players had to literally loosen the screws on their 3DO controllers to improve their inputs.

But as a competitive arcade game that's held up decades later, few games can touch it.

→   DAVE WINSTEAD
        WeaponLord associate producer, Namco Hometek

When it came out? It's kind of funny because we were working on *WeaponLord* at that time, me and James Goddard, and I heard that it dropped at a Keystone on test, which was strange because we always played favourites with Golfland when I was working there. But they chose Keystone this time. [...] I think I got a phone call from a friend that was like, '*Turbo*'s at Keystone.' I'm like, 'Oh my god.' So I told James; we jumped over there at lunch and checked it out. And I will have to say that I was prepared to be disappointed, because I was just so angry still. Like, 'Man, what did you do to our Street Fighter?'

> And I went over there and I just remember having such mixed feelings because like, holy crap. They did everything that I wanted them to do earlier, right? The crazy screen

splash with the [background colour] and everything when you do the super and you hit with it and all that fun stuff was in the design. [...] All that stuff was working really well, and I almost cried, to be honest. I was sitting there going, 'I can't believe it.' I felt kind of numb. Part of the reason was like, 'OK, I left them and they actually did pull through.' I was pretty happy and I went back and then I called Betson Pacific and pre-ordered mine. So I bought a *Super Turbo*. It was day one. I had it when it came out.

→   JAMES GODDARD
         WeaponLord producer, Namco Hometek

When [Winstead] left, I remember he and I went to the arcade to finally see *Super Turbo* on location. So he left before it shipped. That really killed him to do that. But when we first saw the super happen and the big sprite that happens with that [in the background]. [...] He was really thrilled to see that because he was the guy who got that in the game, and he pitched that.

→   TOMOTAKA SUZUKI
         Street Fighter II series combo video creator

I remember when I first played *Hyper Fighting*, I actually thought it was too fast, but then once you got used to it, it started to feel normal. So when *Super* came around, I thought it was a bit too slow. And when *Super Turbo* came out, that's when I started to prefer the faster speed.

→   NORITAKA FUNAMIZU
         Super Street Fighter II Turbo planner, Capcom Japan

Super Turbo was definitely the version that reviewed the best and was the most well received, and it sold a lot of copies. [...] I would say it's because we didn't just add new characters. We also added new moves and new types of data for the older characters as well.

→   SETH KILLIAN
     Super Street Fighter II Turbo tournament player

Super Turbo was the game where the characters' gameplay finally felt as crisp and defined as their famously great looks and backstory. The new super move and juggle systems seemed arbitrary, but otherwise [the game] was full of small-but-thoughtful adjustments, had the most moves per character, and was overall just fast and dirty fun. In the hands of a good player, even the weakest characters in the game were terrifying. That kind of power was fun to dish out on opponents, but it's also thrilling to play against. It gave [the game] the electric feel of a high-wire act, where one second everything is going great, and the next second you're on the brink of total disaster and wondering, *What happened?*

→   JAMES CHEN
     Street Fighter series commentator

Super Turbo definitely improved a lot of things, but this was the point where all the clones were out now, right? This is when, not just Fatal Fury, but we had Samurai Shodown, we had Killer Instinct [...] Mortal Kombat was around. And so, even though *Super Turbo* fixed a lot of the things that a lot of us were frustrated with on *Super*, at this point there were so many fighting games that the player base was really splintered. [...] So Street Fighter had maybe a little mini-resurgence with *Super Turbo*, but it was harder because it was still [...] just another version of the game. [...] The way people talk about *Super Turbo*, you'd think it was like, *Oh my god, this thing just completely reinvented Street Fighter*. No, it was niche, and kind of along the theme that we've been talking about with all the competition out there, it was really hard to stand out at that time.

→ JAMES GODDARD
   WeaponLord producer, Namco Hometek

It stopped the bleeding, but [Capcom] had already lost easily 70 percent of the players that used to be there. [They] lost to Mortal Kombat [...] and other things were happening, right? But it was a great game. I always hear it was one of the most balanced Street Fighters and when I watch tournament play, I agree.

It's a phenomenal tournament game. A really fun game for players. Buggy. There's a lot of weird bugs in that game. I mean, there's famous videos of [characters] just facing the wrong direction. [...] I'll tell you what, though. A lot of cool shit emerged out of that game, and I think it was way beyond its years. And the fact that it holds up to this day in play, even with some of the balance issues and some of the things that happen that make it tough, I think it's definitely one of the best Street Fighters of all time.

→ ZENJI ISHII
   Editor-in-chief, Gamest magazine

Super Street Fighter II Turbo was the game where everything came together. The game had this very distinct Street Fighter II identity to it – all the elements that made Street Fighter II what it was were in there – but especially on a technical level, it was very well made and very well balanced. And I think that's why that game is the embodiment of Street Fighter II for me.

→ CHRIS KRAMER
   Street Fighter II series game counsellor, Capcom USA

Super Turbo today remains not only an important game, but also a super recognizable and fun game. Look at a lot of esports today – if you don't know *League of Legends* inside out, you can't watch LCS because you don't know what the hell is happening on screen. You're listening to people and they're like, 'The jungler is mid-lane and we got an AD Carry situation.' You're like, 'What the hell is going on?'

Street Fighter – in 2007, we did this crazy Comic-Con booth where we built a boxing ring and we were doing all this stuff and we had a huge monitor that was flying over the boxing ring. And there had just coincidentally been a couple of Street Fighter pros in town, and Seth [Killian] had them come and do an exhibition match. He had six or eight of them come and do an exhibition match in the booth, and they were playing *Super Turbo* [...] and we had hundreds and hundreds of people stop to watch, even though that game was ancient at that point. But people were watching because you can watch a [classic] Street Fighter game and you know what's happening. You know when a punch is landing. You know fireballs are being thrown. You can see a big reversal. You can see awesome combos. Even if you don't know how it's being done, you recognize it, and I think that's kind of the magic of Street Fighter.

Seth and I were standing in this boxing ring and we're looking out and there were literally hundreds of people staring up at the screen and they're clapping and they're going 'ooh' and 'ah' like it's a fireworks display, and Seth is like, 'These people could be doing anything right now at Comic-Con. They could be in Hall H learning about the new Harry Potter movie, or they could be in the corner getting Stan Lee to sign a comic book, or they could be meeting William Shatner. But these hundreds of people are standing here right now and they're watching these guys play Street Fighter and they're into it.' And it was just cool to see that game still have that reaction with people, that many years later.

CHAPTER 10

DARK-
STALKERS

In 1991, Capcom put a target on their back.

When Capcom released *Street Fighter II*, they sparked a phenomenon, selling tens-if-not-hundreds of thousands of machines and reinvigorating the arcade business. It was only a matter of time before the rest of the industry wanted a piece of the action.

Soon after, dozens of competitors entered the market. Nearly every game publisher rushed to put a new spin on the versus fighting genre – *Mortal Kombat* went violent, *Samurai Shodown* added weapons, *Virtua Fighter* went 3D – with a notable exception: Capcom. For three years after *Street Fighter II*'s release, Capcom stuck with its horse, releasing four upgrades and a run of console ports but not shipping anything that directly competed with its star.

In 1994, that changed.

After *Super Street Fighter II Turbo* hit arcades, Capcom's laser turned into a shotgun. As it turned out, the company had been working on new projects behind the scenes and thinking broadly about about where they could take the genre, looking into some of the biggest mainstream licences like Dragon Ball and X-Men.

Yet the first game to make it out landed on the opposite end of the spectrum: an original title inspired by classic Universal Movie Monsters.

KING OF THE MONSTERS

For a company with a mainstream hit like the Street Fighter II series, *Darkstalkers* wasn't an obvious next step. Not only were many of the characters based on pop culture icons decades past their prime, but Capcom chose to take inspiration from those characters rather than licence them. The result was a game that impressed players, but also confused many at first glance.

→   JAMES CHEN
         Street Fighter series commentator

When that came out, it was completely random. I was just like, 'Wow, this is weird. They just went with this idea here. [...] Where did this come from?' And obviously back then with no internet and nothing like that, there were no rumours or leaks or whatever to be had. [...] Things just showed up in the arcade. That was how you found out about things a lot of the time, and when *Darkstalkers* came out, seemingly out of nowhere, it was definitely a very weird thing.

→   STEPHEN FROST
         Street Fighter 30th Anniversary Collection producer, Digital Eclipse

Street Fighter is somewhat serious, you know? [It felt like Capcom said] 'We've been doing this for a little while. Let's just do something that's kooky, fun and a little bit different.' And that's fun to watch, right? Because *Darkstalkers* is fun to watch.

→   JUSTIN BERENBAUM
         Darkstalkers customer service manager, Capcom USA

By this time, I'd been at Capcom long enough and played enough versions of Street Fighter where I was just kind of sick of [it], because all the moves were the same, except when they added a new character. It's not like they ever changed Ken's moves or

Guile's moves, so when they put out a new version of Street Fighter, the only thing that really changed was if they added a new character. And the art and the levels. Otherwise, nothing really changed. This was the first time that I really felt like moves changed or the characters were really different.

> I don't know if anybody's going to admit this, but – and this is my gut [speculation] – I felt like it was their opportunity to test stuff without risking anything to the franchise itself. So if they made a character that didn't resonate or they screwed something up or the balance was off or the animations were off, the Street Fighter community wasn't going to get up in arms. I almost feel like this was literally what they started using to open beta the Street Fighter stuff.

→   CHRIS KRAMER
        Darkstalkers game counsellor, Capcom USA

Moving from CPS-1 to CPS-2 was awesome, because with the CPS-1 games you'd get a huge board just filled with silicon and you'd have to rewire everything, but with the CPS-2 system, [it was] essentially a big Super Nintendo so you'd just snap in the B cartridges and turn it on. And what was really cool, for a nerdy Capcom fan in the 1990s, was stuff would just show up from Japan with no labelling on it. [Our liaison with Capcom Japan, Tom Shiraiwa] would just come into the customer service area with a box, and he'd be like, 'All right, you guys figure out what this is.' He'd give us a B board that just had Japanese writing on a white label or something. That was the first time we saw *Darkstalkers* in the US – we got a random B board. We plugged it in. We went, 'Wow, what the hell is this?' It looked very different with all that Bengus art, and it had a very different feel. [...] It was really fast and kind of crazy and not as deliberate and exacting as Street Fighter.

[Ed. note]   Prior to developing *Darkstalkers*, Capcom had
                  been working on a side-scrolling beat-'em-up

inspired by the manga series Baoh. When they cancelled that project, and ideas for a Dragon Ball Z fighting game didn't pan out, Capcom had staff available to work on *Darkstalkers*.

→   ALEX JIMENEZ
        Darkstalkers design support, Capcom USA

You're going to make me go there, aren't you?

OK. For the record. Back in 1993, I was in Japan and they showed me the [Dragon Ball] manga and they explained that it was a very popular manga that sold eight million copies per week. I'm not a huge manga fan so I looked at it and didn't understand a word of it. I'm like, 'This looks really weird. This looks really strange.' And they were telling me how popular it was in Japan. I had no idea what it was. Nobody really did outside of Japan. I said, 'Well, eight million people in Japan is fine. How many of them play videogames? I mean, is that going to be enough to sustain us?' 'What do you mean?' 'Well, I've never seen this. I go to all the comic book shops and whatnot. I have never seen this. How are we going to bring this to America? I just don't get it.' So they kicked it around and it was decided, 'Yeah, OK. We have the opportunity to buy this licence, but if you don't think it's going to make it, then we'll pass on it.' And lo and behold, that was Dragon Ball Z. And looking back on, in retrospect, yeah. Obviously, we probably could have done something outrageous with it, and would have been highly successful. That's only in retrospect, though. I was looking at it from that point in 1993. Who knew it would be that successful?

I explained to them. I go, 'Well, how many of you guys know about X-Men and Spider-Man? How many X-Men and Spider-Man comics do they sell here every week?' And they're like, 'Well, not that many.' It's like, 'Exactly.' It's the same thing, you know? I can make an X-Men game and it would be hugely popular in the States. And lo and behold, a year later, we made an X-Men game. So that might have helped a little bit there. But, yeah. To this day – it's been more than 25 years – I'll go to Comic-Con, see the Capcom booth, and they'll still remind me about that. They'll still throw that in my face. 'Oh, you were wrong about Dragon Ball.' Like, 'Yeah. But I was right about everything else.'

A TRIP TO COMIC-CON

A mash-up of influences, *Darkstalkers* pulled in ideas from around the world – and on the development side, pulled in notes from both Capcom Japan and Capcom USA. Though again, team members recall the origins of the idea differently from one another.

→   KATSUYA AKITOMO
          Darkstalkers concept designer, Capcom Japan

I can't remember the exact year, to be honest, but I was actually sent on a business trip to San Diego Comic-Con. At the time, I think there was a small comic book studio that was making a Street Fighter II comic, so we asked them to get us tickets to the event.

During that trip, [Capcom executive producer Yoshiki] Okamoto asked me to do a few different things. He asked me to visit comic book shops, arcade centres, etc. in California and gather information. So I ended up doing that. And while I was there, I noticed that there was still a lot of merchandise based on the classic Universal Monsters. Universal was still pushing that at the time, even though more than 50 years had passed since things like Bela Lugosi's Dracula and Boris Karloff's portrayal of Frankenstein's monster. It still had a lot of popularity and presence in American pop culture. Seeing that, I got the idea for a versus fighting game that would use those kinds of characters and that kind of world.

So I ended up putting a proposal together and I gave that to Okamoto.

→   NORITAKA FUNAMIZU
Darkstalkers producer, Capcom Japan

Okamoto was trying to figure out how to make new fighting games that used popular characters or well-known characters worldwide that you wouldn't need a licence for. So I think it was Akitomo who, aware of what Okamoto wanted, proposed the idea of using those famous monster characters, which he thought were really cool.

→   ALEX JIMENEZ
Darkstalkers design support, Capcom USA

We went to Comic-Con together. I took a bunch of them to Comic-Con. That was San Diego in 1993. So I took them down there, but I was the one – James and I were the ones who came up with all these good ideas.

→   JAMES GODDARD
Super Street Fighter II design support, Capcom USA

My team originally pitched *Darkstalkers*. [...] We pitched a monster mash-up fighting game like 'Monster Mash'. You know, Frankenstein, Dracula, werewolves. We pitched it and wrote it up and sent it over and it didn't have a cool name. It was much darker. I still have sketches from the nonsense drawings that I was doing back then – I had a Frankenstein with tasers zapping his own nodes just to amp him up, right? So, yeah. We sent all that over there, and we thought it would be great because we could do that to compete against Mortal Kombat and do a dark version. I mean, the version we pitched was dark. Because they're monsters, you could do blood and guts and the whole works, right? Still Capcom style, but we could dismember and the whole [thing]. I mean, let's go.

      And they were very smart in that they later, when we saw it – and I think this again was one of those trips over there, one of my last trips, that we saw the beginnings of *Darkstalkers*, and then it was called whatever the codename was – it was way more cool [with an anime style]. Almost the beginnings of that [*Street Fighter*] *Alpha 2*-style art. Simpler colour palette. And it was like, *Oh, this is really awesome*, though. And so that's the extent of it.

Hey, we pitched a lot of ideas. [Pitching] a monster fighting game doesn't mean you created *Darkstalkers*. It just means we pitched it and they had ideas over there and they had so many teams working on stuff.

Alex Jimenez, to give him some credit [...] was one of the guys behind that idea. [...] So yeah, we just wrote it up and sent it over there. There wasn't much to it. Just some ideas about how dark and violent it could be, and then they hit it out of the park with what they did with it.

→   ALEX JIMENEZ
     Darkstalkers design support, Capcom USA

Darkstalkers was funny, because after the success – I'm sure James told you that they fought him tooth and nail on *Champion Edition*. They did not want to do it. They really did not want to do it. They thought it would be impossible to play-balance. They thought players would not want to play the boss characters. They fought him tooth and nail. [...] But he proved he was right.

So after that, they came to us and they said, 'OK, maybe that was a fluke. So we have this head-to-head fighting system. What can we do with it?' And I remember James saying it – we used to have our offices in the warehouse, basically our desks in the middle there with things going by all the time. He was like, 'What can we do with it?' I just remember looking up and going, 'What can we not do with it? Are you kidding me? This is awesome.'

I started shooting off ideas. 'Let's do Godzilla. Let's do the Toho monsters. Let's do Universal Movie Monsters. Let's do gods versus goddesses. Let's do DC versus Marvel. Let's just pull out all the stops.'

So we wrote all this up, and we couldn't get Godzilla because the Toho licence was prohibitive. It was way too expensive. We couldn't do Marvel or DC because there was no way they'd cooperate. So finally, they [were] like, 'What about these Universal Movie Monsters?' I was like, 'Well, they're favourites of mine.'

→ KATSUYA AKITOMO
Darkstalkers concept designer, Capcom Japan

My initial idea was to have Universal Monsters fighting each other in a fighting game. I loved Dracula and Frankenstein, and watched those old movies a lot when I was little. I was well aware, however, that for a versus fighting game their abilities were too plain. So in my original proposal, I wrote that we should not acquire the Universal IP, but should instead create original monsters that resembled those classic characters. I included some simple sketches and basic notes in my proposal, like what kind of moves they might have, things like that. Really simple drawings.

The thing was, I was such a huge, maniac-level fan of those movies and characters, that as strange as it sounds, I felt it would probably turn out to be a better game if I just gave some hints and ideas to the developers, rather than getting directly involved myself. So for *Darkstalkers*, I wasn't the one who wrote the story or named the characters. That was actually done by an employee at Capcom USA named Alex Jimenez. I think he was the one who took care of all the written elements in the game.

→ ALEX JIMENEZ
Darkstalkers design support, Capcom USA

They were like, 'OK, we like the idea of monsters but we don't want to licence this. We want to make our own. So give us a list of different monsters.' So I wrote up the Darkstalkers. 'OK, let's have a vampire. Let's have the Creature. Let's have Frankenstein.' Let's have all these different things. And I sent that off to them and they liked it. They came back with some artwork, and that afternoon – literally at 6 pm – I was dead tired, ready to go home, but they needed it right away. So I created the Darkstalkers. [...] I made their names and backgrounds and all the rest of that.

→ KATSUYA AKITOMO
Darkstalkers concept designer, Capcom Japan

Alex did put more time into the game than I did, so maybe that's why he would think that he's the one who came up with the idea. Maybe that's why he would misunderstand that. [...] I don't think it's a problem. If I was still doing game planning work, that might be a big problem, but I haven't really done much related to videogames recently, so ...

[Ed. note]   In a 2021 YouTube video, Okamoto credited Akitomo with the idea and proposal for *Darkstalkers*.

→ ALEX JIMENEZ
Darkstalkers design support, Capcom USA

I will say there could have been spontaneous thought on that. And more than likely what probably happened was we sent our ideas in, Akitomo had sent his idea in, and Okamoto looked at both ideas and went, 'OK, there seems to be a consensus here. Maybe we can get these guys to work together for a change.' Because we did have a rather antagonistic relationship with a lot of the devs in Japan. They were, well, how do I put this? They didn't think Americans knew how to make games. Like many developers, they were really protective of what they considered their turf.

James and I fought for the longest time to get the title of designer put on the games for us. We wanted to be listed as designers. And the closest they came was on *Dungeons & Dragons*, they had me listed as 'dungeon master'. They just wouldn't give us that designer title. [...] That kind of bugged us a little bit. Like on *Darkstalkers* and whatnot, we're getting 'special thanks'.

[Ed. note]   *Jimenez's name doesn't appear in* Darkstalkers' *credits, but it does appear in the sequel,* Night Warriors: Darkstalkers' Revenge.]

I'm like, 'Dudes, I wrote the backgrounds for all these characters. I named them.' You look at the copy they're using now. They're using the same copy I wrote back in 1993. So that was a bit of a sticking point. I think that really affected James a lot, too. He really got bugged by that.

A NEW ART STYLE

Part of what made *Darkstalkers* unique was that it combined Western-inspired characters with an anime-inspired art style. That look came about, in part, because Capcom was attempting to streamline their art pipeline and develop a style that required less shading, giving the team more time to to focus on other details and animation – which enabled the characters to move and stretch in all sorts of creative ways.

→   AKIRA YASUDA
      Darkstalkers character designer, Capcom Japan

When we were making Street Fighter, there was a period where my boss, Okamoto, would constantly tell me how cheap the character graphics looked. I mean, these games were huge hits and selling very well, yet he's here saying they look cheap ... wouldn't that make you angry?

So because he said my designs looked cheap in *Street Fighter II*, for *Darkstalkers*, I wanted to take the opposite approach. I don't know if rich and cheap are necessarily the opposites of each other, but I wanted the graphics to look rich. The graphics had been a big part of Street Fighter's success, but even then there was a feeling among everyone that we were capable of much more. Around the time of *Street Fighter II*, there weren't that many talented graphic designers in the company. But by the time *Darkstalkers* came about, our designers had gotten better and Capcom had developed a reputation as being the number one company for 2D pixel graphics, so I felt we should create a game that lived up to that reputation. We were number one when it came to character animation, so we had to create the richest, most beautiful game in the world.

At the same time, Akitomo proposed his idea of doing a monster game, and I thought this could be just the vehicle for us to make a game that would go even beyond what Okamoto had asked for – graphics so rich they'd make your jaw drop.

You know Sega? They had a very strong mechatronics department back then. I don't know if this is true or not, but I heard they had 500 people working there. Capcom didn't really specialize in mechatronics. We had a department for it, but it was only 10 or 20 employees, not hundreds. On the other hand, Capcom did have several hundred pixel artists. Sega only had 20 or 30 pixel artists, from what I was told. When I realized how many people we had, compared to Sega and other companies, it made me want to create a game that would harness that power and communicate it to players and the world. And *Darkstalkers* was that game.

→   KATSUYA AKITOMO
        Darkstalkers concept designer, Capcom Japan

There was a big stylistic change between *Street Fighter II* and *Darkstalkers*. On *Street Fighter II*, the artists put a great deal of effort into the character shading, but in exchange, the character movements were a bit sloppy. If you compare that with *Darkstalkers*, we drew the silhouettes very precisely and used almost no shading. We poured all our energy into the animation. It was [Yasuda]'s decision to take this approach.

→   JUSTIN BERENBAUM
        Darkstalkers customer service manager, Capcom USA

I think the sharp edges were much easier to animate than the round, because the round were – even back then, it was technically 2D, but they almost looked a little 3D. If you look at even the Street Fighter characters from like, 1994, 1995, 1996, especially with the backgrounds, they almost look 3D. And I think the *Darkstalkers* ones were probably simpler overall to create.

→   JAMES GODDARD
        WeaponLord producer, Namco Hometek

[*Darkstalkers* was] beautiful. And I'll tell you what – this is what I did when it came out. I was in the middle of working on *WeaponLord*, and we were doing these super-detailed Frazetta, Bisley-esque sprites with freaking veins, and just so much detail and density within the 16-bit pixels. Here comes *Darkstalkers* and I'm like, *Ah, shit. Simpler palette.*

> I thought what they showed us [when we first saw the game at Capcom Japan] was just the base colourform blockout. I talk about that a lot – make sure everything's broken up so you can track hands and track the fighting against the backgrounds and all that. But no. [The final game] was more detailed but not by much, colour-wise, and it seemed like it had more frames of animation. And I'm like, *Ah, shit. We should have done this with* WeaponLord. *Goddammit. It would have been faster.* So when I saw it, I had a moment of [Goddard hits his head] – because I was comparing it to my first game from scratch and going, *This thing is a masterpiece. This is where this is going. This is going to change everything.* I mean, it was crazy. All the morphing they did, it was so funny.

[Ed. note]   While the concept for *Darkstalkers* started with Universal's Monsters, the development team didn't restrict themselves to that lineup. Early on, the team batted around ideas for traditional Japanese monsters, and they ended up going with a variety of characters that team members felt would appeal to players around the world – with some disagreements along the way.

→   ALEX JIMENEZ
     Darkstalkers design support, Capcom USA

The character Felicia was vastly different than what I wanted. [...] I had originally wanted Felicia to be a Black Panther woman. I wanted her to be this beautiful, tall, Maasai woman from Africa and she'd be this really – think what we have now with [Marvel's] *Black Panther*. Like Okoye from *Black Panther*, you know? That really tall, beautiful woman, kind of a Maasai, really long limbs, who would fight you and during a special attack, she would actually shapeshift into a panther. And lunge on top of you and claw you and bite and whatnot. You know, like [horror film] *Cat People*. *Cat People* was my inspiration.

>   And they took that and they gave me the kitty cat, which I wasn't too crazy about. I was like, 'Seriously?' I was like, 'This really doesn't [work].' But, yeah. 'This is real popular in Japan. This is a real appealing thing. A black female character probably won't sell as well in Japan. It won't go on.' So I argued about it. I made my point. I took my stand, and then [Capcom USA senior vice-president] Frank [Ballouz] wisely said, 'Pick your battles', you know? 'If it's one character out of ten, let them have one.' So that's always something that sticks in the back of my mind because I think she would have been a fantastic character. And it would have gone a long way toward healing our perception of being culturally insensitive.

→   DAVE WINSTEAD
     Darkstalkers design support, Capcom USA

Cultural differences. Yes. Definitely when it came to the female characters, there was always a little bit of a worry. Felicia, for *Darkstalkers*, really caused some problems on the US side. So we went to visit Japan. They bounced [some ideas] off me and [Capcom USA senior vice-president Joe Morici]. And I remember, I stood with him. We were standing with each other. They were like,

'We want to show this to you because we want to make sure we don't offend anybody in America.'

They showed us Felicia, just animating. They didn't have any moves, really, or much in there. She just could walk and animate, and we looked at it. And I'm like, 'No, I wouldn't touch her. She looks great.' I thought she looked awesome. I'm like, 'Well, she's just got stuff that [mostly covers her body]', and this is back before a lot of people were really looking into this [sort of thing and saying], 'You know what? Maybe it's not quite right for kids to see stuff this crazy.' And so I was kind of like, 'I think she looks pretty good', and then Joe Morici walks in and he's just like, 'Oh, for sure. Ship it. No, that's fine.' And that's the story, because if anybody else on the [Capcom USA] consumer side had any say on that, they would have had clothing put on her, probably.

GOLD

As a follow-up to *Street Fighter II*, *Darkstalkers* had a lot riding on its shoulders. As for whether it was a success, like many things, it depends who you ask.

In a 2021 YouTube video, Okamoto said he considered the game a hit but Capcom founder Kenzo Tsujimoto felt otherwise. 'Sometime after the release, president Tsujimoto called me into his office,' Okamoto said. 'I thought he was going to praise me, but instead he said, 'Tell me, Okamoto ... why did this game fail?' I was like ... 'What? How can you call a game that sold over 24,000 copies a failure?' But compared to the earlier Street Fighter series, it wasn't a large amount.'

→   NORITAKA FUNAMIZU
              Darkstalkers producer, Capcom Japan

I thought it sold well. Okamoto thought it sold well. But, you know, Tsujimoto told Okamoto that he did not think it sold well. He made that very clear to us back in the day. In fact, we were just talking about it last week, too. I really don't know why he said that, considering that it did actually sell very well.

→   ALEX JIMENEZ
              Darkstalkers design support, Capcom USA

The first *Darkstalkers* sold very well. It wasn't near the Street Fighter level, obviously. But it did sell extremely well for the first year, and it carried on to the following year.

It sold better [in Japan than in the West]. It's funny. They were able to market it more over there. There was a lot more add-on material to it. [...] A lot of comic books. I've got a shelf-load of some of the manga things they did – I've got a bunch of them here right now, [that I'm] looking at. There was a lot of manga. A lot of hint books. A lot of background stuff. They did a lot more with it over there than they did here. I don't know if it was the appeal of monsters or whatnot, but they seemed to run with it more than we did in the States.

→   CHRIS KRAMER
    Darkstalkers game counsellor, Capcom USA

[It wasn't a success in the West] and weirdly, the PlayStation port was actually done by [British studio] Psygnosis because Capcom didn't have a whole lot of people internally doing development of games for home consoles. And with the start of the 32-bit era, there was a lot of new technology and they ended up just kind of looking around going, 'Well, we need someone to help us make this game. Who can do it?' And somebody had pointed [Psygnosis out to] Capcom Japan, and they're like, 'Oh, the guys at Psygnosis have been making Amiga games and they're really deep in on the PlayStation technology.' So for some reason, they were the ones who did the port.

[Ed. note]   Among players, *Darkstalkers* became a hardcore favourite, with many fans loving the characters and combat that built on the template Capcom had established with Street Fighter.

→   JAMES CHEN
    Fighting game commentator

Darkstalkers was a game that I fell in love with instantly. I played a ton of *Darkstalkers* when that came out.

→   JUSTIN BERENBAUM
    Darkstalkers customer service manager, Capcom USA

I loved that game when it came out. [...] I felt like it was an homage to anime mixed with Street Fighter.

→   JAMES CHEN
Fighting game commentator

What it really, honestly felt like is, it felt like it was Capcom's experiment, because [the developers] started adding crazy inputs into the game. Like Morrigan's air fireball originally was up-to-forward – it was an upside-down fireball.

→   STEPHEN FROST
Street Fighter 30th Anniversary Collection producer, Digital Eclipse

It had been out in circulation a little bit and there [were] already some moves lists for it, and I had printed [one] out on my dot matrix printer, and I distinctly remember in my head, I'm sitting over at the counter [of a nickel arcade in Oregon] paying for admission. I'm holding the FAQ with the moves list and I'm about to race upstairs to go play it. So I enjoyed that series quite a bit.

→   COREY TRESIDDER
Darkstalkers game counsellor, Capcom USA

I'm kind of into gothic music anyway, so I definitely connected with *Darkstalkers*. [...] I think probably the pros were the different colours and themes and just the character variations. [...] It was definitely different than *Street Fighter II*, but I think one of the cons is it was too close to *Street Fighter II*. I think that was probably one of the reasons why it was not that popular, or it didn't really do that well for Capcom, because it wasn't different enough and I think *Street Fighter II* was so popular that everybody just wanted that.

→   NORITAKA FUNAMIZU
Darkstalkers producer, Capcom Japan

We tried [to make something very different from Street Fighter], but I think we failed at that ... too much of it resembles Street Fighter.

→   JAMES GODDARD
    WeaponLord producer, Namco Hometek

This is an example of where, yeah, it's really beloved, but it's kind of niche. Hopefully people aren't offended if they see that quote, but if you think about it, it just never got the widespread love it should have had and it's probably just because of the style of it. I mean, I love that they have really different takes on – and brought in different kinds of – folklore and spirits and monsters.

[Ed. note]   Capcom went on to produce multiple Darkstalkers sequels through the mid and late 1990s, then moved away from the series as Capcom's more popular titles – like their Marvel fighting games – took over.

→   DAVE WINSTEAD
    Darkstalkers design support, Capcom USA

I actually loved *Darkstalkers* [...] I really kind of wish they would make another one. I would love it if they did.

→   STEPHEN FROST
    Street Fighter 30th Anniversary Collection producer, Digital Eclipse

I've always sort of wanted to pitch Capcom a [Darkstalkers collection] but I think just over the years, that series has kind of faded away, and while there's a hardcore audience that still loves it and still plays it, that number is not big enough to sort of justify a collection per se.

→   KATSUYA AKITOMO
    Darkstalkers concept designer, Capcom Japan

I think it's quite an honour that people still like it today. We loved videogames, and our motivation as game developers – and not just with *Darkstalkers* – was to create things we found fun and then share that enjoyment with as many people around the world as possible. And of course I got paid for that, and it supported a lifestyle for me where I could buy the toys and games and stuff that I loved. The fact that we were then able to create games that were loved by so many people, and are still enjoyed today, is a huge honour to me.

DARKSTALKERS: THE ANIMATED SERIES

Following *Darkstalkers'* release, Capcom spent time building the game into a multimedia brand, licensing a manga series, an anime series, action figures and other merchandise – with certain deals specific to Japan, and others focused on international markets. Some of these helped build the property into a franchise and established the characters as semi-recognizable pop culture figures, though not all of Capcom's efforts turned out exactly as planned.

→   ALEX JIMENEZ
      Darkstalkers design support, Capcom USA

We did a Darkstalkers cartoon. An American Darkstalkers cartoon. It was funny. I was informed of this in May of [1995]. It was around the 23rd of May, and I was called into our licensing agent's office, and he said, 'Did you ever work on *Darkstalkers*?' I go, 'Yes, as a matter of fact, I did.'

He goes, 'What did you do?' I said, 'I created the characters.' He goes, 'Oh, that's great, because we just licensed them into a cartoon show.'

Now, this was the time of [Disney's animated series] *Gargoyles* and whatnot, so I was stoked. That was going to be so cool. 'Oh, I love cartoons. This is going to be awesome.' He goes, 'Oh, you want to work on it?' 'Oh, I'd love to', you know? I was all over that. And they were like, 'OK, good.'

I was like, 'So will this be a midseason replacement in January?' He goes, 'No, the first episode is September 9.' I was like, 'How are you going to do a show in three months? An animated show.' He's like, 'The first six episodes are done. We need you to approve them.' 'Well, if they're already done, what is there to approve?' 'Read the script.'

I read the script, and they were horrendous. They were absolutely horrendous, so we muddled through with the first six episodes, which were terrible, and then the next ones we finally got to, actually, before they were animated; we got to look at the scripts and make changes. So from around episode eight up, it started getting a little bit better. We wanted to start making it less episodic [and give it more of a story arc]. I wanted to do *Gargoyles*, you know? I wanted to do something worthy of *Gargoyles*.

So we started making changes, but by then it was way too late, and I looked at the ratings. They had us on at 6 am on Sundays in the Bay Area. I looked at the ratings. Like, *the farm report is getting better ratings than we are right now.*
I knew we weren't going to come back.

I had a phone call from Richard Mueller, who was the lead writer for the show. He's like, 'Well, we've got one more [episode] to do. What do you want to do?' I go, 'Hey, we're not going to come back for a second season, obviously.' He goes, 'No, probably not.' I go, 'Well, let's have some fun with this. Let's go Shakespearean. Let's kill them all.' And he was like, 'You want to kill them? We can't do that.' I was like, 'Of course I can. I created them.'

I'm like, 'I created them. I can destroy them.'
And he started laughing. He goes, 'All right, Madame Medusa, Medea. Let's go do it.' So we wrote this grand battle where they fight it out and fight it out and finally, the kid, the last one standing, with his last ounce of energy, he finally destroys the vampire. He destroys them all. And the energy drain is so much that it knocks him out, and he keels over dead. Fade out. The end. So we typed this all up and we sent it off to Japan, because they always looked at the scripts.

And that morning, 2.30 in the morning, our time, I get a phone call. I'm going to keep this in historical accuracy so you might want to bleep it later.
But I get a phone call at 2 in the morning, broken English. 'Are you out [of your] fucking mind?' Not even 'hello'. Just, 'Are you out of

your mind?' I'm like, 'Wow. Who is this? What's going on?' 'It's me, Tom [Shiraiwa]. Are you crazy? You can't kill the characters. We're still selling the game.' I was like, 'Tom, no one's watching this thing. It doesn't matter.' 'You can't kill them.' 'Well, they're mine. I made them.' Like, 'Yeah, but we're making money off of them, so you can't kill them yet.'

CHAPTER 11

X-MEN: CHILDREN OF THE ATOM

If there's a lesson to learn from *Shaq Fu*, it's that the mid-1990s game industry would turn just about anything into a fighting game. A movie, a TV show, even just a celebrity – drop it into the template, and that was often enough to greenlight a game. So when Capcom started moving beyond Street Fighter and experimenting with other fighting games, it wasn't a surprise to see them take on a licence. This was the company, after all, that made an NES game based on a Domino's Pizza mascot.

For their first licensed fighting game, Capcom went for something a bit more aggressive. As part of an attempt to appeal to a Western audience, Capcom brought together some of the key staff behind *Street Fighter II* to imagine what an arcade game starring Marvel's X-Men could look like.

What they came up with became not only the most successful of Capcom's fighting game experiments, but the start of a 20-plus-year franchise.

HOW IT CAME ABOUT

X-Men: Children of the Atom wasn't Capcom's first game with Marvel. In the days before Capcom became a fighting game factory, they rolled out quite a few side-scrolling beat-'em-ups. And in 1993, Capcom and Marvel released *The Punisher*, a side-scroller in the *Final Fight* playbook. Marvel execs thought the game was too violent and Capcom struggled to elevate it above the sea of arcade beat-'em-ups, but both sides were happy enough to leave the door open for another collaboration.

At the same time, a new employee at Capcom Japan – who was also instrumental in the concept for *Darkstalkers* – started making noise around the office about his interest in Marvel properties.

→   KATSUYA AKITOMO
       X-Men: Children of the Atom advisor and artist, Capcom Japan

I applied for a job at Capcom around the time *Final Fight* came out. Because the game had been so successful, Capcom was looking to hire more staff, and I was in college and saw a job listing, so I applied for a job as a graphic artist, animator and pixel artist. Then I had an interview. I was asked to submit illustrations of the kind of art that I could draw. I remember submitting something Dragon Ball-related. When they saw the materials that I had drawn, they found out that I spoke English and I told them that I really wanted a job related to American comics.

When I joined Capcom, my first project was *The Punisher*. And during my training, while I was learning how to draw pixel art, [side-scrolling brawler] *Captain Commando* came out. At the time, the biggest game market was in North America. North America had 50 percent of the market,

Japan had 30 percent, and 20 percent was other territories. The issue with *Captain Commando* was that even though it was supposed to be a US- or an American-inspired game, it actually looked very Japanized, right? It was a lot like some of the popular things that were around at the time, like *Lupin the Third*, *Speed Racer*, *Battle of the Planets* and *Gatchaman*, right? All of these properties tried to imitate American comic book culture, and sometimes they didn't look authentic. They didn't look quite American enough, and I felt that if you wanted to go for the authentic American feel, you had to properly culturalize things. We were trying to imitate people who themselves were influenced by American comic books, so our creations were twice removed from the original American sources.

So when I joined Capcom in 1991, I felt I needed to introduce the Capcom staff to more of the authentic, original American comic books.

→ TAKESHI TEZUKA
X-Men: Children of the Atom planner, Capcom Japan

Akitomo was always a big fan of American comics, even as a kid before he joined Capcom. I remember when he joined the company, he was always giving American comic books to the designers in order to inspire them. So you could say Akitomo was like the Marvel ambassador inside of Capcom.

[Ed. note]   Akitomo made a strong impression on the Marvel staff, who remember him under a variety of nicknames.

→ DANA MORESHEAD
Head of creative services, Marvel Entertainment

They had a great team [at Capcom]. I believe there was a guy who I only knew as 'Marvel Fan'. Even on his business card, he also had his name written: 'Marvel Fan'. [...] I remember there were a few meetings when – while everybody else was doing business stuff – he and myself and one of the other people were duelling sketches back and forth.

→   JUSTIN MCCORMACK
        Executive vice-president of consumer products, Marvel Entertainment

I remember fondly Dana and I, and I believe one other person – [Marvel creative director] Mike Thomas, I think – going up to [visit Capcom]. They sat us down, and we had a conference room dedicated to us, and they brought in this kid called Marvel Zombie.

[Ed. note]   While Akitomo doesn't take credit for the idea behind *Children of the Atom*, and says he never pitched an X-Men game, team members say that his influence around the office played a role in Capcom pursuing the licence, getting Marvel to trust Capcom with it, and turning many Capcom employees into Marvel fans.

→   KATSUYA AKITOMO
        X-Men: Children of the Atom advisor and artist, Capcom Japan

Officially, the only game I proposed [at Capcom] was *Darkstalkers*. But actually, the whole reason *Children of the Atom* was able to get off the ground was because the comic series *Marvels* had come out. It was painted by Alex Ross and, I think given the content of the publication, this was the kind of comic that could inform people about American culture, right? They could see what kinds of stories were being told, and that comic books could be seen as a reflection of people's views on American culture, so I thought it was very important for me to show this to the staff at Capcom. I even translated it from English to Japanese, and after I did that, I think there was this sentiment growing within the team that they wanted to make a Marvel game, and it turned out that [Capcom Japan executive producer] Yoshiki Okamoto had acquired the rights to use the X-Men in a videogame. We weren't sure at the time what kind of videogame he wanted to make, just that he had acquired the rights. And actually, at the same time, he also told me that we could use all the Marvel characters. [...] So I think in terms of the initial conceptualization of the X-Men game, I can't take credit for that. It would be Okamoto.

→   ALEX JIMENEZ
             X-Men: Children of the Atom design support, Capcom USA

X-Men was something we had recommended [on the US side]. We recommended doing a Marvel [head-to-head fighting] game using superheroes. Superheroes are made to order for that. And we were told to get one of the most popular ones, and at that time – mid-1990s – X-Men, they were on top of the universe.

> The minute I heard [Capcom Japan was interested], I jumped on top of [Capcom USA senior vice-president Frank Ballouz] and was like, 'We got to do this', you know? 'We got to do this. I'm telling you. It's going to make a fortune. It's going to be great. It will cement us. No one else has done this yet.' Data East came out with a side-scroller of [Marvel's *Captain America and The Avengers*]. I'm like, 'We're going to blow them out of the water with X-Men, because I don't know a kid out there in America now that doesn't want to be Wolverine.' So we were just all over it. I pushed it and pushed it and pushed it.

→   SCOTT SMITH
             X-Men: Children of the Atom marketing manager, Capcom USA

It's weird considering where Marvel is today, but Marvel wanted to get into the market in Japan, and I think they were looking for opportunities, and videogames were one of them, to penetrate the market and kind of make their properties a little more well known.

→ KATSUYA AKITOMO
X-Men: Children of the Atom advisor and artist, Capcom Japan

Another thing was that Konami had just released [side-scrolling beat-'em-up] *X-Men*, which was a big hit for them [in America]. I think it was entertaining enough and people talked about it, but the thing is, a lot of players in Japan thought the game was unfair. For a lot of Japanese gamers, fairness is one of the most important elements of the gameplay experience. So because of that, it didn't do well in the Japanese market at all. Also, even though the 1991 X-Men comic had come out by then, Konami's *X-Men* arcade game was based on an animated pilot [from 1988 called *Pryde of the X-Men*]. I think only one episode ended up being made. So by the time Konami's arcade game came out, it just seemed kind of old and the visuals were obviously different from what the comic book had shown us, so I thought it wasn't really that interesting and it was a little too old. So I felt that we could do better.

→ DANA MORESHEAD
Head of creative services, Marvel Entertainment

[Konami's *X-Men* game was in development] right as I came into the licensing group. And you can tell, because honestly, they used clip art [for the arcade cabinet artwork], which I tried never to do on videogame cabinets. [...] A part of it was, we would always have to navigate those aspects – like, which continuity is this project from? Is it from the animated series, which was slightly different than the comics? If it was in the comics, what time period was it from? What can we borrow? Which eras can we borrow from?

→ JUSTIN MCCORMACK
Executive vice-president of consumer products, Marvel Entertainment

I just remember coming in and my boss, [Marvel head of licensing] Jerry Calabrese – great guy, but he was kind of all about the numbers. For the videogames, between Sega and Capcom and I'm trying to remember whoever else, we would do these, like,

December 25th end-of-the-quarter deals, and they would be all verbal and Jerry would just whip these deals out.

> He really shot from the hip. He was a great guy, great businessman. He was just like, 'Make it work. Make it work. We'll do it.' And so again, we'd have these eleventh-hour million-, half-million-dollar deals, in order to make budget. But then it would be like, 'OK. Now you guys sort out the mess that we just created.' So that would be what happened. We would always kind of be bandaging or fixing it up or rehabilitating deals that had sort of been done in the eleventh hour on a cocktail napkin because they were trying to make the quarter.

→ ALEX JIMENEZ
X-Men: Children of the Atom design support, Capcom USA

At that time, luckily for us, Marvel was not doing well financially, you know? They were on the rocks, really on the rocks, and they were more than willing to license us the characters quickly and easily. They were like, 'Oh, sure. Here.' They were desperate for money. They were literally – I mean, they actually did file Chapter 11 in [1996], so they were desperate for cash. So they gave us X-Men, and we took it and ran with it from there. The guys really did a great job with that one.

→ DANA MORESHEAD
Head of creative services, Marvel Entertainment

I think [*Children of the Atom*] happened relatively early on and would have been very, as they say, easy [to negotiate]. I think [the later games] would have been more difficult. That had nothing to do – or very little to do – with Capcom, as much as it was navigating the other deals in existence. [...] I always had a great respect for our sales teams as they had to navigate all that stuff.

We were always touting our hundred – all of our characters. The reality was, obviously Spider-Man and the X-Men were the most popular, but we also had Punisher, which was popular. Silver Surfer – well-known character, but difficult, number one, to render. At that point, the technology wasn't great. We had people coming at us for Hulk on his own. I mean, there were random characters that people could come in and get licences for, because those characters had nothing on the dance card.

NISHITANI'S CHOICE

As Capcom put together the pieces for the game that would become *Children of the Atom*, the company needed someone to run the project. While Akitomo knew the licence inside out, he didn't have experience as a game designer or project leader, so Capcom needed someone else to direct the game. Enter *Street Fighter II* planner Akira Nishitani.

→   TAKESHI TEZUKA
      X-Men: Children of the Atom planner, Capcom Japan

One day, Okamoto called Nishitani and I into a meeting, and he gave Nishitani the option. Okamoto asked him, 'Do you want to work on *Street Fighter III*, or do you want to work on an X-Men game?' Nishitani chose X-Men.

→   KATSUYA AKITOMO
      X-Men: Children of the Atom advisor and artist, Capcom Japan

It was significant, you know? Because Nishitani had made *Final Fight* and *Street Fighter II*. So I thought his presence on this team meant things would go well.

→   TAKESHI TEZUKA
      X-Men: Children of the Atom planner, Capcom Japan

I was happy [he chose X-Men]. When you deal with a franchise like Street Fighter, it's a fighting game, but the characters are basically human, and thus limited to realistic – albeit greatly exaggerated – movements. But with the Marvel series, you're dealing with superheroes who can do anything, and there had been lots of requests to do something different, so I thought it was a good idea. So, yeah. It was Nishitani's decision, but even if I had made the call, I probably would have gone with X-Men anyway.

Also, *Street Fighter III* would have been a lot of pressure, since it's such a huge, popular series, and I didn't have the confidence for that.

→   KATSUYA AKITOMO
            X-Men: Children of the Atom advisor and artist, Capcom Japan

Nishitani had hit a point where he had done everything he could think of with the Street Fighter series. He felt that there was really nothing left he could do without making changes to the fundamentals of Street Fighter, and so if he were to be involved in it, he felt like there would be no point. With X-Men, on the other hand, once Nishitani saw those characters and heard about their powers, he started getting a lot of ideas. For example, if you look at a character like Cyclops, he shoots out these wicked beams from his eyes, right? And it didn't seem like there would be opportunities to do anything like that in the Street Fighter series.

MAKING TWO GAMES IN PARALLEL

Around the time Capcom signed up to make *Children of the Atom*, they also signed up for a Super NES action game, *X-Men: Mutant Apocalypse*, and a second arcade fighting game: *Marvel Super Heroes*. For Capcom's arcade group, that meant planning *Children of the Atom* and *Marvel Super Heroes* in parallel, with one group of artists working on *Marvel* in the background while another group – along with the planners, programmers and other staff – initially focused on *Children of the Atom*.

Capcom ended up releasing *Marvel Super Heroes* to arcades less than a year after *Children of the Atom*, establishing their Marvel fighting game series from the start. Some had differing opinions on whether *Marvel Super Heroes* was a sequel in the traditional sense, though, given the similar mechanics but distinct story and cast.

→   TAKESHI TEZUKA
      X-Men: COTA planner and Marvel Super Heroes director, Capcom Japan

You could say that we made *Marvel Super Heroes* as a sequel to *Children of the Atom* in the same way *Street Fighter II: Champion Edition* was a 'sequel' to *SFII*. But *Children of the Atom* only used X-Men characters, and Marvel had more popular characters from the Marvel universe at the time, such as Spider-Man and Iron Man, so when we were making them, we figured they'd be viewed as different games. It's sort of like, as the creators, internally, we saw *Marvel* as a sequel, but as a commercial product, we wanted to present it as its own distinct game.

→   ALEX JIMENEZ
      X-Men: COTA and Marvel Super Heroes design support, Capcom USA

Marvel Super Heroes came on the heels of *Children of the Atom*. Everyone was expecting us to do an X-Men 2, you know? Everyone was expecting a sequel to that, and instead we came out literally a year, not even a year and a half later [with *Marvel Super Heroes*]. [...] When I got the word on that, I was obviously delighted, but I was like, *Oh, this is a change in pace.* I was like, *Cool. We're not just doing an add-on like* Darkstalkers *[did with its follow-up* Night Warriors: Darkstalkers' Revenge*]. We're doing a whole different game. This is cool.*

[Ed. note]   *Marvel Super Heroes* marked Tezuka's chance to direct a game for the first time. After working as a planner on Capcom's brawler *Cadillacs and Dinosaurs*, he played a support role on *Children of the Atom* while overseeing *Marvel Super Heroes* in the background. Then, as design and programming staff finished their work on *Children of the Atom* and rolled on to *Marvel Super Heroes* – and *COTA* director Nishitani left Capcom – Tezuka took on a larger role overseeing the team. Asked if Nishitani's departure opened a slot for Tezuka to direct *Marvel Super Heroes*, Tezuka says he saw it differently.

→   TAKESHI TEZUKA
      X-Men: COTA planner and Marvel Super Heroes director, Capcom Japan

Actually, it's the opposite. It was decided from the start that I would be the director of *Marvel*, so if anything, Nishitani was allowed to quit Capcom because there was another director ready for *Marvel*.

[Ed. note]   Nishitani and Tezuka are officially listed as planners for their roles on *Children of the Atom* and *Marvel Super Heroes*, due to Capcom's loose crediting practices at the time. Employees often held different titles inside the company than they did in credit rolls appearing in games, and their titles in credit rolls didn't always reflect the work done on those games.

CONTROLLING THE MADNESS

When designing the gameplay for its Marvel games, Capcom made a conscious effort to move away from the Street Fighter template that it had established years earlier. Many fighting games of the era felt like *Street Fighter II* with a different skin – sharing the same moves and character archetypes – but in *Children of the Atom* and *Marvel Super Heroes*, Capcom leaned into what made the licences unique. Characters could leap multiple screens into the air, pull off 99-hit combos, and fill the screen with the sorts of chaos normally reserved for other mediums.

→   AKIRA YASUDA
         X-Men: COTA and Marvel Super Heroes character designer, Capcom Japan

If you compare X-Men to Street Fighter, the X-Men are mutants with special powers. So part of what we had to consider when we were designing the game was how we could take the move system in our fighting games and use it to express the special abilities that the X-Men have. While some of the characters in the Street Fighter series could be said to have superhuman powers, for the Marvel games we did like *Children of the Atom*, all of the characters were defined by being mutants with superpowers, so from the get-go we decided to try and make their special moves more intense and flashy.

→   KATSUYA AKITOMO
         X-Men: COTA and Marvel Super Heroes advisor and artist, Capcom Japan

Children of the Atom was obviously about controlling the madness, and if you have a theme of controlling madness, the result will be something that looks wild, right? Nishitani and Yasuda, I think, were big proponents of this idea of controlling the madness, and I think that that became a very prevalent theme in the game. So at the time, I personally did not have any worries about how that would turn out. In fact, I felt that the more flashy the game was, the more fun it would be, and I think that's what every team member felt as well. I mean, maybe we did too much with the game. Maybe we went too far. But we didn't really know that or feel that at the time.

→   JAMES CHEN
               X-Men: COTA and Marvel Super Heroes FAQ writer

The combo system was so free-form, and it was so revolutionary at the time that nobody knew how to do any of the stuff. You could launch people, go into air combos and all that stuff, and nobody was doing it. But I kind of figured it out after a while because I was obsessed with combos, and that was the game that actually got me started writing my FAQs. I actually got known for writing FAQs at one point, and that was the game that kind of spurred that on.

→   KEN WILLIAMS
               Assistant editor, Electronic Gaming Monthly magazine

It was all about pulling off these combos – especially a bunch of air combos if you can pull them off, and stuff like that. I didn't really care for it. There's not much of a ground game, and I didn't like the variety of it.

→   ALEX JIMENEZ
               X-Men: COTA and Marvel Super Heroes design support, Capcom USA

We got a lot of that with *Children of the Atom*. Because we were doing the double vertical screen, where you had the super jumps going really, really high up. We got a lot of pushback on that. A lot of people didn't like that. They found it too confusing and too fast-paced, and I countered by pointing out, 'Well, you guys loved *Street Fighter II Turbo*, and that was ten times faster than this.' As far as the screen being too high, bear in mind: these aren't martial artists. These are superheroes, you know? So they should be able to go higher, faster. I mean, come on. Half of them fly.

→ CHRIS TANG
Marvel vs. Capcom design support, Capcom USA

Originally, I didn't like [Capcom's Marvel fighting games]. I thought having a beam cannon and doing many, many hits was cheesy. I kind of felt like – because I was really into skill-based fighting games – doing a combo and making the counter go up to a high number, that kind of meant something. If I got a 20-hit combo, I earned all those hits. [...] [Capcom's Marvel games] cheapened it. It was like, you do a beam cannon and, 'Oh, 30 hits just like that, for free.'

→ TAKESHI TEZUKA
X-Men: COTA planner and Marvel Super Heroes director, Capcom Japan

We did do that intentionally, and the reason is because I think everything that came with *Street Fighter II Turbo* and after became more and more focused on hardcore gamers. And more casual gamers ended up getting shut out of that. So for the Marvel games, we wanted to make up for that by putting in a system that even ordinary players could enjoy easily. That's why we put in all the various combos that were easy to access. Unlike *Street Fighter II*, where the different special moves all required their own individual inputs, for the Marvel games we decided to make most of them share common inputs for simplicity's sake. That way even bad players could enjoy the games.

→ MATT ATWOOD
Marvel vs. Capcom public relations manager, Capcom USA

I think the big impact and the multiscreen combos and all that stuff was intimidating, but I think that the licences helped keep people engaged.

THE CAPCOM/MARVEL RELATIONSHIP

When developing *Children of the Atom* and *Marvel Super Heroes*, Capcom and Marvel were simultaneously making games and learning how to work with one another. Though the companies had collaborated before on *The Punisher*, new staff and rising expectations put more focus on the partnership and communication between the two.

→ DANA MORESHEAD
Head of creative services, Marvel Entertainment

We were a very small group back then. My team was a grand total of six people; six people including myself. We worked for marketing but spent most of our time with the licensing sales team, and they came in with the Capcom project. And from there on in, we were connected at the hip to Capcom for the longest time.

This is all pre-internet, so we had developed this very unique, longhand form of working together where we would [look over] the game documents, the character reference [materials], which moves they do, what they couldn't do. [...] We would get these 60-page faxes, or we would get a FedEx or international shipment with a few hundred pages in it [with] the character animations, because it was easier. They would basically handwrite the name. It might be that it was 'Super Piledriver Twist', and then they would sketch it out – an actual pencil drawing of what Omega Red was going to do, or what Wolverine was going to do – and then we would go back in and tweak. Sometimes it would be fine. Other times, we would make little tweaks. And sometimes we'd have to adjust the names because, even though they didn't always appear on screen, the last thing we wanted was sort of an odd name showing up in one of these reference or how-to books. Once we got that process down, it all went relatively smoothly. A huge 'relatively'. So much, so much work.

→   JUSTIN MCCORMACK
        Executive vice-president of consumer products, Marvel Entertainment

My bosses were more concerned about the money, unless there was a backlash creatively. Dana, because he was more of a fanboy and was charged with creative, he tried to be the enforcer, and I was always brought in to kind of help give Dana back-up. You know, yell at people, that kind of thing.

→   NORITAKA FUNAMIZU
        X-Men: COTA planner and Marvel Super Heroes producer, Capcom Japan

We saw *Children of the Atom* and *Marvel Super Heroes* as a natural extension of our previous work on the Street Fighter games – it was like working on 'Street Fighter III' to us. So we started working on them, but the issue was that our character designs were very different from the original American comic designs. We changed their designs a lot, to be more fitting for a videogame. We fought a great deal with the American Marvel offices over this. We just couldn't seem to agree.

→   KATSUYA AKITOMO
        X-Men: COTA and Marvel Super Heroes advisor and artist, Capcom Japan

Because I knew so much about the Marvel franchises, people often came to me and asked me for information, so I ended up being the one who was also kind of in charge of making sure the right ideas were presented to Marvel. Sometimes people came up with ideas that misunderstood Marvel's intentions or what they were willing to allow. But if the idea was good and if the idea would make fans happy, then Marvel would obviously approve it.

I spent a lot of time translating comics for Capcom and consulting with the team. For example, I'd point things out and answer their questions, like explaining the difference in size and weight between Juggernaut and Spider-Man, or explaining how dangerous Juggernaut was and his whole 'unstoppable' thing, or helping them get the right level of pomposity and arrogance for Dr. Doom's lines. Lots of little things like that.

→   TAKESHI TEZUKA
     X-Men: COTA planner and Marvel Super Heroes director, Capcom Japan

I remember going to New York and negotiating with Marvel. [...] What kind of characters we should use, explaining how the game system worked, getting their understanding of that. [...] I remember proposing some characters we wanted to use in [*Children of the Atom*], but Marvel didn't agree to let us use them. The opposite was also true, where they wanted us to put certain characters into the game, but then we turned them down because those characters didn't fit the game system that we were using.

One of the characters I wanted was Venom. We couldn't put him into the game. [...] Well, he was never in *X-Men* to begin with, but he didn't appear in *Marvel Super Heroes* either, so ... hmmm ... Venom was a really major character, big enough that we probably would have had to get a whole separate licence for him, so perhaps Capcom didn't want to make things too complicated. No one ever said that, though, I should add. But the basic reason, I think, was because we based *Marvel Super Heroes* on the Infinity Gauntlet storyline, and Venom wasn't in that.

→   DANA MORESHEAD
     Head of creative services, Marvel Entertainment

[With licensing in general] you'd get somebody that wanted to take an X-Men licence and they would try to throw in members of the Fantastic Four or Spider-Man or just somebody that showed up in an X-Men comic. We're like, 'Well, no. That's not quite who the X-Men are.' And even later, just dividing them up even between the teams – which characters work together, which ones don't. Are they the good guys or the bad guys? There was always a little pushback. People would try to work in characters or properties, even backgrounds that weren't part of the character's universe.

→   ALEX JIMENEZ
      X-Men: COTA and Marvel Super Heroes design support, Capcom USA

We [had a lot of back and forth between Capcom USA and Capcom Japan as well], especially on *Marvel Super Heroes,* more than *Children of the Atom. Marvel Super Heroes* had a lot of debate on the characters, for who we could and couldn't use.

I wanted to have Gambit in *Children of the Atom.*

I remember I wanted to have Gambit, and they wouldn't let me have Gambit. They felt Gambit was a crook. He was a thief, so they didn't want to use Gambit. They didn't want to use Rogue because Rogue's powers would be too difficult to reproduce, you know? Her ability to drain other people and take their powers – they thought it would be a little too tricky to do, especially for basically a 16-bit videogame. [It would have been] a little hard [to pull off].

Marvel Super Heroes was the one I really disagreed with. I really disagreed with using Blackheart. I thought there were so many other characters we wanted to use. I wanted to have The Thing – Ben Grimm and The Thing. And Thor. Those were the main ones I wanted to do. They were like, 'No, can't go with that', so ...

→   DANA MORESHEAD
      Head of creative services, Marvel Entertainment

That part. Sort of sitting around in a room with arcane faxing and emailing back – well, barely emailing – sending notes back and forth about who the team could be was always one of the most interesting parts. I still remember when we were talking about the *Marvel Super Heroes* game, they asked for Shuma-Gorath. It's always interesting, because everybody is familiar with the Marvel mainstays, but when you're in a meeting and somebody in there, on their list of the first asks, has Shuma-Gorath, [it's a surprise].

> Even our team, which was made up of some pretty hardcore – let's be honest – geeks, I think half of them just looked at each other like, 'Who? Is that ours? Is that yours?' On my team, there were three of us that had grown up in and around comics, and we all were just like, 'The Doctor Strange villain? The squid with one eye?' 'OK, sure. By all means, you can have Shuma-Gorath.'

→ TAKESHI TEZUKA
X-Men: COTA planner and Marvel Super Heroes director, Capcom Japan

Unfortunately, Marvel Comics had very little visibility and awareness in Japan at the time, and so I remember when we were trying to select the characters for inclusion in the game, we wanted characters that Japanese gamers could easily identify with as well.

→ DANA MORESHEAD
Head of creative services, Marvel Entertainment

In some cases, we had other existing deals. Especially Spider-Man. Spider-Man had videogames long before X-Men did, so there were existing deals we needed to sort of navigate around. And even when they branched out to do a *Marvel Super Heroes* game, we needed to make sure that the characters were not only balanced from a performance and play point of view, but from an intellectual property point of view. [We didn't want the cast to be] three-quarters Spider-Man characters.

→ JUSTIN MCCORMACK
Executive vice-president of consumer products, Marvel Entertainment

Gameplay was also an issue, right? Because there were plenty of parents' groups that were, at this point, kind of hot about the violence in videogames. And so that was something that was really the only reason I had to be involved, because I was the one person on our side who had the business clout to say, 'No, you can't do that.' But Capcom was always pretty compliant.

> The Japanese, the Japanese companies [...] they kind of did what they wanted to do and they would, a lot of times, just go ahead and then ask for apologies later, you know? Or apologize later, or pretend they didn't understand what we were talking about. They would just sort of forge ahead. And that's kind of how the *Punisher* game came out so violent. Somebody was asleep at the wheel on our side, and it was just like, *Wow. This is a pretty heavy game.* And it's a great game, you know? I loved that game. But it was [more violent than the game industry was accustomed to at that point].

[Relatively, though,] Capcom was chill. We had a good relationship with them.

[Ed. note]   Marvel's approvals commonly centred around character choices and visuals, though towards the end of *Children of the Atom*'s development, Capcom and Marvel came across another challenge – getting the right voices in the game.

→   ALEX JIMENEZ
       X-Men: COTA and Marvel Super Heroes design support, Capcom USA

One thing that was funny was, [Capcom Japan] called me up in a panic [...] literally less than two weeks before the game was supposed to be shipped. They called up in a panic saying that Marvel had turned down all the voice [actors] they'd come up with.

> All the voice-over and audio for the game had been rejected except for the Silver Samurai; that was the only one they accepted. 'They rejected all the others. What are we going to do?' I was like, 'Well, who did you get to do the voice-overs?' 'Oh, we got English-speaking people.' I'm like, 'Were they Japanese? They have accents, you know.

You can't have Wolverine with a Japanese accent.
It doesn't work.'

So they were in a panic. They wanted me to talk to Marvel and get Marvel to go with it. I'm like, 'Look, they're not going to, no matter what you do, so let me see what I can do.' And I called up the head of licensing at Marvel at the time, a gentleman named Joe Calamari. He was the president of licensing. I said, 'Joe, who does the voice-over work for the animated X-Men cartoon?' And he's like, 'Oh, it's a group up in Canada. They're really helpful', bop-bop-bop. He goes, 'You want me to set you up?' I'm like, 'Yeah, please. May I get their number?' So I called them up. I told them who I was, what I was trying to do, and the woman up there was wonderful. She was the head of – it was called Dome [Productions], up there in Toronto.

And they said, 'OK, which ones do you need?' And I told her which characters I need. 'OK, well, we can get you these characters plus the studio time. Would $5,000 be too much?' $5,000 for all the characters and the studio time? Canadian? I was like, 'Oh!' And I immediately set it all up, and I called [Capcom localization manager Tom Shiraiwa] in Japan. I said, 'Hey, tell the guys to pack their bags. We're going to Canada.' He's, 'What do you mean?' I go, 'We're going to go this Thursday.' 'Are you sure they're going to approve these voices?' I go, 'Yeah, because we're using the characters they actually have already, so they're already preset. Joe Calamari has already assured me they are preapproved.'

So they were delighted. We got to work with the actual X-Men, and we actually used that as one of the sale points that we were using. We were connecting it directly to the animated series. We were using the actors from that.

→   DANA MORESHEAD
       Head of creative services, Marvel Entertainment

I do remember [that situation]. I don't remember it as quite that big a time crunch. But yeah, they submitted, and really what wound up happening is, that first game was very much – it was a lovely trial by fire where all of these creative people, both on our side and their side, were used to working in our own very special and unique ways. Suddenly, we're working together, trying to get a game done. You know, their team, maybe they had three or four people that spoke English. We didn't speak any Japanese. So we literally, with the first release, [we] were trying to pioneer the way that we were going to hopefully do more.

> I do remember the voices coming in and that basically the path of least resistance was for them to just essentially employ the [actors from the animated series]. And I don't remember if they got all of the voice actors, but some of the voice actors. They hired the voice-over studio in Canada to do the voices. [...] And I remember it was quick. I don't remember it being quite two weeks. But I'll still give them the benefit of the doubt. It makes for a good story, right?

THE START OF SOMETHING BIG

When *Children of the Atom* hit arcades in late 1994 and early 1995, it made an instant impact on players. There had been licensed fighting games before, but it was the first to break through to competitive fighting game fans and show that licensed games could stand up well next to hardcore favourites like Street Fighter.

While Akitomo remembers the arcade game selling very poorly in Japan and below expectations in the US, those we spoke to on the US side recall the game being one of Capcom's biggest successes of the mid-1990s.

→   DANA MORESHEAD
              Head of creative services, Marvel Entertainment

We couldn't have planned it better if we tried. [...] It was a huge seller. It's when the X-Men animated series had come on the air. [...] So it was a huge, huge – I mean, it exceeded everybody's expectations.

→   CHRIS KRAMER
              X-Men: Children of the Atom game counsellor, Capcom USA

That was the 1990s, dude. That was the X-Men era. That cartoon was on and making Marvel more money than they would make until the movies started, right? So that was Marvel's bread and butter at that point in time.

→   TAKESHI TEZUKA
              X-Men: COTA planner and Marvel Super Heroes director, Capcom Japan

Of course, the Marvel games were developed primarily targeting overseas markets, but in Japan, the fact that a Japanese company like Capcom was making those games was obviously its own marketing point. In terms of the American comics market in Japan, I think Capcom's games helped Marvel become more popular.

→
ALEX JIMENEZ
X-Men: COTA and Marvel Super Heroes design support, Capcom USA

[Capcom] banked on the popularity of X-Men. They took a bit of a gamble; I've got to give them credit for that. They took a bit of a gamble on it. *Children of the Atom* was their first hero-licensed game with Marvel, and they took a little gamble on that, and it paid off extremely well. *Children of the Atom* was a very, very popular game. Very successful title.

[Ed. note]   Following *Children of the Atom* and *Marvel Super Heroes*, Capcom took the series in a different direction with their first crossover fighting game: *X-Men vs. Street Fighter*. As the series grew, it eventually transformed into Marvel vs. Capcom and became one of Capcom's long-running staples with multiple sequels – and the only one of Capcom's fighting game franchises, apart from Street Fighter, to last more than 20 years.

→
DANA MORESHEAD
Head of creative services, Marvel Entertainment

Generally what would happen is, we would have a deal for one or two arcade games. If that went well, [the licensee] would come back and we would figure out [what to do next] – you know, Capcom would come back and say, 'We want to do more.' And we would say either yes or no. And the Capcom relationship was unique in that it really did grow exponentially. So we went from trying out one game to being very happy with the results. And then going to another game, and another game, and another game.

But each time they would expand, they would – we'd try to add more stuff. So, it snowballs. It starts with one and then goes to two if everybody performs. Goes to three and four, and then, when it became relatively easy to port that motherboard over from the arcade game to make the home version, then all the brakes came off, because suddenly we were able to take their area of expertise, which really was the stand-up game, and bring them home.

[When we got to *X-Men vs. Street Fighter*], I don't think that we had ever done a character crossover before in licensing. [...] It was a big deal.

They're like, 'We want to do this.'

And we're like, 'Let's try it. Let's try it.'

CHAPTER 12

STREET FIGHTER ALPHA

In the early 1990s, Capcom had started to develop a reputation. In a world before games became services, the company had a thing for incremental upgrades.

It started small, with *Street Fighter II: Champion Edition*. The idea that designed itself. Millions of fans wanted to play as the bosses, and *Street Fighter II* had been enough of a sensation that they were happy to get anything new.

Then came *Hyper Fighting*. Again, it made sense, as a reaction to hacked versions of *Champion Edition*. And many loved the speed, despite minimal other changes.

When *Super Street Fighter II* came around, the naming convention started to get a little silly. And by *Super Street Fighter II Turbo*, it all felt like a bit of a con. But players loved the games, so they kept putting in tokens.

Behind the scenes, Capcom had business considerations players weren't aware of. They had excess hardware to clear out and, as the series took off, a development pipeline they needed to keep running. Publicly, though, players saw Capcom pumping out upgrades and spinoffs, rather than moving forward to the next numbered Street Fighter sequel. So when the time came for the next Street Fighter game after *Super Turbo*, many assumed the next step would be *Street Fighter III*. Capcom had drawn out *Street Fighter II* for three years,

so the obvious move was to finally take a proper
step forward.

Instead, Capcom announced a detour and
went back in time.

A GAME OF CONVENIENCE

Street Fighter Alpha: Warriors' Dreams wasn't a remake, though it had traits of one. Falling early in the Street Fighter timeline, the game brought back two characters from the original *Street Fighter* and two characters from *Final Fight*, and folded them into a game that played like the next incremental step after *Super Street Fighter II Turbo*.

With popular characters like Chun-Li and Akuma on board, and a new look that added a youthful, anime-inspired style, Capcom put together a game that bought themselves time before the next proper numbered Street Fighter sequel would be ready – and again allowed them to use up leftover arcade hardware. This time, Capcom had stockpiled large quantities of their CPS-1 boards, so it began developing *Alpha* for the legacy tech rather than the newer CPS-2. But partway through development, the company's priorities shifted, moving the game to CPS-2 without much time to take advantage of the new hardware. Capcom ended up releasing two versions of the game: the main release on CPS-2, and a slightly compromised version for their CPS Changer hardware (which was essentially a CPS-1 designed for home use).

→   NORITAKA FUNAMIZU
        Street Fighter Alpha planner, Capcom Japan

To explain the whole story of how the Street Fighter Alpha series came about, there were a few different factors at play. First off, one of the sales tactics that we used to sell CPS-2 boards was that we offered to buy back the leftover CPS-1 boards that a lot of arcades had. And we had done enough of that that we were building up a big stock of CPS-1 boards.

> By this point, [we had been doing this for a while and] I was personally sick of hearing about problems of excess inventory, and I pretended not to know anything about it. But there was this warehouse where they kept all of them, and they were just kind of stacking up over time.

→ HIDEAKI ITSUNO
Street Fighter Alpha planner, Capcom Japan

Yeah, initially we were working on trying to get rid of the CPS-1 boards, but then halfway through the process, we realized we had a decent amount of CPS-2 boards left over as well, so it was this combined inventory ... we were trying to figure out how to get rid of all that. [laughs] In terms of the exact numbers, I don't remember, but considering there was such effort put into getting rid of them, I imagine we had quite a lot.

→ NORITAKA FUNAMIZU
Street Fighter Alpha planner, Capcom Japan

So that's kind of the first factor that led to *Alpha*.

> The second factor was, we had a lot of freedom in planning the game, and we started thinking there were a lot of players whose skill and technique were incredible. It was a problem because normal players couldn't go into an arcade and play anymore. Everyone was too good. So we wanted to create a game that would lower that threshold.

Also, at that time some new designers joined Capcom, and they were recruited for [*Street Fighter II* planner Akira Yasuda's] new design group. That design team had Kinu Nishimura and [Naoto] Kuroshima, whose pen name was Bengus. His first job was to illustrate drawings of *Street Fighter I* characters, but reimagined in a modern style. It was for a gaming magazine, which I can't remember the name of. They were really great, though. I kept saying over and over how amazing they were. Eventually [Street Fighter II series programmer Seiji] Okada heard this, and he said to me, kind of off-handedly, 'Hey, if they're good, why don't we try making a Street Fighter II game with these *Street Fighter I* characters, like you've been talking about?'

My first impression was one of slight panic: 'Oh god no, not again. Don't make me deal with this again!'

Anyway, we ended up deciding that we'd make a game based off those designs of Kuroshima's. And it was partially a way to use up the CPS-1 inventory that I mentioned. Plus, we had all these new employees – I mean, a lot of them – to train. Also, [Street Fighter II series lead programmer Shinichi] Ueyama had been leading the programming team for a long time – which is to say, not 'leading' a team; it was just him at first – but around this time the leadership passed to Okada and his team for this project. With Okada in, I decided to throw my hat in too, and agreed to be a part of it. What I was not prepared for, though, was the impossible three-month deadline we were then given.

→   SEIJI OKADA
       Street Fighter Alpha lead programmer, Capcom Japan

Yeah, I learned that the *Alpha* team had been given a three-month deadline to make the game. So even though I was working on something else, I thought to myself, *There's no way they'll make it without my help.* That's how I ended up joining the team. [...] I had been doing research on the PlayStation, and it was my first time learning about 3D. But then, just as I was starting to understand it, I had to switch over to *Street Fighter Alpha.*

→   NORITAKA FUNAMIZU
       Street Fighter Alpha planner, Capcom Japan

Yeah, we had a three-month deadline. I mean, it was initially three months, although I guess the game really took six months in the end.

It did come out of nowhere. It showed up really fast, and it was at a point in time where there was already concern – like, 'Hey, do we have too much Street Fighter in the marketplace?' You know, the Super Nintendo version of *Hyper Fighting* came out in 1993 and then *Super Street Fighter* came out in 1994 and all these [console] games were just coming on top of each other, and the arcade games were getting either updated or were getting new versions, and I was like, 'Oh no, another Street Fighter game. What are we going to do here? Are we oversaturating the global market with this brand?' And I think there was initial hesitation just across the board from people going, 'Oh, do we really need a new Street Fighter?' But then when it showed up, it was very different. So once people saw what it was, there was less hesitation around the game. I think people were like, 'OK, it looks fairly different.' The art style had moved to a much more anime style, and they were doing different things with the gameplay, and it's like, 'OK. We get what you're doing.'

A BIG BREAK

On top of the short timeline, one of the biggest challenges the *Street Fighter Alpha* team faced was their lack of experience. While the game was led by Funamizu – a series veteran who had overseen multiple Street Fighter II games – the team also consisted of a number of younger members, including planner Hideaki Itsuno.

At the time, Itsuno was new to Capcom, having worked on a couple of obscure quiz games, and *Alpha* served as a turning point in his career. Following *Alpha*'s release, Itsuno moved into various leadership roles, overseeing Capcom's first attempts at 3D fighting games, working on key 2D fighting games like *Capcom vs. SNK*, and eventually heading up the Devil May Cry and Dragon's Dogma action franchises and becoming one of Capcom's most popular game directors.

He says it all started when Funamizu noticed him playing a game from Capcom rival SNK.

→   HIDEAKI ITSUNO
         Street Fighter Alpha planner, Capcom Japan

They were short on staff, and my boss [Funamizu] saw that I came into the office early every morning to play the Neo Geo – I was playing *King of Fighters '94*. So my boss was like, 'Hey, how about you become the new planner for Street Fighter Classic?' 'Street Fighter Classic' is what *Alpha* was called at the time; it was abbreviated 'SFC'. This was around the time Super Famicom was released. Since it had the same abbreviation as 'Super Famicom', we were confident the game would eventually be ported over to the Super Famicom, right?

So when I was given that opportunity, I was like, 'Yeah, absolutely. I want to have an opportunity to work on this.' Internally, I was freaked out. I had absolutely no confidence I could make this happen. But how many times do you have a chance as a new employee, being given this great opportunity? I felt like, *If I back down now, then I'm not going to be able to do anything in the future,* so I jumped on the opportunity.

→   NORITAKA FUNAMIZU
          Street Fighter Alpha planner, Capcom Japan

I apologize to Itsuno for saying this, but I can't actually remember working on *Street Fighter Alpha* with him. I saw Itsuno mention it in an interview recently and I was like … oh, OK.

→   HIDEAKI ITSUNO
          Street Fighter Alpha planner, Capcom Japan

I was still a fresh new employee at the time, so it was one of those things that anything that I did was very much training. You're talking about working on the biggest franchise, Street Fighter, so I did a ton of research. It wasn't just researching Street Fighter games. I would go out and research whatever was in the genre, and of course I studied the source code of prior Street Fighter games, looking at the way the hitboxes work. [...] Yeah, I spent a lot of time researching, and I feel like that was the foundation of how I was able to build myself up.

→   NORITAKA FUNAMIZU
          Street Fighter Alpha planner, Capcom Japan

You can say that he was part of that next generation [of staff who worked on the game].

Funamizu is not one to dish out compliments too often, so I can't remember a single time I was ever complimented during my work on Street Fighter. [*laughs*]

> The most memorable thing that [Funamizu] said to me was ... he pulled me aside and he told me, 'Man, you've got no talent.' He would also say, 'You have no sense.' I started to hate the word 'sense' just because I associated it with being told that.

I learned a lot from him, though. One of the things that he taught me was, 'Every move has a purpose.' Nowadays I've morphed that into 'every concept has a purpose', but at the time when we were making the game ... for example, a crouching mid kick: for some players, that may feel like a useless move they don't use too much, but when we were developing the game, I was told, 'Look, every single move that you create has to serve some kind of purpose. And the player senses that it's fun because there is a purpose. It can't just be a throwaway move, so regardless of what you're creating, make sure that there is some kind of purpose associated with it.'

A CONSOLE-LIKE GAME

With only three months scheduled to develop the game, and the need initially to make it run on Capcom's dated CPS-1 hardware, the *Alpha* team had to cut certain corners to make the game work, leading to a lot of experimentation. As Itsuno remembers, *Street Fighter Alpha* marked a time Capcom allowed themselves to break their own rules.

→   HIDEAKI ITSUNO
                Street Fighter Alpha planner, Capcom Japan

Thinking back to making arcade games, our mentality at the time was that we wanted to make games that were impossible to port to home consoles. We wanted to take advantage of the hardware and push things as far as we could. But for *Street Fighter Alpha*, because we were still working with the CPS-1 board, we felt like the specs were low enough that ... we had this idea: *This is going to be a game designed for porting.*

The initial thought was, *Let's make it for Super Famicom,* but when it was time to actually start the porting process, it was decided that we would be porting it over to PlayStation. So it wasn't a matter of 'this is going to be designed to port to this specific platform'. It was more that it was designed to be ported in some form or fashion based on the board that was being used. It just so happened that when it came time to decide where to port it, Capcom decided to put it on PlayStation.

→   KEN WILLIAMS
                Assistant editor, Electronic Gaming Monthly magazine

It really felt like it was made for consoles. It didn't look like it was taking advantage of the arcade technology at the time, but it played well. That was the important thing. Back in the day, it wasn't really about the graphics and all that other fun stuff. Because it was very cartoony. But if it played well, it was gonna be a hit. If it felt smooth and the action was there and the variety was there, I mean, I could play that endlessly.

→   STEPHEN FROST
        Street Fighter 30th Anniversary Collection producer, Digital Eclipse

For me, personally, no, I didn't feel that [it seemed compromised] because I was so enamoured with the art style and stuff like that. I mean, they made new backgrounds and character designs. They had […] new abilities for the characters and things like that, plus some new characters. So I didn't feel that. I didn't feel it at all.

→   JAMES CHEN
        Street Fighter series commentator

I hadn't ever thought of it [as a game designed so it could be easily ported], but, yeah, that definitely makes sense. I know a lot of people really appreciated the nice anime style, the graphics and everything like that, but the gameplay was just so, so simplified.

When *Street Fighter Alpha* came out, at the time I don't think we realized it, but subconsciously we realized it – it was really Capcom's first attempt to kind of dumb down Street Fighter, right? It's simpler to play because we had the chain combos, alpha counters, air blocking. They really put in a lot of concessions to try to make the game easier for beginners to play.

→   CHRIS KRAMER
        Street Fighter Alpha public relations associate, Capcom USA

We knew from the get-go that it was more of a prequel, which was kind of a weird decision because it was like, 'Well, why aren't you just making "Street Fighter III"?' But it took a while to see that. They were kind of splitting the Street Fighter series, right? *Alpha* was going to be the more new-player-friendly one because arcade operators were saying, 'Hey, look, the only people who are playing Street Fighter II games are these hardcore guys, and they can put tokens in and stay on that machine for an hour. And new players don't want to put money in because it's so overwhelming: you have to know moves and counter moves for everything.' So that's why *Alpha* had air block and counters and combos and stuff in there that were a lot more friendly, and the input timing is a lot more forgiving than *Street Fighter II* as well. So they really did kind of look at it as a split within the Street Fighter games in order to make a game that would be easier for new players to get into, slightly less intimidating to learn.

→   HIDEAKI ITSUNO
       Street Fighter Alpha planner, Capcom Japan

The thing is, Capcom – and this is still the case today – has always been a maker of 'hardcore' games. They've never been about simply trying to suck up to and curry favour with players. The developers have a strong artisan's disposition; they make games for experts, and for maniacs ... that is, when it comes to making games, they have a lot of pride. However, the development period for *Street Fighter Alpha* was very short, we were using inferior hardware, and we had a bunch of new hires on the team. In addition, this was a time of experimentation with new visual techniques at Capcom. Drawing extremely detailed pixel art is very time-consuming, but if we compensated for that by going overboard with the animation, we could still make the tight production deadline.

Specifically, for *Darkstalkers*, what we did was decrease the colour palette but increase the frames in the animation to portray a sense of higher quality. But for the Street Fighter Alpha series, we cut back on the number of colours and decreased the number of frames per second of animation and cut down on development time. We were rushing to make everything as fast and low-cost as possible. But thanks to that approach, we were able to make not a game that pleased only the expert or hardcore fans, but something that appealed more to what casual fans wanted, full of flashy moves and designs. This was the only time we were allowed to experiment like that.

There was also the benefit of me not having been in development for years and years. I was still very much a fresh new recruit that could be seen as someone from a consumer perspective. They were like, 'Use that to your advantage. Use the fact that you're still new and you still have that consumer mindset. We want to tap into that – we want to know, hey, what do the consumers want to see?' So I came up with a bunch of moves along those lines. Street Fighter teams were always made of veteran developers who wouldn't accept any other way of making the game. I was lucky to fall into the team that wanted to hear my ideas. And coincidentally, this approach just happened to succeed, and it was because of this experimental mentality within the team.

DAN HIBIKI

Since the mid-1980s, a rivalry had been brewing between Capcom and SNK. To some, it felt tense; to others, playful. And as the years went on, the companies started referencing one another in their games and marketing materials.

In a spring 1993 issue of Capcom USA's newsletter, the *Capcom Craze Club*, for instance, a comic shows Ryu mistaking Ryo from SNK's *Art of Fighting* for Street Fighter's Ken. The two proceed to fight because their names sound alike, and they match each other's moves one to one until Ryu comes up with a unique attack to win the fight: a Burning Dragon Punch. 'It took all my strength and power but I finally defeated him,' says Ryu. 'Funny though, the only move he couldn't match was something original.'

Street Fighter Alpha marked a new stage for the rivalry, as Capcom adopted an anime-influenced art style that looked more like SNK's games and brought back fighters created by staff that had gone to SNK. The most scrutinized element, however, came with the secret character Dan – whose design looked like two characters from *Art of Fighting* mashed together, and whose weak strength and goofy personality made him more of a joke character than a serious competitor. Dan wasn't the first example of the two companies referencing one another, but quickly became the most popular.

→   JAMES CHEN
Street Fighter series commentator

It was pretty clear right away that Dan was a way for them to poke fun at SNK. He was Robert Garcia's head on top of Ryo's body.

At that point in time, that 'rivalry' was pretty big. And so it was clear that they made him as a character to say, 'Hey, look. This character sucks and he's from the Art of Fighting series.'

→   CHRIS KRAMER
        Street Fighter Alpha public relations associate, Capcom USA

There was that feeling that SNK had stolen away a lot of Capcom talent in that era, and I think there was some bitterness there because a good chunk of the *Street Fighter* team had gone over to SNK for various reasons. And so Dan was 100 percent their opinion of what SNK fighters were versus Capcom fighters at that time.

→   NORITAKA FUNAMIZU
        Street Fighter Alpha planner, Capcom Japan

That might have been the case for the person who designed the character and brought him to me. But I didn't think of Dan as a mockery of SNK's characters.

> I think the person who came up with Dan wanted to put in a character who wasn't so strong, physically speaking. The whole idea was you could use this character, and even though he wasn't very strong, you could use him and win battles – I remember noticing that about the character. Because we had added a super-powerful character in Akuma, I thought it would be cool to have a weak character like Dan, too. I thought it would feel satisfying for more skilled players to win fights with a weaker character like Dan.

→   JAMES CHEN
        Street Fighter series commentator

He was funny, and at the time – because nobody was winning tons of money on these games – it was OK to have a character kind of uselessly taking up a spot to be non-competitive. So it was pretty funny, and as a result, I do think he was kind of popular in a way, and a lot of people did try to win with him because he was bad.

[Ed. note]   While Yasuda didn't design Dan, he illustrated a piece of promotional art showing Street Fighter's Sagat holding Dan by his head – an image that many saw as further evidence of Capcom displaying their superiority over SNK.

→   AKIRA YASUDA
        Head of illustration group, Capcom Japan

I didn't think that it would catch that much attention from people. I remember the deadline was pretty close anyway, so I was just trying to figure out what would work. [...] I just thought it would look cool to show how much stronger Sagat was than Dan. I wasn't trying to mock or make fun of the character or anything. [...] Maybe it's sort of referencing a pro wrestler's performance on a microphone. You know, they'd speak on the mic and say, 'Oh, I'll beat you up.' [...] I mean, if anything, maybe there could have been elements of Capcom parroting the SNK character, but there was no intention to belittle SNK or make fun of them. But if that's what people think, then, I guess, what can we do?

→   TOYOHISA TANABE
        King of Fighters series director, SNK Japan

This is just my personal opinion, but I always felt Capcom was one step ahead of SNK. So when Dan came out, it was like, 'Oh look! They're noticing us! They based a character on us!' Personally, I was happy about it. There may have also been people at SNK who thought they were making fun of us, but I was happy they were referencing us like that. Actually, in the King of Fighters games I was involved in, we inserted some Capcom references as little jokes. I wonder if Capcom wasn't, in part, responding to those. I felt that Capcom and SNK were very aware of each other during that period.

As to whether I was ever involved in the creation of these jokes ... I can't deny I was. I worked on the series from *King of Fighters '94* through *King of Fighters '98*, and ... well, I don't know if I should say this, but there's a character in those games named Yuri Sakazaki. Her background story says she learned her amazing moves and abilities in a very short period of time. I can't deny; I did give her some of Capcom's special moves.

Yuri Sakazaki originally was a character in *Art of Fighting*. In the first game, she's a weak girl who can't fight at all. In *Art of Fighting 2*, she learns Kyokugen Karate and becomes an extremely strong character. That was her background, and well, honestly, I did this out of respect for the character, but I added my own interpretation where she learned all those special moves very quickly. And I started adding more and more moves from other characters to her. Then it kind of occurred to me – again, really just as a joke – 'Oh, hey, what if she could use Capcom's moves too?'

A DRAMATIC BATTLE

Despite *Street Fighter Alpha*'s short development cycle, the team at Capcom were able to include a number of bonus features, ranging from secret characters like Dan and Akuma to a hidden Dramatic Battle mode – a two-on-one fight where players controlled Ryu and Ken in a confrontation against M. Bison, mirroring the battle at the end of 1994's *Street Fighter II: The Animated Movie*. As it turns out, the Dramatic Battle mode came about in part because of a song.

→   NORITAKA FUNAMIZU
        Street Fighter Alpha planner, Capcom Japan

It all started because there was a Street Fighter anime in Japan that had a theme song sung by a famous Japanese idol. I think she's pretty famous now; her name is Ryoko Shinohara. In the movie, there's a scene where Ryu and Ken face off against M. Bison towards the end, and this song plays over that fight. I really wanted to put that fight into the game, so I went to Okada and said, 'Go make it so players can play two-versus-one in the game.'

→   SEIJI OKADA
        Street Fighter Alpha lead programmer, Capcom Japan

Yeah, then I said, 'I could do it, but I won't,' right? [*laughs*] But I told Funamizu, 'If you put Ryoko Shinohara's ending theme in the game, I'll do it.'

→   NORITAKA FUNAMIZU
        Street Fighter Alpha planner, Capcom Japan

What we had to do was, we had to put JASRAC's seal with the song's registered number on the arcade board, and there were hardcore users who looked at the arcade board, found that JASRAC number and then looked it up, and discovered it referred to that particular song.

[Ed. note]   JASRAC is a collective management organization that oversees copyright for musicians in Japan.

→   NORITAKA FUNAMIZU
      Street Fighter Alpha planner, Capcom Japan

The big breakthrough was figuring out how to have a character both receive and deal damage at the same time. To see that in action with multiple characters simultaneously ... that [worked out very well].

→   SEIJI OKADA
      Street Fighter Alpha lead programmer, Capcom Japan

It wasn't so difficult, actually. I think it took a week or two. Maybe one week. I mean, I had the concept in my head already, and so I got the most important things down on the first day. Then it just took about a week or two to kind of get that running. I don't think it was terribly difficult.

→   NORITAKA FUNAMIZU
      Street Fighter Alpha planner, Capcom Japan

Yeah, I don't think it was hard to actually do it. And I told him, 'Well, this is a hidden mode, so even if it's glitchy, it's not a problem.'

MEETING DEMAND

After Capcom released *Alpha,* fans were split. While some thought the game felt too simplified and unrefined, *Alpha* appealed to an audience that wanted a new version of the game that wasn't overly demanding to play and brought back familiar elements from previous games. The peak days of Street Fighter II were behind Capcom, but *Alpha* kept the pipeline flowing.

→   STEPHEN FROST
         Street Fighter 30th Anniversary Collection producer, Digital Eclipse

I think for those of us who had been playing since *Street Fighter II* and just playing it religiously and were on our Super Nintendos playing *Super* over and over again, which is what I did, we were getting a little burnt out of Street Fighter. And I think when *Alpha* hit, it was sort of a breath of fresh air, and it sort of rejiggered a bit of excitement and joy again.

→   SETH KILLIAN
         Street Fighter IV special combat advisor, Capcom USA

I do think *Alpha* was ambitious on a systems level, but the new mechanics undercut two essentials that had made Street Fighter II so enduring: delicate positioning, and a tight risk/reward relationship. The strength of the easy chain combo system made the characters feel flat, and downplayed the unique character nuances that had made the Street Fighter series such a global sensation.

    I was also personally feeling frustrated because it seemed like the *Alpha* systems had been designed as a direct response to a simplistic description of what had frustrated players in Street Fighter II. 'Combos are too hard,' [they said,] so we got chain combos with loose timing. 'I don't like feeling trapped by fireball/uppercut patterns,' [they said,] so we got the ability to roll on the ground and block in mid-air. Both air-block and chain-combo systems were done well in later games, but *Alpha 1*'s versions felt under-baked, and threw the baby out with the bathwater.

→ KEN WILLIAMS
   Assistant editor, Electronic Gaming Monthly magazine

It was a new way of seeing the game. [...] And if you go into the console [versions], the console games were some of the best games they ever put out, with the different modes and so forth. So it was one of the first games that really – it translated well to consoles. Like, really well.

→ CHRIS KRAMER
   Street Fighter Alpha public relations associate, Capcom USA

It was the first Street Fighter game to get on the new console cycle, right? So it was the first Street Fighter game for PlayStation, and *Alpha* was on there pretty early in the PlayStation life cycle, too. So it definitely felt like a win because it was a newer game. It was on the brand-new console that everybody was super excited about. There was just so much hype around the PlayStation at that point in time. So I think the first *Alpha* did really well because it was early in the console cycle.

→ HIDEAKI ITSUNO
   Street Fighter Alpha planner, Capcom Japan

Of course, Funamizu was responsible for the success of the game, but one of the things Funamizu said at the time is, 'Young people need to taste success in order to grow.' And for me, having just worked really hard on the title and it getting all that positive reception afterwards, it was a great feeling. It was nice to be able to put in all that effort and then get that positive reinforcement back. And having been able to experience that very early on in the industry definitely helped reinforce that hard work pays off. It was a great moment.

As far as I can recall, we were successful in getting rid of all the arcade boards, especially the CPS-2 boards, with the success of *Alpha 2* and *Darkstalkers*. I think we even had to reorder more CPS-2 boards to meet the demand.

[Ed. note]   In a 2021 YouTube video, Capcom's former executive producer Yoshiki Okamoto said that *Alpha* did not help Capcom clear out many of its CPS-1 boards, as the game's primary release was the CPS-2 version, rather than the CPS Changer version that ran on leftover CPS-1 hardware. Capcom eventually brought the Alpha series to Super Nintendo with a port of *Street Fighter Alpha 2* in late 1996, but ended up ordering more cartridges than it could sell, leaving it – once again – with leftover product piling up in a warehouse. It was one of a few Super Nintendo games that put a financial strain on the company.

→   JUSTIN BERENBAUM
         Street Fighter series customer service manager, Capcom USA

I was involved with finding third parties to take the games that were sitting in the warehouse off our hands, because at that time the cost of goods on a Super Nintendo game – especially because these games required so much memory – was anywhere between 25 and 40 bucks a cartridge. So if you over-manufactured by a hundred thousand cartridges, you're sitting on $4 to $5 million in inventory cost. And I do remember the warehouse, because the shipping warehouse was right next to the Capcom offices. And I remember the warehouse was just being loaded with pallets and pallets of the game.

I remember dealing with some companies that we would ship them to, and then they would guarantee to ship them out of the country so they didn't get resold back into retail. That was a really common practice back then. [...] This was, like, a legitimized grey market to sell off stock without destroying the retail market in the US [...] They would sell

it to distributors who promised to take it south of
the border. And back then, it was all grey market south
of the border, for the most part, but they needed content.
So we sold at a loss, but they were contractually obligated
– if those units came back into the US, they would be
fined. That's one of those dirty secrets that nobody really
talked about.

We cut these deals for a pallet full or two pallets full for these
companies. And they were good deals because they were cash
in advance, so we didn't ship until the [wire transfers] would
come through. And then literally, they would show up with a
box truck, and we'd load the pallets onto the box truck and they'd
drive them off.

[Ed. note]   Capcom followed *Alpha* with two numbered
sequels, as well as numerous home ports and
upgraded versions, with follow-ups piling on
characters and bonus features. By the time
Street Fighter Alpha 3 Max hit Sony's PlayStation
Portable in 2006, Capcom had built the game's
roster to almost 40 characters, and had turned
a series that was invented out of convenience
into one of the most densely packed franchises
in the industry.

→   SETH KILLIAN
         Street Fighter Ⅳ special combat advisor, Capcom USA

SFA1, *2* and *3* are very different games, but as a series I think the
Alpha games are best understood as Street Fighter's R&D division.
A lot of experimental new mechanics got introduced, and though
the results were mixed, it seemed like the teams were learning a lot.
This led up to *SFA3*, which was an oddball masterpiece that showed
Capcom's ability to synthesize signature mechanics from Street
Fighter's history alongside cool new stuff like the Guard Meter.

SFA3 also introduced the mostly forgotten 'blue blocking' mechanic, which served as a trial run of the system that would come to define Street Fighter's next numbered iteration: *SFIII*'s infamous parry.

→   SHINICHI UEYAMA
             Street Fighter series programmer, Capcom Japan

With *Street Fighter Alpha*, remember [Okada and Funamizu] were talking about the two-versus-one system? That went into the first game, and then we thought about a new system for *Street Fighter Alpha 2*. And I think that's where we came up with the Custom Combo system, where you could press buttons however you wanted to make your own combos. Though in *Street Fighter Alpha 2*, we didn't really use that system to its potential. It wasn't until *Street Fighter Alpha 3* where I feel like we were able to go all the way with the concept.

→   STEPHEN FROST
             Street Fighter 30th Anniversary Collection producer, Digital Eclipse

I thought [*Alpha*] *3* was amazing. The World Tour mode [was fantastic]. Especially the home version of *Alpha 3* was incredible with how much content that they had packed in for at-home people, and it was one of the few times – or one of the earliest times – that companies started [saying], 'OK, the home version of this game, we need to pack with additional content and different things to keep them playing. It's not OK just to port it over and that's it, or have some simple versus mode and things like that.' And I felt that *Alpha 3* really, really did that.

→   MATT ATWOOD
             Street Fighter Alpha 3 public relations manager, Capcom USA

In my mind, *Alpha 3* was the perfection of Street Fighter. The response time and the movement was so smooth. I could play, and then I realized how bad I was fairly quickly. Watching people play became like … *Alpha 3* was cool.

There was a tournament that I put on for Capcom, and it was the North American champion Alex Valle against Daigo [Umehara] from Japan. We flew him out, and watching those two play was really interesting to see because Daigo, he was the Japanese champion, and he looked like he was almost typing because his movement was so crisp and so emotionless. And then you had Alex Valle, who was very animated. You know, the crowd was crazy and he was very much into that. So he played with a little more emotion.

So I think in the end, *Alpha 3* [...] it's definitely my favourite, even [including] the originals. The originals, of course, have nostalgia, but I think *Alpha 3* was a huge accomplishment for the dev team. It was perfect.

CHAPTER 13

STREET FIGHTER: THE MOVIE

By late 1994, Capcom had been through a lot on their first live-action film.

A challenging shoot starring Jean-Claude Van Damme. Cultural differences. Script issues. Drug problems. Injuries. Delays. Actors who didn't know martial arts. An association with MC Hammer, fresh off a controversial rebranding. Even the illness and death of co-star Raul Julia. The movie, which began as a pet project of Capcom founder Kenzo Tsujimoto, had become a series of compromises for many involved, and it showed on the screen.

But Capcom had a film to promote, so towards the end of the year, they organized a premiere at their US headquarters in Sunnyvale, California, inviting local media and putting together a Q&A session with actors from the movie. Taking place in a Silicon Valley office park, the event lacked the spectacle of a Hollywood opening, with second-string celebrities filling out the space.

'Van Damme, of course, wasn't there, and Kylie Minogue wasn't there,' says former Capcom PR rep Chris Kramer. 'Wes Studi was not there. Raul Julia was definitely not there. But it was all the other guys, you know? It was, like, the dude who played Honda.' Then MC Hammer drove into the parking lot in a convertible, blasted the song he recorded for the soundtrack, and drove off, fulfilling his appearance quota. As Kramer says: 'MC Hammer did a drive-by.'

Such was the state of Capcom's *Street Fighter* movie, an earnest fumble that landed somewhere between tribute and parody. Capcom even ended up in a lawsuit over the soundtrack.

And without all that, we'd never have gotten one of the most bizarre games in Street Fighter history.

For a brief period in the mid-1990s, fighting games starring digitized actors were having a moment. As Street Fighter's popularity began to fade, Mortal Kombat became the industry's new favourite target – with some taking inspiration from its over-the-top violence, and others copying its visual style.

At the same time, Capcom was in an experimental phase, following a dip in Street Fighter sales. They opened a console development studio in California. They kicked off development of *Resident Evil*, which went on to define their next decade. And they kept trying new fighting game concepts, from *Darkstalkers* to *X-Men: Children of the Atom* to *Street Fighter Alpha* – even a robot-themed game called *Cyberbots*.

Continuing their experiments, Capcom decided to take a shot at a digitized fighting game of their own. They had actors lined up, on account of the movie. They had the deepest fighting game expertise in the industry. They even had Van Damme, who the creators of *Mortal Kombat* originally wanted to star in their game.

Capcom's US arcade division was also evolving, as Capcom and licensor Romstar were building a pinball and redemption factory in Illinois called GameStar. Romstar founder Takahito Yasuki, an old friend of Tsujimoto's, ran GameStar for a short period before Capcom merged the office with their existing US arcade video operations and turned the combined group into Capcom Coin-Op.

To develop the game, Capcom hired Illinois-based studio Incredible Technologies, located near GameStar/Capcom Coin-Op and not far from the team making Mortal

Kombat at Midway. Under their Strata brand, Incredible Technologies had been developing arcade fighting games for a couple of years at that point. But, as former team members recall, that didn't mean the team was ideally positioned to take on the game.

→   KATSUYA AKITOMO
          Marvel Super Heroes artist and advisor, Capcom Japan

I think the whole reason this project got started was because the president of Capcom at the time, Kenzo Tsujimoto, was a big movie fan, and he actually had always dreamed of making a movie out of one of Capcom's properties. The movie was a dream come true for him, and he felt very attached to it. And because Tsujimoto wanted a game for the movie, even though [Capcom Japan executive producer Yoshiki Okamoto and illustration group head Akira Yasuda] probably didn't think it would be very financially successful, they realized it was extremely important to Tsujimoto, so they probably had no choice but to go along with it.

→   JOE MORICI
          Street Fighter series senior vice-president, Capcom USA

If I remember correctly, Capcom Japan wasn't very high on the idea of doing the movie version, so we chose to start the development for the movie version because Capcom didn't really want to do it in Japan. So we took it over here and went to Incredible Technologies.

→   RALPH MELGOSA
          Street Fighter: The Movie art director, Incredible Technologies

We were a really small company. [...] At the time, Incredible Technologies was maybe 32 employees, and of those employees, I'd say maybe half were actually game developers. Other people were administrative, accounting, whatever. Tech support. So Richard and Elaine, the owners of the company – Richard Ditton and Elaine Hodgson; they were married at the time – but they were approached by Capcom to do this game.

→   ELAINE HODGSON
       Street Fighter: The Movie president and CEO, Incredible Technologies

We were working with Capcom at the time – or trying to get work with them, because at that time we were going off to various companies to try and do development work for them. We had some games we were working on for our own IP, but we were trying to make money to keep the company afloat. So I know I went off to Capcom and proposed different game ideas to them. But then they came back and said, 'We have a job that you could do. We're making a movie and we want to make a game based on that movie.' And we also had some expertise with digitizing pictures and that kind of thing. So they looked at our skill set and thought that we would be able to do it.

→   RALPH MELGOSA
       Street Fighter: The Movie art director, Incredible Technologies

We had experience in the past. We had done a digitized football game, and a basketball game called *Rim Rockin' Basketball*. The football game was called *Hard Yardage*, where we digitized the characters, but the tools we had were very, very primitive to do that. But since we had some experience with digitizing characters, and we had done [violent fighting game] *Time Killers* and another game called *BloodStorm*, [they thought we'd be a good fit].

> *Time Killers* was a big hit for us. It came out on the heels of *Mortal Kombat,* so it was really successful for the company. For a company that small, we sold a lot of units, which made us a lot of money. For a small company of 32, it was, it was a home run, you know? [...] We sold about 7,000 of them, which, now – you've got to understand, the size of our company was really small. That was huge.

[After *Time Killers*], the company had been struggling a bit. You know, we had kept our head above water, but the owners had seen this also as a higher-profile project and to bring money in to seed some other stuff we had going on. Among them was the new version of Golden Tee Golf, which is still going on, right? So Street Fighter kind of helped fund *Golden Tee 3D*, which became a huge, huge hit for us.

[Ed. note]   While Capcom had ignited the fighting game boom a few years earlier, some saw their decision to hire Incredible Technologies to make a *Street Fighter: The Movie* game as a sign that the company was no longer leading the genre, but following their competitors.

→   ELAINE HODGSON
      Street Fighter: The Movie president and CEO, Incredible Technologies

They were definitely trying to find an American audience. They had success with their own Street Fighter [games], obviously, and then when they were doing this movie for an American audience, they were looking to us to be more Americanized.

→   RALPH MELGOSA
      Street Fighter: The Movie art director, Incredible Technologies

Well, they wanted to compete with Mortal Kombat, right? They wanted to take on Mortal Kombat, which is why they came to us. Midway and WMS, Williams, they were massive. They were huge. We were the little guy. They were always laughing at us, right? They were always like, 'Oh, you're nothing.' I mean, really. If anything, that was the feeling, that we were the little guy. But yes, it gave us motivation: *We've got to compete with these guys*, right? They all had better hardware. They always had more people. They had better tools. Bigger staff. More money to develop the products. They were just better at it, you know? Them, along with these other companies. We were a little guy. Our bread and butter was making cheap, affordable kits that you could put into old cabinets.

→ CHRIS KRAMER
Street Fighter: The Movie public relations associate, Capcom USA

I made an unfortunate comment on Usenet [about *Street Fighter: The Movie* when it was in development] and I got in trouble for that. [...] I think I tried to say something very neutral where I was like, 'Oh, the Street Fighter movie game is not being done by Capcom and so it's being done by this company that did a game called *Time Killers*, so I can't really comment on it', or something like that. I think I tried to say something that I thought was fairly neutral, but it was pretty clear to people that I was like, 'Don't expect this to be any good.' And at that point in time, no one in Japan was on Usenet, but it turned out that some of these guys who were making the game were on Usenet, and they saw that and made a complaint to Japan. So I got in trouble, and then those guys came out to have a meeting with me to show me the Street Fighter movie game to convince me that it was going to be as good as any Street Fighter game.

→ RALPH MELGOSA
Street Fighter: The Movie art director, Incredible Technologies

By that time, *Mortal Kombat II* or *3* – I think maybe *3* – was out. The competition was fierce, right? I mean, it was with fighting games, and [*Street Fighter: The Movie*] wasn't a very good game, honestly. I mean, I know what we had with it, which is why sometimes it's painful to talk about this, because it was a tough game to work on.

THE AUSTRALIA TRIP

With the deal signed, Incredible Technologies mapped out their approach, figuring out a visual style and which characters to implement. Before long, the team was off to Australia to visit the movie set. The plan was to get in, capture each of the actors performing moves for the game, and get out. But the team ran into a few complications along the way.

→   RALPH MELGOSA
              Street Fighter: The Movie art director, Incredible Technologies

We were a small crew, man. In Australia, to film, there were basically three of us and then the owners of the company, right? So there's a crew of five.

→   ELAINE HODGSON
              Street Fighter: The Movie president and CEO, Incredible Technologies

I went because I was in charge, but the real worker bees were [game designer Alan Noon, project manager Leif Marwede and art director Ralph Melgosa], and Richard went as well, and we had some programming help. But really, the real work was Leif Marwede and Alan Noon doing the choreography for the [actors]. They knew what moves they wanted to digitize for the different actors, and then Ralph did a lot of the heavy lifting as far as being behind the computer with the camera, and capturing and making sure we had the assets that we needed back home.

→   RALPH MELGOSA
              Street Fighter: The Movie art director, Incredible Technologies

We rented camera equipment here in the US and brought that over with us, and we stayed just a few miles away from what I believe is Warner Bros.' studio in Brisbane, which was kind of like an amusement park. Like, they have tours and stuff there. That [was next to us].

[On the *Street Fighter* set], they set up a blue screen studio, which was right next to the special effects building, which was really cool because we got to hang out with special effects guys and make props and models and stuff, and I was into that stuff when I was a kid. I loved that stuff. So just to hang out with those guys and the model makers and all that, I loved it. I absolutely loved it. But yeah, the blue screen room was pretty much just an empty studio. We had our equipment in there. We [had access to] the commissary or wherever they had catering set up for the actors, and we could just stroll over there and eat. So, many times, you'd see actors and the director. Some of the actors' families would be there, watching the filming of the movie. So that was kind of fun.

→   ELAINE HODGSON
      Street Fighter: The Movie president and CEO, Incredible Technologies

The original idea was that we were only going to be there for maybe two weeks, and that was the schedule, to get the actors in there when they were in costume while they were shooting. So then there was a big meeting with everybody there while we started the process, and the president of Capcom at the time got up and was talking about the success of the franchise and how Street Fighter had made the company, Capcom, over a billion dollars and all this stuff. And then all of a sudden, the actors determined that they wanted more money.

I mean, this is probably the most interesting part. So they were now not wanting to come and digitize, necessarily, until there was a negotiation on them getting a royalty for being in the game. These were the very early days of videogames using real actor images, and nobody in that field had really thought about the videogame part. So him getting up in front of everybody, saying how much money the franchise made, I think made the actors and their agents rethink it. So what [was supposed to be] like, ten days, two weeks in Australia eventually turned out to be about six weeks.

Capcom footed the bill for us to stay, with additional lodging, and we would wait in the blue screen room for the actors to come as they were negotiating these things. So there was actually a lot of time where we were waiting and not working. Sometimes we got to go into the shooting of the movie, which was interesting to see how tedious that process was, because I'd really never done that before, and how they kept having to reshoot the same thing over and over again. And we got to see the likes of Jean-Claude Van Damme perform, and Raul Julia and Ming-Na Wen. I actually got to know Ming-Na Wen a little bit. We went to dinner with her and her husband, I believe. She's very nice. Kylie Minogue, we didn't get to interact with her very much except for the digitizing part. So there were interesting people there to observe and meet. But we had to wait for them to renegotiate the contracts with some of these people before we could get them off.

→   RALPH MELGOSA
     Street Fighter: The Movie art director, Incredible Technologies

That was our first night we arrived in Australia. We were invited to this dinner. All the actors are there. Got to meet Van Damme for the first time. I'm 5 foot 7 inches without a haircut, and he was probably just maybe an inch taller than me. I mean, he's not that big of a guy.

But yeah, Tsujimoto came out and talked about the millions of dollars that Street Fighter had made, and, 'Now we're making this movie and this movie is going to make millions of dollars and now we're going to make a game based off the movie and that's going to make millions of dollars.' And all the actors were looking at their agents saying, 'Hey, wait a minute. It's in our contract, but we should probably be making more money because it's not just the movie, but it's a game as well, right?' So they were all holding out, just renegotiating. Which turned our – it was supposed to be an 11-day shoot, into almost a month that we were there, in Australia.

→   ELAINE HODGSON
          Street Fighter: The Movie president and CEO, Incredible Technologies

I thought Capcom treated us well when the issue came up that we had to stay longer. So that could have been a big mess, because there we were in Australia – that's where it was shot – and that's a long way from home. Luckily, Richard and I had his parents watch the kids, and we had the ability to do that. But it was a long time, and they did treat us with respect and financial assistance, so I did feel Capcom was good to us.

→   RALPH MELGOSA
          Street Fighter: The Movie art director, Incredible Technologies

[Most of the actors] were good [to work with]. It's funny because they were all required to work out and have martial arts training, even while they were filming the movie. And one of my favourite things I remember of Damian Chapa is walking by the exercise room, and he's walking on a treadmill. Not running, but walking extremely, extremely slow, eating a Snickers bar. So it's like, *All right. Way to work out, buddy.*

But we did go out socially with these guys sometimes, and they were great. Grand L. Bush, he and his wife took us out for dinner one night. We went to a club with Kylie Minogue and ... who played Dee Jay? I can't think of his name now.

[Ed. note]   Miguel A. Núñez Jr.

He was a good guy. Very nice people. Ming-Na Wen was nice. She didn't want to come to the set. [...] We didn't even shoot her until she ended up coming back to Chicago so we could film her. Gregg Rainwater never even showed up.

→   ELAINE HODGSON
               Street Fighter: The Movie president and CEO, Incredible Technologies

Ultimately, the game was OK, but it wasn't extremely successful. I don't even know how many units they sold, ultimately. [...] I don't think the royalties ended up to be gobs of money for these actors.

→   RALPH MELGOSA
               Street Fighter: The Movie art director, Incredible Technologies

No, not at all. Not at all.

→   ELAINE HODGSON
               Street Fighter: The Movie president and CEO, Incredible Technologies

But they were taking care of themselves, as they should.

[Ed. note]   As the star of both the movie and game, Van Damme reportedly made out better than the rest of the cast. In 1994, Variety reported he would get between $7.5 million and $8 million for the role. A representative for Van Damme didn't respond to an interview request for this book.

→   ELAINE HODGSON
               Street Fighter: The Movie president and CEO, Incredible Technologies

I did understand that he was the marquee draw and Capcom paid a lot of money to him to be in the movie. And that's how they got him.

→   RALPH MELGOSA
               Street Fighter: The Movie art director, Incredible Technologies

It was his biggest payday at the time. I know that. I remember – I thought it was more than $7 [million], to be honest with you. [...] I thought it was $20 [million].

→   ELAINE HODGSON
     Street Fighter: The Movie president and CEO, Incredible Technologies

I remember him making sure that he could see his image at the same time we could, so he could see how he would look in the scene. And how he was probably, without a doubt, the most professional at knowing where every part of his body was in these moves, because that was important to us. We were taking snapshots, basically, of these people while they were moving, and he, more than anyone, probably knew exactly how he would look to the camera.

And he had a lot of control over his body and he could do these poses – he could stand with his leg straight out to get that move, you know? Without having to do it while it was in motion, because he had that kind of muscle control. The crazy guy could stand and do the splits in midair, you know? Most of the other actors didn't have that physicality. And so, oftentimes, Leif would hold some of the people in position while they were digitized, and then Leif would have to be erased out of the scene. [...] But, yeah. Jean-Claude Van Damme didn't do that, and I remember going, actually, to his dressing room while he was getting ready to do this, and I was kind of starstruck, actually, and he was very gracious. But we only had limited interaction with any of them. So it was nice. It was good.

→   RALPH MELGOSA
     Street Fighter: The Movie art director, Incredible Technologies

The guy was such an asshole. He wasn't pleasant to work with. [...] I literally remember – we'd have to wait for the actors to become available to work with them in the blue screen room, and so, if we had downtime and there were no actors available, we are allowed to just go walk the set and watch them film the movie.

So one day, they were filming the big fight scene between Van Damme and Bison at the end, and Van Damme's fighting Bison's stunt double, and here you've got the crew, you've got everyone around, catering, all the other actors. And they're fighting, and this actor's hat keeps falling off, and you see that it's not Raul Julia. It's the stunt double. And after about three times, Van Damme said, 'I'm not coming back until you staple or glue this guy's hat on his head', and he went into his trailer and sat and drank beer for, like, an hour and a half, and wouldn't come out. Everybody's waiting, and I just thought – and I saw this firsthand, and I'm sure this happens all the time, and he was the star of the movie – but I just thought, *What an arrogant prick*, you know?

When we did finally work with him [...] he was good only because Leif constantly was stroking his ego while we were working with him. [...] Leif worked with the actors really, really well, in particular Van Damme. He just had that personality and presence that can get a little bit more that we needed out of these actors. He just knew how to schmooze. Leif was a huge martial arts fan. Huge Van Damme fan. He knew every one of his movies, every one of his moves, so when he finally worked with him, Leif would say, 'Oh, in this movie, you did this type of a move. Can you give us something like that?' And Van Damme totally, totally ate it up.

[Ed. note]   While in Australia, the Incredible Technologies team not only captured footage for their game, but also for a console version of the game being developed at Capcom Japan – which played quite a bit differently.

It wasn't until we got to Australia where we actually met with [staff from Capcom Japan]. There was a group of, I think it was three or four people from Capcom that we dealt with almost on a daily basis while we were there. [...] They were in charge of overseeing the PlayStation version of the game. Originally, they were going to have a separate camera set up. We were going to have the actors film our moves, and then they were going to do their moves. And then they decided they would just piggyback off of what we set up, and they just gave us [an] additional move set list for each actor. So they piggybacked off us that way.

> They just kind of hung around and watched. [...] From my perspective, it was intimidating because they were so big and there wasn't a lot said. So I'm just like, *Do they like this or not?* Like, *What do they want?*

→ ELAINE HODGSON
Street Fighter: The Movie president and CEO, Incredible Technologies

Leif Marwede and Alan Noon were the choreographers, and they knew exactly what kind of moves they were going to have in the game, what special powers and all that, and I know that the [Capcom Japan team members] were there and they were not necessarily loving it. They weren't necessarily loving the moves because they weren't traditional martial arts moves. And so there was a little conflict there, that they did want it Americanized and they did hire us because we did stuff like *Time Killers*, which had the bizarre [style with] chainsaw people in there and all kinds of stuff. So we were trying to be Americanized and different, but the [Capcom Japan] designers were not loving it. But that was our charter, and that's what they allowed us to do, so it was different, by design.

→ RALPH MELGOSA
Street Fighter: The Movie art director, Incredible Technologies

I'm from a small town, so seeing the whole culture dynamic between us and Japanese culture and development was pretty eye-opening. But overall, I look back at it fondly, right? It was a lot of work. [...] We had fun. It was a good time. I spent my 30th birthday there. Richard had gone out and he was gone that whole day, and I remember being pissed off, saying, 'Shit, I'm here working on my birthday and he's off having fun.' He came back at the end of the day and gave me a cake, because he was running around getting stuff for my birthday. So it was kind of neat. But yeah, it was a pretty wild experience.

WAS IT ORIGINALLY CALLED STREET FIGHTER III?

Released under the title *Street Fighter: The Movie* –
even though the movie itself was called *Street Fighter*
– Incredible Technologies' game had a bit of a naming
problem. Yet for some, the title issues went deeper.
In 2007, Noon posted on fighting game site Shoryuken.com
that he remembered the game, at one point, going by
'Street Fighter III'.

> 'Perhaps this is all my perception, but looking
> back, I remember that there was some amount
> of confusion as to what it was we were making
> exactly,' he wrote. 'It could have been the
> international game of "Telephone", but somewhere
> along the communication chain from the Capcom
> Japan guys to the Capcom USA guys, to our
> management, down to the team, there seemed to
> be mixed signals. I distinctly recall that originally
> during the pitch process the game was billed as
> Street Fighter III.'

Noon wasn't alone in his confusion. In early 1995, Kramer
took to Usenet newsgroup alt.games.sf2 to clarify that
Street Fighter: The Movie was not Street Fighter III, due to
various articles that had reported it that way – including a
story in the official *Street Fighter* movie magazine.

> And years later, Noon dug up a design document
> for the game with the name 'Street Fighter III'
> printed on it. So we asked around to find out
> how widespread that name was at Incredible
> Technologies and Capcom at the time.

[Ed. note]   Noon declined to participate in this book.

→   ELAINE HODGSON
       Street Fighter: The Movie president and CEO, Incredible Technologies

I do not [remember hearing it called 'Street Fighter III']. Because I don't think they ever thought this was part of the original franchise. In my view, it was *Street Fighter: The Movie: The Game*. [That] was all I ever heard it referred to as. [...] [Alan is] younger than me. His memory is better. He was there. But I don't remember it called 'Street Fighter III'. But, you know, maybe he was in a conversation I was not privy to.

→   KATSUYA AKITOMO
       Marvel Super Heroes artist and advisor, Capcom Japan

I haven't heard anything about this myself.

→   AKIRA YASUDA
       Head of illustration group, Capcom Japan

I don't remember, but I don't think that would have been possible.

→   TAKESHI TEZUKA
       Marvel Super Heroes planner, Capcom Japan

I mean, it was obviously supposed to be a spinoff game and it was obviously designed in such a way, so I'm kind of wondering how they came to that conclusion.

→   HIDEAKI ITSUNO
       Street Fighter Alpha planner, Capcom Japan

This is definitely the first time I've heard that.

→   KATSUYA AKITOMO
       Marvel Super Heroes artist and advisor, Capcom Japan

If Capcom was going to make a Street Fighter III, it would have obviously been a big, important project. They would of course want it to be the highest possible quality. At that time, everyone at Capcom knew we were the number one maker of versus fighting games in the world, so it's impossible for me to think they would subcontract out the development of Street Fighter III.

→   RALPH MELGOSA
           Street Fighter: The Movie art director, Incredible Technologies

It was not a name that was approved by Capcom. I think it was just more kind of a local, internal development [name]. But that's how he envisioned it. [...] If you'd seen what Alan had in his concepts and his proposal on what he [originally wanted to do with the game, it] was a much greater scope, which was actually a really cool thing. And he's a super passionate guy about game design and about Street Fighter itself. I mean, he was totally, totally into it. So when you see what we ended up with compared to what he had started out with, it's disappointing, but it's not because of him at all.

> You know, the scope was [originally] much different. The first script we got for the movie was totally different. It was Ken and Ryu, almost like a buddy flick – or not even a buddy flick, but the story centred around them, right? And Ken was kind of the miscreant, the roguish character getting them into trouble. Ryu was the honourable guy that was kind of helping his buddy get out of these messes. So it was a little more interesting. Then it turned out to be something totally different.

THE ILLINOIS TRIP

For much of their time on *Street Fighter: The Movie*, Incredible Technologies kept to themselves, pushing forward without outside interference. Internally, team members ran into some tense disagreements, such as whether to make the game feel more like a classic Street Fighter game or more like Mortal Kombat, but for the most part they hashed out these issues among themselves.

While the team saw staff from GameStar and Capcom Coin-Op from time to time, and they spent time with Capcom Japan team members while in Australia, they didn't have the sort of daily or weekly progress check-ins that might be more common in 2022. So when a group from Capcom Japan flew in to visit Incredible Technologies and check on the game late in development, the trip stood out in a few ways.

→   KATSUYA AKITOMO
        Marvel Super Heroes artist and advisor, Capcom Japan

[Okamoto, Yasuda] and myself, we went to Chicago to spend a month with the developers in order to give them some guidance on the game. Obviously, the graphics looked like digitized versions of the actors, but we did some pixel adjustments to them. I think Yasuda was in charge of that at the time. And Okamoto made suggestions regarding the game's balance and hitbox settings.

→   AKIRA YASUDA
        Head of illustration group, Capcom Japan

I think [Capcom producer Tetsuya] Iijima was there as well. It might have been four people. [...] I think I was there for two

weeks. I saw the game, but it didn't look like it would sell very well.
I think Okamoto was pretty much angry the whole trip.

→   KATSUYA AKITOMO
                  Marvel Super Heroes artist and advisor, Capcom Japan

Okamoto had a lot to say, and I was the interpreter for the project.
But my English isn't that great, so I remember it being a very tough
job. In particular, Okamoto is the kind of person who always has to
be making jokes and teasing people. He was constantly harassing
the people around him, the kind of behaviour that today would
probably cause a lawsuit. And since there weren't a lot of staff and I
was the lowest man on the totem pole, I got the lion's share of it. It
was extremely stressful!

→   AKIRA YASUDA
                  Head of illustration group, Capcom Japan

When Akitomo was interpreting for Okamoto, he would often try
and soften or downplay Okamoto's anger, which actually had the
effect of making Okamoto angrier. The thing was, the game was
mostly done and we couldn't make any big changes at that point,
so there was an atmosphere of futility to the whole trip. Still,
I had nothing else to do, so I tried to at least fix up some of the
graphics, and I messed around with those a bit, making some small
improvements. It was all I could do, but unfortunately, even then,
the game wasn't really any more fun.

→   ELAINE HODGSON
                  Street Fighter: The Movie president and CEO, Incredible Technologies

I don't remember them being angry. I don't know. Maybe I put
it out of my memory. [...] I thought they were gracious, but once
again, they were not convinced that what we were doing was
what they wanted.

→ KATSUYA AKITOMO
Marvel Super Heroes artist and advisor, Capcom Japan

Well, actually, maybe it's not so much that he was angry all the time. It was just more like, Okamoto's the kind of person where, if he's not making fun of people around him, maybe his life has no meaning, or he just can't live without giving somebody some kind of flak, right? It's kind of like Loki, the trickster god, how he just always has to be acting like that. So, you know, you can call it harassment. You can call it fooling around. But basically, it's like he had this innate need to give people a hard time in order to enjoy his life.

→ RALPH MELGOSA
Street Fighter: The Movie art director, Incredible Technologies

It was tense. I would say that, but from my perspective, it was all intimidation. We had Capcom there. I mean, these guys were huge, right? We're this little guy.

> Okamoto, I'll say one thing about him. He was different than any other Japanese person I've ever met. He was so outgoing and he made such an effort to communicate, and if he couldn't say it audibly, he would use gestures. He would try to act out what he meant, and he went through great efforts to do this. And I found him to be a personable guy. I actually liked him. I thought he was really, really different and unique and creative and kind of inspiring, actually, you know? But I did also hear some offensive kind of comments from him as well, which I thought was very odd. Different times.

→ AKIRA YASUDA
Head of illustration group, Capcom Japan

Okamoto was so angry with the game that the CEO of Incredible Technologies tried to patch things up by inviting us over to her home. The house was humongous – it had a basement area, a huge 200-inch projection screen TV, a game room …

Seeing that house actually made my heart sink further, just with how big it was, and how little money I had myself. I mean, we'd created this huge hit with *Street Fighter II*, but I didn't get rich off of it. It wasn't until much later, long after the development of *Street Fighter II*, that we actually started to see some money come in. It wasn't until it looked like we all might quit, and then Capcom brought in a consulting group and we were finally given raises. But before that, we didn't see a lot of money from the games we made.

→ ELAINE HODGSON
Street Fighter: The Movie president and CEO, Incredible Technologies

We had the house that Golden Tee built. [...] [Later on], that house was collateralized to the bank for a loan that we had at the time when things didn't go well, so it was part of the building of the business.

→ RALPH MELGOSA
Street Fighter: The Movie art director, Incredible Technologies

It was an interesting relationship because, especially the guys that were with us in Australia, they were there to give us help somewhat, but there was a part of them where they're like, *We're not going to help you. We're going to let you do it on your own.* So it was an odd relationship where they're kind of looking over your shoulder, but not saying anything. And they came out once. That same crew flew out to Chicago and stayed here for a few days and hung out at the office. But it was that same type of thing, where they're just kind of looking over your shoulder but not really saying anything, right? And there's times, it's like, 'Hey, is this what you like? Do you want us to make any changes', right? And I'm not sure if that's just part of their culture. So that was kind of a head-scratcher.

→ DARRYL WILLIAMS
Street Fighter: The Movie video department supervisor, Capcom Coin-Op

So the guys from Japan – I'll tell you a story about that. The guys from Japan – they saw the version we did, and three of the top producers flew out, and they're like, 'Darryl, we have a problem with the game.' And I'm like, 'OK well, what's the problem?' They're like, 'Well, this flip move doesn't look real. This jump move isn't how Zangief does it.' And then they told me the fireball looks wrong. So then they sat there at my desk and edited the fireball sprite. [*laughs*] Which I thought was interesting, but I'm like, 'No problem. It's all cool. This'll be a story I can tell people.' So the guys sat there. They edited the sprite and sent it back.

→ RALPH MELGOSA
Street Fighter: The Movie art director, Incredible Technologies

They were relatively hands off. When it came to things like effects and the fireball effects, then they'd come in and say, 'No, it should be like this.' But for the most part, even with the moves and stuff, they were pretty distant.

> It was weird, in a way. And I don't want to make excuses – it is what it is – but I do feel in some ways like they kind of wanted us to fail. Because Street Fighter was their thing, and then this American company is given their franchise to do this, and I think there was a little chip on their shoulder over that. Like, *Hey, this is our baby.* I totally get that. I don't fault them for that whatsoever.

→ KATSUYA AKITOMO
Marvel Super Heroes artist and advisor, Capcom Japan

I mean, I didn't think the game turned out to be much of anything. I was more surprised at, like, *How did I end up spending a month with these two very important people* [Okamoto and Yasuda]? *What was the point*, you know?

A QUIET LAUNCH

In mid-1995, *Street Fighter: The Movie* shipped to arcades, approximately six months after the movie hit cinemas. It arrived alongside Capcom Japan's *Street Fighter Alpha*, which featured a number of references to *Street Fighter II: The Animated Movie* – making for a convenient parallel of a Western studio making a fighting game based on the Western movie and a Japanese studio making a fighting game with ties to the Japanese movie. (Capcom also released a multimedia game directly based on the animated movie in Japan towards the end of the year.)

When the games arrived, however, *Alpha* turned out to be far and away the more successful of the two, regardless of territory.

→ ALEX JIMENEZ
  Marvel Super Heroes design support, Capcom USA

When the game came out, we looked at it. I looked at the graphics of it and whatnot, and I'm like, 'OK. You realize this has been done already much, much better', you know? 'Mortal Kombat has already done this system and they've done it way better than us', you know? 'I don't think this is going to work', you know? I was criticized for being too negative. 'Oh, you're being too negative. You're not supporting the company.' I was like, 'I won't support the company while they're flushing cash.'

→ JAMES CHEN
  Street Fighter series commentator

Boy, I still remember being at the UCLA arcade when the game arrived. I used to get to campus before the arcade opened, so I would just basically sit there until it opened and go play *Darkstalkers* by myself, one player, just to have some fun. And I still remember one morning, I showed up and *Street Fighter: The Movie* was being set up, and a whole bunch of people were sitting outside the arcade. We're like, 'Oh my god, there's this new *Street Fighter: The Movie* game.' We were all just sitting there, waiting to play the game. And the arcade opened. They turned the game on, and we looked at it, and oh boy ... oh boy. Yeah. That's the best way I could describe it. It was so bad and kind of almost laughable – you know, we just kind of laughed at the game, really, and instantly nobody took it seriously.

The funny thing is, we were all eager to play on that first day. [But] I don't have any recollection or memory of actually playing it, weirdly enough. That's how little I cared, that my memory of the game has basically all but vanished.

→   STEPHEN FROST
     Street Fighter 30th Anniversary Collection producer, Digital Eclipse

Digitized graphics, for the most part, were a little bit silly. Even though I played a lot of [the games], I never got into the whole digitized movie stuff in the early days – Sega CD and things like that. I always felt it was kind of bad, and I always felt that digitized content didn't play very well and things like that. And so when I first saw [*Street Fighter: The Movie*] before I played it, I was like, *Oh man, this is going to be horrible. I don't see how this is going to be fun.* Because you can look at Mortal Kombat, and Mortal Kombat works within the system, but it is a very rough kind of a game as far as how it looks and how it plays and some of that. It plays a very specific way, and it kind of goes against how Street Fighter plays, and so I was a little bit concerned about that.

→   KEN WILLIAMS
     Assistant editor, Electronic Gaming Monthly magazine

I actually found that game fun, if I [didn't] take it seriously. I actually found it pretty fun. And part of it was, we got to go to the offices when they were making it. [...] I just remember going in there, because I remember the movie was so bad. [*laughs*] We went to play it, and we were like, *It actually plays fairly well*. I mean, it's not really Street Fighter. But it's just funny to see how they translated it from the movie to the game. And I thought it would be a lot more Mortal Kombat-ish, but it actually played a lot more like Street Fighter than you would expect. So it was actually – because our expectations were so low – we were actually pleasantly surprised.

→   CHRIS TANG
     Primal Rage II designer, Atari Games

It's better than *Real Battle on Film* – the home version [of *Street Fighter: The Movie* made by Capcom Japan]. But I admire them for digitizing those actors the way they did. It played better than any Strata/Incredible Technologies game had any right to. But it's not something that I wanted to play competitively.

→   DARRYL WILLIAMS
     Street Fighter: The Movie video department supervisor, Capcom Coin-Op

Everybody's like, 'Street Fighter: The Movie sucked.' I'm like, 'Yeah, but we were trying to do like Mortal Kombat, and we got it done.' The guys who developed it were great guys. They knew what they were doing. But obviously, trying to make a game similar to Mortal Kombat – if you don't know the secret sauce, it's a lot more challenging than you realize. [...] So we tried really hard to get the feel right. Between trying to get the feel right and trying to make it Mortal Kombat-esque, we got close enough but we didn't quite hit the mark. And so, that's kind of how it goes in the games world. Sometimes you get a hit, and sometimes you don't.

→   RALPH MELGOSA
     Street Fighter: The Movie art director, Incredible Technologies

I mean, we wanted the game to be so much more, and we were really limited by what we had to work with on the set of the movie. [...] We did what we could with what we had to work with.

→   ELAINE HODGSON
             Street Fighter: The Movie president and CEO, Incredible Technologies

I don't remember there ever being talk of a sequel. That would have to have been contemplated while we were actually digitizing the characters, obviously. I mean, if there had been a movie sequel, maybe. But I didn't hear that spoken of.

→   RALPH MELGOSA
             Street Fighter: The Movie art director, Incredible Technologies

[A sequel] to *Street Fighter: The Movie*? No.

→   ELAINE HODGSON
             Street Fighter: The Movie president and CEO, Incredible Technologies

Kind of after that, we found our footing with increased Golden Tee and other things. So we didn't have to go out to do third-party development for others. We started just doing our own development.

[Ed. note]   Golden Tee went on to become one of the biggest arcade videogame franchises of the 1990s and early 2000s, giving Incredible Technologies a unique level of success in a struggling industry.

→   RALPH MELGOSA
             Street Fighter: The Movie art director, Incredible Technologies

There's a handful of us that have been there for over 30 years. And Richard and Elaine are really good people to work for. Multiple times they could have sold the company for a ton of money, but they know that this is our livelihood and we're passionate, so they want to keep it going. They've made a lot of money, so they're like, *What else are they going to do?* They'll keep the company going.

338   Like a Hurricane

CHAPTER 14

STREET FIGHTER EX

While on a business trip to Illinois in the mid-1990s, Capcom Japan executive producer Yoshiki Okamoto got a phone call. Okamoto was in town to meet with Incredible Technologies, the studio developing *Street Fighter: The Movie*, and he wasn't happy with the progress being made. But suddenly, he had a more pressing concern.

Akira Nishitani, one of Capcom's most successful developers, wanted more money. Because of his track record designing hit games like *Final Fight* and *Street Fighter II*, Nishitani felt he was due a cut of Capcom's profits. And he was considering leaving the company if he didn't get it.

Akira Yasuda – Nishitani's partner on *Street Fighter II* and other games – was on the trip with Okamoto, and remembers hearing about this while thinking about wages himself. As Capcom had seen success, the profit hadn't trickled down to many of their key developers.

Shortly thereafter, Capcom went on to introduce a system to pay producers and key staff based on the success of their games. But before that happened, Nishitani's situation ended up leading to the first 3D Street Fighter game.

NISHITANI LEAVES CAPCOM

In late 1995, Nishitani left Capcom. He broke away and started his own company: Arika – his first name spelled backwards. Rather than open the company in Capcom's backyard in the Osaka area, Nishitani took his talents to Tokyo, and over time, brought along many of his former co-workers.

→   AKIRA YASUDA
             Head of illustration group, Capcom Japan

At the time Nishitani quit the company, he was pretty high up in terms of the hierarchy, but he wasn't at the top. [Capcom managers] Okamoto, [Noritaka] Funamizu, [Akio] Sakai and [Tokuro] Fujiwara were above him. And I think by that point, Nishitani had made a name for himself doing *Street Fighter II*. He'd worked on *Champion Edition*. He hadn't worked on *Turbo*, but you know, he had made a name for himself by this point, and I think he felt that he had hit the ceiling as far as his potential at Capcom was concerned. Once you put out a hit like *Street Fighter II*, it gets you to think, what else could you do? So I think he kind of felt this sense of something between loss and despair regarding his position in the company, because he couldn't really move up.

      I had gone to America with Okamoto, actually, and while we were there, Capcom called us and told us about an incident that had occurred. Basically, I think Nishitani had gone to management and told them, 'I demand that you pay me 1 billion yen' [$10 million]. He asked Capcom to pay him that money because he felt that he had helped the company.

He was looking for some kind of a bonus or dividend, even though back then Capcom didn't have that sort of system. Obviously, they weren't going to give him that, because they didn't have that kind of policy in place. But I remember hearing about that while Okamoto and I were in America on a business trip. And actually, I remember Okamoto asking me, 'Do you think we should give him 1 billion yen?'

And I remember thinking, *Yeah, why not?* You know, he'd made a couple of successful games. And I thought maybe I could get some of that money, too. But, obviously, that's not what ended up happening.

→ ALEX JIMENEZ
  Marvel Super Heroes design support, Capcom USA

They didn't [pay him enough]. His bonus – I'm serious; I'm not joking around – his bonus for *Street Fighter II* was he got a Super NES cartridge. And they sent him to the States for a few months, ostensibly to do research. So, yeah. They severely underpaid him. He was the genius behind all of that.

→ NORITAKA FUNAMIZU
  Street Fighter series producer, Capcom Japan

Nishitani had wanted to leave the company for a long time but [initially] Okamoto stopped him from doing so.

→ AKIRA YASUDA
  Head of illustration group, Capcom Japan

I think really he asked for that 1 billion yen because he wanted to see what kind of value Capcom saw in him. When it became evident that he wasn't worth that much to them, then his path after that was set. [...] So Nishitani quit and he started his own company, and I honestly think it was inevitable something like that would happen. There really wasn't much that could be done to change that particular outcome.

I thought, *What can you do?*

→   TAKESHI TEZUKA
       Marvel Super Heroes planner, Capcom Japan

I felt like I had lost something when he announced that he was going to leave. You know, he announced it so suddenly, and I found myself wishing that he had told me earlier.

→   KATSUYA AKITOMO
       Marvel Super Heroes artist and advisor, Capcom Japan

I think it was pretty unfortunate, but I also think that Nishitani is a genius, and I think it's really hard for someone of that level of talent to stay in the same place forever.

CAPCOM'S SHIFT TO 3D

Originally going by the name 'Stronger', Arika's first prototype as an independent studio took the shape of a 3D fighting game in December 1995. Nishitani didn't stay away from Capcom for long, though, as Okamoto signed a deal for Capcom to publish the game soon after. Over the next year, Arika turned that prototype into *Street Fighter EX*, the series' debut in 3D.

> As it turned out, Okamoto wasn't interested in Arika's game simply because of the prototype and Nishitani's history. Capcom was also playing catch-up in the game industry's shift towards 3D graphics. With Sega and Namco investing heavily in 3D arcade games, and PlayStation taking over the home console market thanks in part to its 3D capabilities, the industry was changing. And Capcom, as a company that had built its brand on 2D artwork, was slow to transition.

Internally, Capcom had dabbled in 3D research projects, one of which became the fighting game *Star Gladiator*, a weapons-based game inspired by Star Wars. But *Star Gladiator* looked dated next to its competitors, and ended up shipping approximately three years after Sega released *Virtua Fighter*.

> Much like how *Street Fighter: The Movie* had trailed Mortal Kombat, Capcom now found themselves chasing Virtua Fighter and Tekken.

→ NORITAKA FUNAMIZU
Street Fighter series producer, Capcom Japan

The whole reason we were late to the party was because we didn't have the hardware.

→ TAKESHI TEZUKA
  Marvel Super Heroes planner, Capcom Japan

I think the reason why Capcom was a bit late was because they didn't have the development tools necessary to make proper 3D games, and I think the company had enjoyed so much success up to that point making 2D games that there was a bit of inertia in the transition to 3D.

> Before *Star Gladiator*, we simply didn't have 3D-capable boards to work with. If you compare Capcom to a company like Sega, for example, they developed their own 3D-based videogame hardware, so they were obviously in a position to put out more titles compared to Capcom. So I would argue there were a lot of technical considerations that made it impossible for Capcom to jump in earlier than it eventually ended up doing.

I think it's also worth noting that making a 3D game is very different than making a 2D game, right? When you make a 2D game, you can animate assets in a very specific manner, but for 3D games it's different. I think for us, there was a lot of trial and error involved in the process of making 3D games, because it was just so different from what Capcom was used to.

→ HIDEAKI ITSUNO
  Star Gladiator director, Capcom Japan

Of course, we were late to the train. And the reason was simply, we had a lot of people that didn't recognize the validity of 3D games. Even when *Virtua Fighter* was released, despite there being a lot of people within Capcom that liked the game, there was a general sentiment that was just like, 'This doesn't compare with Street Fighter.' A lot of it was because most of the veterans at Capcom, most of the higher-ups, were experts in the 2D space, and the people that were interested in the 3D space were those who had just joined the company, like myself. I was very much interested in the 3D space. But there was just a general sentiment that you couldn't translate Street Fighter's gameplay into 3D, which is why it took a much longer time for us to enter that space.

→   NORITAKA FUNAMIZU
       Street Fighter series producer, Capcom Japan

I guess the real discussion began when the PlayStation was announced, and Sony visited the office and pitched us on it. They told us that Namco was developing an arcade board based on PlayStation hardware, so Sony asked us if we wanted to make a 3D arcade fighting game of some sort. That's how *Star Gladiator* got started.

> Then with *Street Fighter EX*, we decided ... with Street Fighter, there's a storyline, right? And we wanted to see what would happen in the future if we made Street Fighter in 3D, while the mainline [2D] games stayed in their own universe. We wanted to see an alternate future where Street Fighter became a 3D game. So we ended up offering that to Nishitani, and with *Street Fighter EX* being by him, that gave a certain degree of validity to the idea as well.

→   HIDEAKI ITSUNO
       Star Gladiator director, Capcom Japan

Nishitani was actually an advisor on our team for *Star Gladiator* before he left the company. And when he left, he took along a bunch of other Capcom staff to Arika. So it didn't feel like we were really collaborating or competing. It was just like, well, here's *EX* made by a lot of former Capcom people, and we're making *Star Gladiator*, which had been advised by this guy who just left recently and knows our game in detail.

> From my perspective at the time, Nishitani was way up there, seniority-wise. So it didn't feel like we were competing [...] just that we were coming out around the same time.

AKIRA YASUDA
        Head of illustration group, Capcom Japan

Arika, you can say, was a company that was created along the
lines of Capcom's particular culture or style, so there were a lot of
similarities in that regard. The vice-president of Arika, [Ichirou]
Mihara, actually, I remember him calling me one day and saying,
'We need a new design for Chun-Li. Can you make this for us?' And
I remember doing so, but then Funamizu came to me after and said,
'You're not supposed to do that. It's a different company.' I wasn't
sure how it was supposed to work.

[Ed. note]   While Nishitani got Arika up and running,
                    Yasuda stayed at Capcom, working on art for many
                    of Capcom's games, including *Star Gladiator*.

→   AKIRA YASUDA
        Star Gladiator character designer, Capcom Japan

Star Gladiator, that was a tough project to work on. [...] I joined
the *Star Gladiator* team in the middle of development. I think
what made it such a different project from anything that came
before it was the fact that I had to work closely with a programmer
during development. On previous games, I could just show them
the illustrations and then they would take care of everything else,
but with 3D games, I had to talk regularly with the programmer to
figure out what we could do and what we could not do.

> I think it might have been tough because I didn't get along
> with that programmer very well, and it probably didn't help
> that I joined partway through. I was still in the middle of
> studying and learning about 3D, but the development just
> kept moving forward. I felt like I couldn't do everything
> that I set out to do with that project. I didn't do the
> animations, either, so we had to ask somebody else to do
> those. I felt like the animations that I had wanted in the
> game, personally, were not reflected in the final product.

So, yeah. *Star Gladiator* was a project where I wasn't really able to do what I wanted to do or what I envisioned that I wanted to do. I think the animator [I was working with] on *Star Gladiator* actually left the team midway and went to the *Street Fighter EX* team. I remember because *Star Gladiator* wasn't going as planned for me, and I remember seeing the progress that the *Street Fighter EX* team was making and I felt a little bit envious about how much better they were doing. I prefer my games to be very responsive to button inputs, so if I press down, I want the character to, for example, duck right away, right? And I felt like *Street Fighter EX* had managed to do that but not *Star Gladiator*.

> With 2D pixel art games, I was able to get the animation to respond how I wanted to design it, but when the system changed over to 3D polygons, because I had to work with someone else, it didn't become what I wanted it to become. For example, if you think about the purpose of a joystick in fighting games or action games, you would think it's supposed to be for moving characters, right? But actually, the whole point of a joystick is so the player can feel like they're interacting with the game directly.

With *Star Gladiator*, you can move the characters, but it's like you're using a switch. So you can't really do an emergency evasion or dodge. You would think if an enemy is approaching a character, you should be able to run away from it as quickly as possible, but in *Star Gladiator*, you couldn't really do that. So if you're the player and you try playing the game for the first time, you might think, 'Why did I die? I have no idea why I died. I don't get this.'

> I think the reason why the game didn't turn out so well for me was because I didn't do the proper research that I needed to do regarding the game's motions. So because of that lack of research, I feel like some of my worst memories as a game creator come from having worked on that game.

I guess you could say I was capable and good at doing 2D games, whereas with 3D games, I couldn't directly control what would eventually be created. It got so bad when we moved into 3D games that I thought maybe I should just quit game development altogether.

THE FIRST 3D STREET FIGHTER

Street Fighter EX hit arcades in late 1996. Due to the off-the-shelf hardware and the team's limited 3D experience, Arika was never going to push visual limits along the lines of Sega's Virtua Fighter series, which ran on expensive custom hardware. But as Arika's first game, developed from scratch in about a year, it showed Capcom another way forward for the genre. The game built a reputation for a lighthearted tone and extensive combo system, and established an alternate universe path for the Street Fighter series.

→   JAMES CHEN
           Street Fighter series commentator

It really did feel like they were experimenting at that point. Like, 'Oh, should we take Street Fighter to a 3D level? But we don't want to spend our time on this, so we'll get to this company called Arika and have them make it.' Even though we didn't have as much information back then as we do now, it was still pretty obvious that it was a farmed-out game, so to speak, and so it didn't feel like it was being taken as seriously. It felt like Capcom was like, 'Yeah, let's just farm this out. Let's see how this does. Let's see if they can figure out a way to make it work in 3D.'

→   TOMOTAKA SUZUKI
           Street Fighter II series combo video creator

I actually quite liked the Street Fighter EX series because even though they were using polygons for the graphics, the gameplay was pretty much *Street Fighter II* at its core, and it felt very familiar to me.

→   JAMES GODDARD
     Tenth Degree designer, Atari Games:

It was awesome to see it in 3D. I was really happy for Nishitani, that he had managed to leave Capcom and go do his own thing, because I thought he was going to be there for life. And I think that was important, to stay loyal, but at the same time, you need to be able to do your own thing. So I was really excited for it.

It was slow, so you kind of know where this is going. I was like, 'Goddamn, I want to play it. I love that there's all this crazy stuff like [skeleton-costumed businessman] Skullomania.' I mean, it was really an impressive game, but it just played slow and so I struggled with playing it just because I found it to be not at the pace I wanted. [But] it showed that it could be done in 3D and that there was a way to do it. [...] *EX* was an important moment for me playing it, because I saw what could be done in 3D. [...] It just shows that Nishitani's a boss. He, to this day, is the inventor of the way fighting games should feel, even if I don't agree with the pacing sometimes.

→   COREY TRESIDDER
     Street Fighter EX Plus a manual writer, Capcom USA

It wasn't a real popular game, if I recall correctly. Capcom was just doing games all the time so there [were] definitely some games that [our team] probably – if we'd had the ability to make the decisions – we probably wouldn't have released. Japan [was] definitely wanting to get as much revenue out of every product they put money into to develop. [...] We played it a little bit and we just weren't feeling it.

→   JAMES CHEN
     Street Fighter series commentator

EX was very weird. When that game came out, a lot of people didn't really take it seriously competitively because it was just very weird. It was different. It was a fun one-player game. I still remember the thing that really made the game as popular as it was, was the Expert Mode trials [in the PlayStation version]. They're like, 'do this combo, do this combo', and as a person who was obsessed with combos, that was super fun. I really enjoyed that. I got it on the home version specifically for that.

→   DAVE WINSTEAD
        Tenth Degree designer, Atari Games

I actually liked *Street Fighter EX*. [...] I played it a little bit when it was in the arcades, but I wasn't super into it. We knew that this was Nishitani working on this stuff and so we were kind of excited to play it, but when it came home, that's when it opened our eyes to really loving the game. [...] The whole training mode that they added in there was just outstanding. We sat down playing that game for, like, two days straight, just going through all the training and just doing all the crazy combos and unlocking stuff. It was a lot of fun.

→   CHRIS TANG
        Primal Rage II designer, Atari Games

I like it better than *Street Fighter IV* and I like it way better than *Street Fighter V*. I'll tell you what I like about it: you can cancel a super move into a super move into a super move, so being able to Super Hadouken someone into a Shoryureppa. I really like being able to combo into the combo into the combo, because you store up that meter and you try to get something going. Boom, boom, boom. Then you nail them. *Boom, super, boom, super, boom, super.*

The other thing I really like is Zangief destroying the universe with his Level 3 Final Atomic Buster. [...] It's the most epic fighting game finish ever. Basically, what happens is if you do Level 2, he does the Final Atomic Buster and then I guess there are these asteroids that come down and the planet explodes. If you do Level 3, it zooms back from the Earth and the entire galaxy explodes – and he's doing the Final Atomic Buster coming down. I really liked the creativity and the over-the-top-ness of it.

[Ed. note]   While *Street Fighter EX* didn't reach the heights of Nishitani's earlier titles, either critically or financially, it did well enough to justify multiple spinoffs, console ports and sequels. Following *Street Fighter EX3*'s launch in 2000, and seven Street Fighter EX releases in less than four years, Capcom and Arika put the series on hold.

CHAPTER 15

STREET FIGHTER III

In the mid-1990s, *Street Fighter III* was a mirage. After *Street Fighter II* blew up, a numbered sequel was inevitable, yet – following more than a dozen upgrades and spinoffs – it was nowhere to be seen. For six years, in the absence of genuine news about sequel plans, fans drank the sand, latching on to whatever rumours and gossip they could find.

'Here's the exclusive first news on Street Fighter III,' wrote *Diehard GameFan* magazine in its April 1993 issue, as teased on the cover.

'This new version will incorporate only two of the original cast from part two, Ryu and Sagat. You know what that means … 14 new characters! Now, when Ryu does his fireball, he has an aura around him, and Sagat can now do a tiger knee helicopter kick. Instead of 3 special moves per character, there are now 5, and there is no more lag time after throwing a fireball, you can now automatically connect it with a dragon punch. And there's no more charging to do moves like Guile's sonic boom or Blanka's spinning ball from part 2. There will also be one command that all the characters can use. As far as new characters, we know about two so far, Chun Li's younger sister, and Bison's mentor (who will be the last boss), his name is Shadow Lu. Street Fighter III is only a working title (even the name may change). This new game will incorporate two new 16 bit processors created by Capcom, which will be running parallel to each other (parallel processing). We'll have more info for you next month and maybe a big surprise. Remember you heard it here first.' Hardly any of that turned out to be true.

On the Usenet newsgroup alt.games.sf2, players posted prank links promising non-existent screenshots and test site details.

At a Software Etc. in Torrance, California, employees signed customers up for imaginary pre-orders.

Throughout magazines like *GameFan*, *VideoGames* and *Electronic Gaming Monthly*, reports and rumours circulated that the game would have 3D graphics, that it might be developed in the US, that it would run on Nintendo's Ultra 64 arcade hardware, and that it would be exclusive to Nintendo's next home console.

In arcades around the world, players told the same joke: 'Can't Capcom count to three?'

SIX YEARS LATER

As it turned out, for about half of that six-year stretch, Capcom had been working on *Street Fighter III* – they just hadn't told anyone.

In 1997, Capcom released *Street Fighter III: New Generation*, showing their work by underlining the word 'Three' front and centre on the game's arcade marquee.

Flying in opposition to market trends and most of the circulated rumours, Capcom delivered a 2D game with highly detailed art and animation – which led to many calling it one of the best-looking 2D games on the market. The development team made subtle changes to the series' mechanics, added a parry system that allowed players to counter attacks, and took a bold chance by wiping clean the character roster, only bringing back series mainstays Ryu and Ken. (Giving *GameFan* a consolation prize.)

But as quickly became clear, the market Capcom entered in 1997 was very different from the one they had dominated in 1991.

→   NORITAKA FUNAMIZU
        General producer, Capcom Japan

Street Fighter III was the point when I said I would no longer do this. I think I'd just been so involved in the Street Fighter series that Capcom initially assumed, *Yeah, you've got to make* III *as well*. I said no. [...] At that point, I just wanted to make my own game.

→   CHRIS KRAMER
        Street Fighter series public relations representative, Capcom USA

At that point, the Street Fighter brand was kind of in a rocky place. You know, sales hadn't been good on home versions.

The US arcade market was dying. And everybody was looking at what was happening on PlayStation and Saturn. They were like, 'OK, 3D games – this is the future.' And Capcom was leaning in way hard on traditional 2D animation with *Street Fighter III*. So it was like, 'OK, this looks great, but it also looks like more Street Fighter.'

→   AKIRA YASUDA
          Street Fighter Ⅲ artist, Capcom Japan

Virtua Fighter had already come out by that point, right? I mean, there was no way 2D graphics could win against that. If we were going to beat Virtua Fighter, we had to make something that would go down in the annals of gaming history. I knew it was a battle we weren't going to win, but we had to fight it anyway.

→   MATT ATWOOD
          Street Fighter Ⅲ public relations manager, Capcom USA

Virtua Fighter and Tekken were the big ones, and they were tough because it was something different. There was a significant group of people who loved Street Fighter that were also like, 'What's next in the category?' [...] It felt like, from a promotional standpoint, *How can we compete?*

→   JAMES CHEN
          Street Fighter series commentator

I still remember, and this used to make me so mad when I was younger, the magazine reviews would come out and like [...] you had to be 3D or people thought your game was ugly. [...] It was like, 'Wow, they're really sticking to this, huh?' Even despite how beautiful the game animation was. But 3D – even the freaking PlayStation 1 ugly polygon kind of stuff – was the thing at the time. And so yeah, a lot of people were disappointed that it was sprite-based, because 3D was such a fad at the time.

→   NORITAKA FUNAMIZU
General producer, Capcom Japan

Street Fighter III was always intended to be a 2D fighting game that would take 2D to its limit, and home in on the 2D aspect. And part of the idea was it was going to be made by a new generation of creators, so I think, for both myself and for Yasuda, we felt that we didn't want to say anything that would interfere with the direction of the new generation.

→   AKIRA YASUDA
Street Fighter III artist, Capcom Japan

It's a bit of a complicated story, but [Tomoshi] Sadamoto, the director of [Capcom's side-scrolling brawler] *The King of Dragons*, initially conceived of making an original fighting game that wasn't part of the Street Fighter series.

→   SHINICHIRO OBATA
Street Fighter III planner, Capcom Japan

Yeah, that's true. But it was only an original game at the very beginning of the project.

→   AKIRA YASUDA
Street Fighter III artist, Capcom Japan

I remember seeing the initial concept of Sadamoto's game and thinking, *You know, they're probably going to want to turn this into a Street Fighter game anyway.* The characters didn't seem to have a lot of personality, so I proposed that they add Ryu and turn the game into a Street Fighter game. [...] At the time, there were team members who weren't really open to or supportive of that idea.

WHAT TOOK SO LONG

Capcom kicked off *Street Fighter III*'s development in 1994 – originally as a new IP – using a small team led by producer Sadamoto. The team expanded in 1995 as more staff became available, yet it took until early 1997 for Capcom to ship the game to arcades – an anomaly at a time when most of Capcom's fighting games took a year or less to develop, and a counterpoint to the fast-tracked *Street Fighter Alpha*.

Street Fighter III was to be a showcase of Capcom's technical abilities and new CPS-3 arcade hardware, with extensive resources poured into the game's 2D visuals. But as Obata says, that wasn't the only reason the game took so long to make.

→ SHINICHIRO OBATA
Street Fighter Ⅲ planner, Capcom Japan

After working on [vertical-scrolling 2D shooter] *19XX*, I was trying to figure out what kind of project I should do next, and my boss at the time, Funamizu, asked me to try designing a new kind of shoot-'em-up. But it just so happened that at the same time, *Street Fighter III* had already been in development for two to three years, and, just honestly speaking, it wasn't looking very interesting, and I didn't think the team was making good progress with the title. There also weren't enough game designers on the team, so I ended up joining the team in order to help them. [...] More than two years had passed, so the game was in its third year of development.

To explain what happened, there was a big structural change at Capcom at the time. Prior to that point, the company didn't have a system where a different producer led each project. [Capcom executive producer Yoshiki]

Okamoto had been producing pretty much every game Capcom released. But then Capcom solicited the services of a consulting company that recommended Capcom introduce a producer system in order to streamline the flow of development.

[Ed. note] Around this time, Okamoto established an independent scenario and development studio called Flagship, with funding from Capcom, Nintendo, and Sega. Capcom acquired Flagship shortly thereafter, and Okamoto continued to oversee Capcom's game lineup during this period.

So when that change happened, the people who had been the lead game designers or directors ended up becoming the producers of Capcom's projects. In the case of *Street Fighter III*, it was originally spearheaded by someone who worked on it as a lead designer or director, and then he became the producer. But the thing is, a lot of these people had only done game design, so they didn't know how to produce games. And when he became the producer, Capcom had to find someone to take his place as the lead designer, and they assigned that job to someone who was pretty junior at the time.

The thing about *Street Fighter III*'s team was that, surprisingly, even though it was Capcom, which was known for fighting games, 70 to 80 percent of the team members had no experience making fighting games. Why that was the case, I honestly have no idea. But there were people in the team who were quite inexperienced. I think more than half of them – mainly the planners and programmers – weren't really familiar with fighting games at all. By this point, a lot of the old guard, the people who had worked on fighting games beforehand like [*Street Fighter II* planner Akira] Nishitani, had already left the company. And even among those of the older Street Fighter games who were still around at Capcom at the time, most of them were not on the *Street Fighter III* team. They had all the knowhow, but they were all on the *Street Fighter Alpha* team. And the *Street Fighter Alpha* team and the *Street Fighter III* team never really shared much information with each other.

So by the time I came around, [the team] didn't really have a very clear concept of what to do with the game. [...] They had created a lot of animation patterns, and they wanted the hits to feel like they had a real heft behind them, to make it look cool when you took damage. But the problem was the team had no idea what kind of mechanics should go into the game in order to make it an interesting fighting game. There was no plan for that, and there weren't enough moves for each character. So I ended up joining the team when the game was in that kind of state.

[Ed. note]   Others point to a variety of issues slowing down development – some technical, as Capcom were working on new hardware and creating a game with a level of art and animation detail that was new for the company. Capcom declined an interview request to speak with Sadamoto for this book.

→   AKIRA YASUDA
     Street Fighter III artist, Capcom Japan

I think [one] reason why development was so protracted was because of the lack of well-developed tools for the CPS-3 hardware we used for the game. One palette in the game could use up to 256 colours, right? But in order for us to exploit that palette, we needed tools that we just didn't have. When developing for the CPS-3, we had to make a choice between having a high colour count or having more pixels – a higher resolution, that is. When it came time for us to make that choice, we went with having a higher colour count.

A month or two before I left [Capcom, localization manager Tom Shiraiwa] took me in a room and locked the door and showed me a tape of *Street Fighter III* test animation. He's like, 'What do you think? Will this be successful in the US? Will American gamers like this?' [...] And really, it was just like idle animation, or here's Ryu on a stage jumping or punching, and stuff like that. And you could see how much more was going into the game, in terms of animation and movements, and the art style was definitely light-years beyond Street Fighter II. But it was always going to be a huge thing for them and they had to do it absolutely right. So I think they went through some stops and starts before kind of landing on what they eventually released.

It was hard to say [whether I thought it would be successful]. I think my initial feedback was, 'It looks amazing.' He was like, 'Yeah.' And [he] told me, he's like, 'Oh, this will be CPS-3 so we'll have all-new arcade hardware', and he's like, 'They'll never be able to do this for the PlayStation, because the PlayStation won't be able to do all the animation correctly. So it's really a showcase for the CPS-3 hardware and shows how important arcades are.' Because that was always a big deal. The arcade guys always wanted to make the ultimate arcade experience, even though realistically, the line was like, 'Hey, put it out in the arcades. It gets popular and then six, eight months later, it comes home and then the sales explode from there.' But the arcade guys were definitely always looking to showcase how they could do things at a high end of the scale, because it had infinitely more RAM than a home console did at that time. They could do a lot more clever stuff on their dedicated hardware.

→   SETH KILLIAN
       Street Fighter Ⅳ special combat advisor, Capcom USA

SFIII was before my time at Capcom, so my only insight into why it might have been a long dev cycle is based on my general perspective as a developer who has worked on many fighting games. *SFIII*'s sprite animation work is considered one of the finest achievements in the genre, but nothing about it scales. Because those animations are all carefully hand-drawn, and made by a shrinking pool of pixel-artist talent, even a small change to an attack might require redoing a lot of work, which slows down your ability to experiment and iterate. This is especially tough because *SFIII* probably needed to iterate more than any game in franchise history. The parry system was both very different from previous Street Fighter games, and also very delicate – a few frames in either direction could make it impossible to attack. Finally, in addition to the regular surprises you get during any game development, the decision to make it a Street Fighter title sets expectations that are both high and specific, which can be a hard place to work from creatively.

[Ed. note]   Obata says that not all of the development challenges led to an extended timeline – some came with other issues.

→   SHINICHIRO OBATA
       Street Fighter Ⅲ planner, Capcom Japan

Another problem, in terms of the game balance, was that the balancing and adjustments for the characters were done by separate people, so the balance was all over the place. One person would design their character to be more traditional and Street Fighter-like, then another would do it in the Darkstalkers style. There was no unity.

Up to that point, all the Street Fighter II games – specifically, *Turbo, Super Street Fighter II, Super Street Fighter II Turbo* and, though it's a different series,

Darkstalkers too … almost all of the balancing – that is, how strong the characters are, how strong their moves are, the level design – almost all of it had been done by one person, an extremely skilled programmer named [Yasunori] Harada. He had been handling everything, but for *Street Fighter III*, we changed it so that everybody would handle their own specific characters. There are pros and cons to that kind of approach.

[Ed. note]   Ultimately, Obata says he saw the game make large strides over time, with features like super moves added late in development.

The *Street Fighter III* team was passionate but full of very inexperienced people. But I think things started to pick up a bit when a guy named [Kazuhito] Nakai joined the team. He was a very knowledgeable programmer, so development kind of sped up at that point. I came up with the idea for the 'super cancels', where if someone does a Hadouken and then you input a super right after that, it will cancel the move. That type of cancel was my idea, and Nakai was able to program it for me. So while that was going on, I also homed in on the blocking and the parrying aspects that needed implementation and polish.

Also, one more thing worth mentioning was that five to six months before the game's development was completed, a game designer named [Hidetoshi] Ishizawa joined the team. He had worked on *Street Fighter Alpha 2*. He was my *kohai* [subordinate employee], but he ended up joining the team and I think he was very interested in the parry system, so he focused most of his energy on adjustments and balancing for that system. Nakai and Ishizawa gave us a much-needed boost, and we were able to make the attacks and moves more fun and interesting, have better game balance, new systems and so on.

The biggest takeaway from all this is that the team was very indecisive and really had no idea what they wanted to do early on in development. But the thing is, there was so much pressure from within the company and from other teams, because this was *Street Fighter III*, right? You know, this was the sequel or what came after the legendary *Street Fighter II*. So there was just no way this game would be allowed to fail, and the team themselves – they were feeling that pressure, but they also felt the sense of obligation to complete what they were trying to do. So there was a lot of indecisiveness. There was a lot of back and forth discussion on what to do. And eventually they figured out, *Yeah, maybe we should do this, this, and that.* But it took a lot of time for the team to gather its bearings.

THE NEW GENERATION

One of Capcom's boldest decisions for *Street Fighter III* was to drop most of their established characters in favour of a new cast led by a new main character: a wrestler named Alex. While Capcom reversed course on producer Sadamoto's initial idea to release the game as a new intellectual property, the game still ended up with ten new characters alongside Ryu and Ken, shifting the balance considerably.

This proved controversial, both because fans were disappointed to see their favourite characters missing, and because the new cast didn't resonate with players in the same way as the original roster.

→   CHRIS TANG
      Street Fighter Ⅲ design support, Capcom USA

They sent us documents [showing the characters via fax]. My first reaction was like, *OK* ... I was a really, really big fan of Capcom, and I thought they could do no wrong. And the first time I saw the character designs for *Street Fighter III*, I didn't think they were real. I thought this was some other game. The first time I saw Oro, I was like, 'Did something happen? Did they fire everybody? Does [Akira Yasuda] still work there, or what?'

So I did not have a favourable opinion of the designs when I first saw them, especially when they were, like, in a black-and-white fax. But later on, we found out they had a lot of frames of animation. They were able to leverage that to make them kind of cool. But my impression of the designs was not that favourable.

→ AKIRA YASUDA
   Street Fighter Ⅲ artist, Capcom Japan

On previous projects I had a lot of input on how the characters were envisioned, but on *Street Fighter III*, Sadamoto's opinions were obviously a very big driving force on how the characters were eventually designed. I wanted more freedom, but I couldn't veer too far from Sadamoto's character designs. In most of the games I'd been involved in, people came to me for guidance on the designs, but *Street Fighter III* was Sadamoto's show, so I was relegated to brushing up his original designs.

> I remember being there to put pressure on the team to do good work. For some of the characters, I would set the basics of the design early on. I would give the team directions and so forth, and they would kind of take care of things on their own. When there were certain parts of the design that weren't going well, I would step in and maybe fix up a few things, but I didn't really have such a concerted involvement in the game.

→ SHINICHIRO OBATA
   Street Fighter Ⅲ planner, Capcom Japan

If we're talking about what [Yasuda] did, I think he might have forgotten this, but originally, Ryu and Ken's pixel art and animation were done by a different person. But that person hadn't been able to produce those animations at the quality needed, so [Yasuda] actually went back and fixed a lot of the issues. [...] So, that's why they hold up so well today.

→ JAMES CHEN
   Street Fighter series commentator

It was interesting, because it was all new characters except for Ryu and Ken, and nostalgia is one hell of a drug, and so a lot of people were like, 'I don't care about these new characters. What is Oro?' Like, 'What is this?' You know, it was weird. [...] I know a lot of people didn't like the game much at all, and [...] I think it had to do with the fact that a lot of the returning characters didn't come back.

→ KEN WILLIAMS
Assistant editor, Electronic Gaming Monthly magazine

The fact that they pretty much killed the cast [was a bummer]. It was like, 'Who are all these characters?' I'm like, 'I'm still expecting to see the primary cast.' Even if you age them, right? [...] And Alpha is guilty of that too, because it spoiled us in that way, bringing a whole bunch of characters into the mix.

→ SHINICHIRO OBATA
Street Fighter III planner, Capcom Japan

If you look at games like *Street Fighter Alpha*, *Alpha 2* and *Alpha 3*, they sold very well. And as you already know, they had familiar characters like Zangief, Blanka and E. Honda that the fans really wanted to see. Just having those legendary *Street Fighter II* characters was enough for those games to sell very well. But because *Street Fighter III* had started out as an entirely different game, they had a totally new cast of characters, which nobody liked. The problem was that the characters had very uninspired designs, and I would say they were quite strange in comparison. If you think about the fact that we moved on to the CPS-3 arcade hardware for this game, I think people wanted to see Vega, E. Honda, etc. created on that new hardware with the technology it offered.

→ KEN WILLIAMS
Assistant editor, Electronic Gaming Monthly magazine

Having all new main characters really threw me off on the storyline. I had no problems with any of the new characters, but having Alex be the new main guy, I was like, 'He's never going to be my main, ever. That's never gonna happen.'

→   AKIRA YASUDA
       Street Fighter III artist, Capcom Japan

I think it was lacking characters with traditional martial arts styles like judo and karate. I mean, come on. To have a guy with stretchy arms and he's an Indian yogi, OK, that's believable; that's recognizable. But a guy who's just straight rubber … ? It's like they were almost sci-fi. It didn't really feel like an authentic Street Fighter game. I don't think the game had characters that felt like they belonged in a Street Fighter game. I mentioned Necro [the character made of rubber], and I personally like Necro as a character, but that's not Street Fighter.

[Ed. note] Asked if he thinks it would have been better had *Street Fighter III* remained an original property, so the characters wouldn't feel out of place in the Street Fighter universe, Yasuda says he'd prefer another way of changing history.

Actually, if I had to change the past, I'd rather just not have worked on that game at all.

[Ed. note] Since the early days of Street Fighter, Capcom has faced criticism over their stereotypical character designs, which often incorporate exaggerated cultural aspects and use them to define character personalities. According to Capcom USA design support staff team member Alex Jimenez, these stereotypical designs often led to tense conversations between team members at Capcom USA and the designers in Japan, particularly with how the games represented black characters such as Dudley in *Street Fighter III*.

→   ALEX JIMENEZ
           Street Fighter Ⅲ design support, Capcom USA

We were working on *Street Fighter III* and one of the characters was a black character. When I looked at the artwork for him, it was a black gentleman dressed in a suit. He looked like an old English boxer. I thought ['Dudley' seemed like a good name]. And I wanted to make him this 1890s-style old English boxer, you know? The kind of guy that holds their fists at face level, all the way extended outward, like the old-time boxers.

> I thought this would be great. I'm going to make him Sir Dudley. He's going to be a gentleman. He's going to be a noble in England. He'll be a specialist in biomechanics. He'll be really, super, super smart, and he's entering the Street Fighter tournament because boxing is the noble art, you know? Boxing was originally called the noble art. So I was like, *Perfect. We can work that angle in there with this being the noble art. He's going to show the world that a gentleman can fight.* [...] I had this whole thing of him being this brilliant, brilliant guy, you know? Brilliant Englishman with a style and whatnot.

And they took that and threw it all out and they lowered his IQ by about 60 points and they had his reason for being in the tournament so he can get this really fancy car so he can pick up lots of girls, you know? And his speech pattern was really, you know, dumbified. That would be the best word for it. So I looked at that and was like – I just got so frustrated at that point – 'I can't believe you guys are still doing this', you know? And the fact that I've been here for five frickin' years and I haven't convinced you to stop doing it really annoys me, you know? Really, really bugs me.

→   JAMES CHEN
           Street Fighter series commentator

When Dudley first showed up, I immediately loved the fact that he wasn't the stereotypical kind of [character]. I loved that he was anti-stereotype. So hearing that that's what they originally wanted him to be makes me very, very sad. [...] I've heard stories about some other characters' origins and stuff like that, that kind of fit in with that narrative and really disappoint me.

I mean, even if you look at *Street Fighter IV*, and when you look at a character like [Mexican wrestler El] Fuerte, that character is already questionable in how they designed him. [...] And, for example, Birdie. What they did to Birdie I was always really disappointed with, [because he wasn't] African American in *Street Fighter I*. Clearly a white guy. Not that I have any problem with them changing him to a different ethnicity, but by the time they hit *Street Fighter V*, they turned him into a kind of joke character all of a sudden, and he was fat and slobby and all this stuff. I was always really disappointed in how they handled Birdie.

→   JUSTIN BERENBAUM
        Street Fighter series customer service manager, Capcom USA

[There was the whole thing in *Street Fighter II* of] Blanka being from South America, right? [...] I mean, let's not forget that we all have our racial biases, but Japan was pretty racially biased, especially in the 1990s. [...] [You could see that aimed at] African Americans and Latinos in particular, and honestly, you got the sense even working there sometimes that we were just the stupid gaijin. Sometimes if we'd provide feedback on a game and just say, 'Hey, this is great, but there's this thing that doesn't make sense in English' or whatever, oftentimes we would get feedback saying basically, 'You're stupid. You know nothing.' But they would make the change. But we wouldn't be given any props for suggesting to make the change.

→   CHRIS KRAMER
        Street Fighter series public relations representative, Capcom USA

Japan doesn't have the connection to the understanding of the day-to-day of racism that we have in the United States. So there was a lot of just random stuff that was making its way into Japanese culture, still, even in the 1990s. [There were] weird caricatures of people who were black and it was the sort of stuff that had no cultural connection for them and was no different from the idea of Zangief being a big hulking Russian or Dhalsim being a stretchy yoga master, right? They were kind of looking for quick ways to identify a character and a setting with the limited tools they had. So yeah, I think there have been issues with race and depictions of different races throughout Japanese gaming. But again, they just are not connected to the understanding of that history there and that cultural sensitivity. So I think it's one of those things that would have to be explained pretty regularly at every Japanese company.

But yeah, there were [issues]. The first time somebody pointed out to me in *Street Fighter II*, it's a white guy that punches out a black guy in the attract mode before the logo comes up – honestly, I'd never even thought about that, right? And that was one of two African Americans shown in *Street Fighter II*. So not exactly a good look, but the idea of that cultural sensitivity just didn't exist in the Japanese mindset at that time.

THE CLOSEOUT

When *Street Fighter III* hit arcades, it proved to be a tough
sell. The game showed Capcom's 2D animation at its best,
which gave the series a fresh coat of paint and a distinct
identity among other fighters, but it arrived sandwiched
between *Virtua Fighter 3* and *Tekken 3*, leading some
players and arcade operators to disregard it. 'The great
mystery is why Capcom called this *SFIII* instead of leaving
that honor for a more powerful and revolutionary 3D title,'
wrote *Next Generation* magazine in their review.
Fold in the unrecognizable cast and the deep roster
of other fighting games competing for attention,
and many were quick to dismiss Capcom's game.

→   KEN WILLIAMS
        Assistant editor, Electronic Gaming Monthly magazine

I actually went to Capcom to look at it for the first time [...] and it
was a little awkward because I didn't like it much. To be honest, I
really didn't. [...] It was too slow. It didn't play well. It felt more like
a gag, parody version to me. It just didn't play the same. [...] 'It didn't
really feel like a Street Fighter game' is probably the most damning
comment I could have made to them. Because it didn't play the same.
It really didn't.

→   SETH KILLIAN
        Street Fighter IV special combat advisor, Capcom USA

I thought it was beautiful. I was blown away by the animation and
the obvious care that had been poured into the game. That said,
while it felt like an exciting new Capcom fighting game, between
few returning favourite characters and a parry mechanic that gutted
SFII's full-screen fireball gameplay, it didn't feel much like a Street
Fighter game to me. The mind games around parries created iterated

rock/paper/scissors games that were exciting, but that felt closer to Virtua Fighter gameplay than SFII's positional tug-of-war.

→   CHRIS KRAMER
                Street Fighter series public relations representative, Capcom USA

You can't feel how *Street Fighter III* plays so differently from Street Fighter II just by looking at it. If you look at screenshots, you're like, 'Well, I guess that looks better', but you don't understand how different those games are until you actually get in and start playing them. I can't play *Street Fighter III* at all. I can't play that game. I'm useless. Even though it's a joystick and six buttons, I can't get anything in that game. Street Fighter II, I still have the same ingrained muscle memory for that, and that didn't really translate across into *Street Fighter III*.

→   SHINICHIRO OBATA
                Street Fighter III planner, Capcom Japan

It became much harder for casual players to enjoy. The ability for beginners to compete had been very important to Street Fighter II – the idea that, as long as you blocked and made simple attacks, you'd be OK. Hey, you might even win. That casualness was lost in *Street Fighter III*. Now if you fought a good player, you couldn't do anything. They'd block all your attacks. And the cancels were difficult, and there were lots of other highly technical aspects to the game. Of course, high-level players loved this, but casual players didn't play it at all. The characters weren't interesting to them, the gameplay was difficult and unintuitive, and you had no chance in hell against a better player. So basically only hardcore players loved *Street Fighter III*, but for them, it offered a longevity and depth that's kept them interested for decades now. It turned out to be a very special game, in that regard.

You know, there are many different approaches you can take to game design. One approach, which we took in *SFIII*, is to design your game around 'unanswerables'.

I think with any game, players will search for the best tactic, the best strategy ... like, if X happens, you should always do Y; if you do this here, you'll always win. There's competitive games like that, where the match is essentially a confrontation of theoretical knowledge that each player has built up. But *SFIII* is a game that, by design, doesn't have fixed answers to those questions. There is no 'best' tactic; you can spend your whole life trying to find the perfect theoretical approach to a situation in *SFIII*, but it will never be quite right. You always have to be reading your opponent in the moment; you can't just fall back on your theories. It's a game that lets you search for answers forever. And that was the opposite of Street Fighter II.

→   BRIAN DUKE
           Street Fighter Ⅲ director of national sales, Capcom USA

I just remember, once again, being rather disappointed that it was so similar in play [on the surface], and I think that's the time that I went to Japan and [...] they told me it was coming, and I was like, 'My god, guys. Why do you keep doing this?' And that's when they gave me the analogy of hitting a single or double rather than a home run.

→   MATT ATWOOD
           Street Fighter Ⅲ public relations manager, Capcom USA

For me, that was the time it felt like they'd done a bunch of revisions and put in some new characters – I just felt like that was a time when we were looking and going, in my mind, *Is that one we need?* [...] I think you were starting to see fatigue.

→   JAMES CHEN
           Street Fighter series commentator

For me, it was cool that there was a new Street Fighter. They finally hit the number 3, as the joke was. I do remember going to Southern Hills Golfland and playing in tournaments over there for the game.

So it was cool that we finally got a new Street Fighter. And so, there was a little mini resurgence at that point, but the game wasn't particularly balanced, and the parries actually turned out to be kind of too strong. It was a good resurgence for the fans of fighting games, but in terms of pop culture, in terms of appealing to the masses, it was actually not particularly successful.

→ SHINICHIRO OBATA
Street Fighter III planner, Capcom Japan

I personally felt that the game was incomplete. You know, there were three versions of Street Fighter III, and I think the first one in particular felt unfinished.

[Ed. note]   When selling *Street Fighter III*, Capcom knew they were facing an uphill battle, in part because arcade sales were struggling as console sales were erupting. 'It's not going to be as big as Street Fighter II,' Funamizu told *Edge* just prior to the game shipping. 'The games market had real power at that time, it's flat now by comparison.'

→ AKIRA YASUDA
Street Fighter III artist, Capcom Japan

The initial version of Street Fighter III saw shockingly low sales. I remember seeing the numbers and just being really surprised at how the game just wasn't selling. [...] It felt like we'd created the worst-selling game ever at Capcom. It felt awful.

Remember when I had to point out the bad aspects of [Street Fighter creator Takashi] Nishiyama's game *Avengers* back in the day? Well, *Street Fighter III* only sold maybe twice the number of copies as *Avengers*. *Avengers* sold around 500 copies, and I think *Street Fighter III* only sold 1,000. So I felt like I was experiencing the same problem that Nishiyama had faced a decade earlier.

Street Fighter II had sold 55,000. *Street Fighter II: Champion Edition* had sold 75,000. And one unit cost 240,000 yen [roughly $2,000 in 1997]. Back then, just to compare, you had to sell 3,000 arcade units in order to be considered a success. Before Street Fighter and *Final Fight*, 3,000 units of an arcade game sold was considered a success.

When *Final Fight* came out, that sold 30,000 units, and then after that, *Street Fighter II* came out and sold 50,000 units. So the standard had gone up from selling thousands of units to selling tens of thousands of units.

[And *Street Fighter III* sold] 1,000. That's terrible, right? I mean, it was terrible because look at how much we had invested into the game's development.

→   SHINICHIRO OBATA
                     Street Fighter III planner, Capcom Japan

Yeah, the game didn't sell well. I think it cost around 1 billion yen [$8 million] to develop, which back in the day was a very, very high budget. I think in terms of profit and loss, it might have been around zero in the end. It might have been a zero-sum project. Just barely not incurring a loss for the company. When we released *2nd Impact* and *3rd Strike*, I think the overall project became more profitable at that point. I remember the producer at the time saying we were lucky that the game didn't bring us into the red. But yeah, I don't know if it only sold a thousand units. I imagine we sold a bit more than that.

So, you know, it used a CPS-3 board, and each unit cost 200,000 to 300,000 yen [$1,600 to $2,400]. For a single board, that was quite expensive. And so I think the president of Capcom at the time had wanted to sell 50,000 to 60,000 units, because that's what *Street Fighter II* was able to sell. But of course, we weren't able to make those numbers with *III*, unfortunately.

I think worldwide, I'd guess it sold more than 10,000 units.

→   BRIAN DUKE
      Street Fighter III director of national sales, Capcom USA

It definitely was not more than 10,000 [in North America]. I guarantee you. It may not have been 1,000. It may have been 2,000. But I don't think that we moved that many. In fact, if I remember correctly, I think that's one of the few games that we did a closeout on, and it was all because we had [excess] inventory.

→   CHRIS JELINEK
      Street Fighter III vice-president of sales, Capcom USA

Closer to the 1,000, from what I remember, than the 10,000. Not anywhere near 10,000. Nowhere near. I mean, unless they produced that many and dropped them in the ocean somewhere. No, it didn't do 10,000 units. [...] I'm thinking worldwide. [I worked in North America but] I had visibility to it.

[Ed. note]   Former Capcom Coin-Op sales manager Drew Maniscalco estimates that Capcom sold 300 units of *Street Fighter III* in the US. 'Overseas, I'm sure it was much better,' he says. Multiple former sales reps say that Capcom's biggest arcade game of that time in the US was *Marvel vs. Capcom*, which Maniscalco estimates sold 3,000 units.

→   CHRIS JELINEK
      Street Fighter III vice-president of sales, Capcom USA

I wouldn't blame it so much on the game, although you can attribute some of it to the game. I mean, they were subtle iterations. But I think the big thing is that the arcades had just taken such a hit, right? [...] Even the machines in places like 7-Elevens and all of that were getting pulled, right? So there was a complete shift as people expected that same experience at home.

→   BILL GARDNER
           Street Fighter III president and CEO, Capcom USA and Capcom Eurosoft

Would I say it was a disappointment? Only in the sense that all of coin-op was a disappointment [at that point].

> I just remember that [Capcom founder and CEO Kenzo] Tsujimoto was very upset. He would scream and pound the table when we had our monthly meetings because sales weren't where he expected them to be, but he was looking at it from a totally different perspective. He was looking at it from the past.

[In the early days], coin-op was so much bigger than consumer. Just, a number of times bigger. And they were selling a lot of coin-op over here. That was the mainstay of the Capcom business, was coin-op.

> And, you know, they made, and they still do make, a lot of money on coin-op in Japan. So as *Street Fighter III* came out, the home console business was starting to really take off. I mean, really take off. And so when we made our monthly reports in Japan, we'd go over and I'm reporting on a million-unit seller on home console, right? And coin-op was going and saying, 'Well, we sold 450 units this month,' or something like that, you know? And Tsujimoto was just – he was beside himself. He was convinced they weren't working, and he wasn't quite in touch with the revolution that was taking place.

→   SHINICHIRO OBATA
           Street Fighter III planner, Capcom Japan

I feel like *Street Fighter III* was one of those projects where just a bunch of unfavourable results came together into one game. [...] If we had had good leadership and followed a clear vision from the beginning, I feel like it would surely have been a hit.

DELAYED REDEMPTION

Despite *Street Fighter III*'s slow start, Capcom continued to invest in the series with follow-ups *2nd Impact* and *3rd Strike*. The new versions brought back beloved legacy characters Akuma and Chun-Li, and refined many of the series' mechanical and balance issues. While neither of the entries reached the sort of commercial success Capcom had seen in the early 1990s, both went on to earn significant critical acclaim, with *3rd Strike* in particular becoming a cult favourite.

Over time, Street Fighter III's reputation shifted – what was once a series that many felt was behind the times because it couldn't match 3D standards went on to become appreciated as a rare premium run of 2D games.

→ SHINICHIRO OBATA
  Street Fighter III planner, Capcom Japan

After [*Street Fighter III*] came out, Capcom had a postmortem regarding what worked with the game and what didn't, and they realized that the design needed to be put into the hands of an experienced designer. So that's why Ishizawa became the lead designer of the project and took it forward.

The end result of that is *3rd Strike*. *3rd Strike* was made under his careful direction, and [was] where it really came together, I think.

→ JAMES CHEN
  Street Fighter series commentator

You know, even though a lot of people talk about how *3rd Strike* is, like, 'This is the pinnacle of Street Fighter. This game is so great' – when that game came out, nobody cared. Like, it was just the same thing again. Chun-Li was clearly overpowered, and a lot of people were really mad about that. You could just hit back heavy punches all day, and it just killed half the characters in the game, and nobody really cared. So a lot of people have this assumption that *Street Fighter III: 3rd Strike* came out and just resurrected it. Nowadays everyone talks about it as this gold standard. But honestly, during that time, nobody really [batted] an eye on it. It was not that popular of a game in the arcades.

→   SETH KILLIAN
         Street Fighter Ⅳ special combat advisor, Capcom USA

The difference between [*3rd Strike* and *New Generation*] was mostly just time. It's no accident that the best Street Fighter games in a series tend to be the last ones. Developers understand their own systems better over time, and in conversation with their most dedicated players. There's almost no debate among those core players that *3rd Strike* was the best of the SFⅢ series, but there was also no magic ingredient – *3rd Strike* is just a beautifully refined game. Its interest is limited to a small group of experts, but the magic of parries made it feel like glorious victory was always just one good read away, even for the game's many underpowered characters. That's intoxicating.

CHAPTER 16

CAPCOM vs. SNK

The late 1990s weren't kind to arcade fighting games.

When *Street Fighter* director Takashi Nishiyama left Capcom for SNK in the late 1980s, he set in motion a series of events that built the fighting game genre and gave a much-needed jolt to the amusement industry. For a few years, many forgot about the business's gradual downward trajectory, thanks to games like *Street Fighter II* and *Mortal Kombat* (as well as non-fighting game hits like *NBA Jam*).

By the late 1990s, though, the industry's momentum caught up to it. While games like *Tekken 3* and *Marvel vs. Capcom* kept up appearances, the business was changing. Console games were exploding, the fighting game boom was over, and Capcom and SNK's arcade divisions were left trying to scrape the last pieces of candy out of the piñata.

Fortunately for Capcom, they had managed to grow their console game division in the meantime, finding success with the Resident Evil series, among others.

SNK failed to find the same level of success outside of fighting games, trying their hand at a CD version of their Neo Geo home console, new 3D arcade hardware and a Neo Geo Pocket series of portable game machines. Nishiyama, who served as the head of SNK's development group, says this marked a tough time for him personally, in part because he was opposed to the release of the Neo Geo Pocket, which SNK invested heavily in.

Soon after, SNK was acquired and filed for bankruptcy, and Nishiyama left and started his own independent studio. But before departing, he left behind a parting gift – one that neatly tied a bow on his past decade.

MENDING FENCES

Often friendly. Occasionally contentious. Rooted in executive frustration yet resembling a playground flirtation, the rivalry between Capcom and SNK played out in many forms throughout the 1980s and 1990s. Privately, some spoke of a feud between Capcom founder Kenzo Tsujimoto and SNK founder Eikichi Kawasaki, while publicly, fans saw the companies trying to top one another while constantly referencing each other in their games.

> 'Capcom and SNK spent the 1990s in a kind of call-and-response dance,' says veteran fighting game developer Seth Killian. 'Capcom had Ryu, so SNK made Ryo,' he says. 'Street Fighter added a parry; SNK introduced the Just Defend. You got T. Hawk? We got a Tizoc.'

Nishiyama sat in the middle of this, having developed the original *Street Fighter* at Capcom before joining SNK and overseeing the Fatal Fury and King of Fighters series. While he says he didn't directly participate in the back-and-forth, he couldn't help but notice it. And in the late 1990s, he hatched an idea to bring his franchises together: What if the two companies put all this history to good use?

→ NORITAKA FUNAMIZU
General producer, Capcom Japan

The way the idea came up to begin with was because Nishiyama – I think he and [Capcom executive producer Yoshiki] Okamoto had lunch or dinner together one day, and then out of the blue, Nishiyama suddenly said, 'Yeah. Why don't we make a "versus SNK" game?'

→   TAKASHI NISHIYAMA
    Head of development group, SNK Japan

The way this came about was, Okamoto had become the top of Capcom's development division and I had been the top of SNK's development division, and we ended up meeting one day. We talked about putting the past behind us, and the idea came up of combining our forces and using each of our companies' characters in a collaborative project. And Okamoto thought that the idea was very interesting. So I told Okamoto to convince Tsujimoto to make that happen. I would convince Kawasaki to make it happen. I think this discussion happened right before I ended up quitting SNK.

Actually, it wasn't that difficult to convince Kawasaki. [...] I think you could say they'd put the past behind them. Kawasaki was a businessman, so I think he realized there was a lot of potential to benefit from this kind of collaboration.

→   MATT ATWOOD
    Capcom vs. SNK public relations manager, Capcom USA

I remember thinking, like, *Really? SNK?* I always thought it was crazy that these two rivals were actually working together.

→   TOYOHISA TANABE
    Capcom vs. SNK pixel art supervisor, SNK Japan

I was extremely surprised but also extremely happy.

→   NORITAKA FUNAMIZU
    General producer, Capcom Japan

Before we started talking with SNK about a project, Tanabe, [planner Hideaki] Itsuno and I had started hanging out together. And it was a few months later that the whole SNK vs. Capcom thing came up. So yeah, I think we were getting along pretty well by then.

→   TOYOHISA TANABE
            Capcom vs. SNK pixel art supervisor, SNK Japan

At the time, it's not as if SNK and Capcom never talked to each other or anything, but I had the impression that there was some bad blood between the two. When I heard Capcom and SNK would be collaborating, it felt like, *Ah! Spring is here!* Like there was a thawing of relations between the two companies. For me personally, it previously felt kind of difficult to approach people at Capcom, but thanks to that collaboration, I got to know the people there. Our relationships improved, and we would go out drinking together and stuff. We used to do these Capcom vs. SNK drinking parties together.

> Aside from drinking, you know the card game Yu-Gi-Oh!, right? That was actually quite popular back in the day, and there were a lot of people at SNK who loved playing it. They would play during their lunch breaks, for example. It turned out there were Yu-Gi-Oh! fans at Capcom as well, so we ended up throwing Capcom vs. SNK Yu-Gi-Oh! tournaments.

→   MATT ATWOOD
            Capcom vs. SNK public relations manager, Capcom USA

I think it was a good opportunity for [SNK because] they were starting to quiet down some, where Capcom had been able to hold its own and do series behind Street Fighter. And really, SNK was really starting to slide. [...] You had the arcade folks who were like, 'Yeah, of course we remember SNK games. We love them.' But broader appeal? They didn't know these characters.

→   TOYOHISA TANABE
            Capcom vs. SNK pixel art supervisor, SNK Japan

I wasn't directly involved in the negotiations or the process that led to them collaborating, so I don't know anything about it for sure [...] but I think it might have been the release of the Neo Geo

Pocket that led to the two companies initially collaborating. When SNK decided that they were going to release the handheld system, they approached various companies to see if anyone would develop games for it, and I think the company spoke with Capcom at the time. I think it was those conversations which sparked the idea to create a game with licensed characters from both Capcom and SNK. So on the SNK side, there was *SNK vs. Capcom* on the Neo Geo Pocket, which was a card game. And on the Capcom side, there was *Capcom vs. SNK*, which was the fighting game. I'm not sure but I think that's how it all got started.

→   TAKASHI NISHIYAMA
               Head of development group, SNK Japan

I don't think everything was necessarily decided in that initial agreement. It proceeded more gradually, step by step. It was like building up a new business, and we had to figure out precisely who would do what.

CAPCOM VS. SNK

With an initial agreement in place, both companies planned out their crossover games.

SNK kicked things off in 1999 with two titles for their Neo Geo Pocket Color: card game *SNK vs. Capcom: Card Fighters Clash* and fighting game *SNK vs. Capcom: Match of the Millennium*. Both earned critical acclaim and fleshed out the portable console's library to help it compete with that of Nintendo's Game Boy, though many players wondered why SNK didn't produce an arcade fighting game instead. In 2001, SNK followed with a Card Fighters Clash sequel, which ended up being the final Neo Geo Pocket Color game, as SNK gave up their portable console ambitions.

Capcom, meanwhile, went straight to their bread and butter in 2000 with *Capcom vs. SNK* – a 2D arcade fighting game running on the same hardware as *Marvel vs. Capcom 2*. The concept proved popular around Capcom's offices, with some staff like planner Itsuno begging to work on it. To accommodate multiple styles of play, Capcom developed a ratio system – where players could build a team of fighters of different strengths – and a groove system, where players could choose between Street Fighter or King of Fighters mechanics.

It was the game fans expected from the Capcom/SNK collaboration, with a few caveats.

→ 	NORITAKA FUNAMIZU
	General producer, Capcom Japan

I had heard of King of Fighters, and just from the title, I had my own impression of what kind of game it would be. It sounded really cool. The Neo Geo had all these different fighting games, you know, so wouldn't it be great if you mixed all their strengths together in one single game? That's what I imagined King of Fighters to be. But when I actually played it, it turned out to be totally different. So when we were making *Capcom vs. SNK*, I wanted to make it more like the King of Fighters I had imagined in my head.

→ SEIJI OKADA
Capcom vs. SNK series programmer, Capcom Japan

I actually had never played an SNK game before, so I had no knowledge about anything, or even the names of the characters in the game, so I had to do a lot of research for that. At first impression, the way the games played felt totally different from Capcom's fighting games, which was refreshing.

→ JAMES CHEN
Capcom vs. SNK series FAQ writer

[*Capcom vs. SNK*] definitely felt like it was more Street Fighter [than King of Fighters], because even though there was the SNK groove, it wasn't very good. [...] For the most part, it felt like the SNK characters were put into a Street Fighter game.

→ STEPHEN FROST
Street Fighter 30th Anniversary Collection producer, Digital Eclipse

I think [the SNK characters] played better [than they had in previous games], if you can say that, right? I think that they handled a bit better. They felt a little bit more responsive in comparison to [how they had] in the past. So I thought they blended in well, and I thought [the developers] found a nice middle ground between matching Street Fighter and the SNK stuff.

→ TOYOHISA TANABE
Capcom vs. SNK pixel art supervisor, SNK Japan

I thought Capcom's staff liked SNK's characters and handled them with great care. I felt they poured a lot of love into the pixel work they did for them. According to what I heard, when they were making *Capcom vs. SNK*, the Capcom designers were all vying for the opportunity to design certain characters. 'Let me design Iori Yagami!' 'Give me Mai Shiranui!' So no, I wouldn't say that it was hard to blend together or anything. I think SNK felt comfortable putting these characters in the hands of the Capcom designers.

→   JAMES CHEN
      Capcom vs. SNK series FAQ writer

Man, the SNK characters [looked] awesome. It was refreshing to see the characters look so cool. It was also just really awesome that it was actually made. That this finally [happened], this dream match, [after all the Dan jokes] and the Yuri clapbacks from SNK. And it was really just cool to see these two companies that had this rivalry finally coming together and making a game like this.

→   TOYOHISA TANABE
      Capcom vs. SNK pixel art supervisor, SNK Japan

I had worked on the King of Fighters games at SNK, and those were kind of the big party titles where a bunch of different characters came together, but *Capcom vs. SNK* took that festive party atmosphere to the next level by transcending the company's boundaries. In many ways it was like a dream game for me. It was so nice seeing the characters that we had designed get reinterpreted by the people at Capcom. And as a game, too, I really loved it. At the time, it felt like the only way we could ever top this would be if we made a truly Olympic-scale fighting game ... something crazy like Sega versus Namco versus SNK versus Capcom.

[Ed. note]   Prior to Capcom and SNK collaborating, Tanabe says he and other team members at SNK liked the idea of a crossover game so much that they developed one themselves – as a limited internal hobbyist project.

> I have a secret to tell you, and I don't know if this is something I really should be saying, but: [...] Two years before *Capcom vs. SNK* came out, we made *King of Fighters '98,* and we actually had a little bit of time after we finished development. So the team ended up making a build of the game with Ryu and Ken in it. This isn't something that a lot of people know – I think only the developers know about it, and I've never told anyone myself – but yeah, just for fun, before *Capcom vs. SNK* was a thing, I was playing as Ryu and Ken in *King of Fighters '98.*

I doubt [a version of it still exists anywhere]. We did this on the development hardware, so of course it was never on a physical cartridge. Also, I'm just remembering this now, but it wasn't only Ryu and Ken that we ended up playing around with. We put in Dragon Ball characters, like Son Goku, as well.

[Ed. note]   While *Capcom vs. SNK* made headlines for its concept and Capcom released an upgraded version, *Capcom vs. SNK Pro,* many say the series wasn't fully realized until Capcom released *Capcom vs. SNK 2* a year later. Featuring an expanded roster and more variety and polish, *Capcom vs. SNK 2* marked the series' turning point from a novelty to a tournament staple.

→   JAMES CHEN
      Capcom vs. SNK series FAQ writer

When [*Capcom vs. SNK 2*] came out, that to me felt like this was the next great Street Fighter game, because they added all the grooves. *CvS1,* if people don't remember, [put player attacks on] four buttons.

And that didn't feel very Street Fighter-y, and I know a lot of people didn't like that.

And so when *CvS2* came out and it went back to six buttons – I mean, I wrote [FAQs] for both of those games, and you can kind of see it in my FAQ for *CvS2*. I just keep talking about the fact that it's six buttons again, and how wonderful it is. I was so happy that it was six buttons, and the graphics were so good. The gameplay was really solid in it. It really felt, to me, like, *This is where Street Fighter needs to go.*

In the FAQ, I'm like, 'You've got to play this game. Please play this game because it's so good. Let's make this game popular', you know? I'm practically begging readers to play the game because I was so enamoured with it at the time and I just thought it was going to be the next big thing.

→ SETH KILLIAN
   Street Fighter IV special combat advisor, Capcom USA

Compared to previous games, *CvS1* did offer a big cast and a lot of system choices, but most of the options presented were just bad choices. As players realized this, the result was long matches between low-powered characters, filled with as many as *seven* breaks between rounds. *CvS1* was not a bad game, but its slow, low-stakes style created a black hole where hype went to die.

CvS2 felt like a game that said 'yes' to pretty much every dumb idea that designers suggested, and yet somehow [made] it all work. It was simultaneously traditional and wild – a return to classic 2D Street Fighter-style combat, but with a huge roster, the widest and wildest system mechanics in Capcom history, plus the chance to mix them all to taste.

A return to the Capcom-style six-button controls added an essential dose of extra moves. The match flow got tightened up, limiting players to three characters per team, but the system mechanics went bananas, offering players a choice of six entirely different flavours (C, A and P grooves, as well as S, N and K options) for each of their favourite characters. Grooves didn't just swap super moves; they changed everything from defensive options on down to core movement mechanics. Combine that amount of choice with 48 characters, and you've got a huge space for players to experiment and explore.

[Ed. note]   Between *CvS1*, *CvS Pro*, and *CvS2*, Capcom released three crossover games in the span of a year. Former sales manager Drew Maniscalco estimates that Capcom sold 400 arcade kits of *Capcom vs. SNK* in the US – just above *Street Fighter III*, as he recalls. *Capcom vs. SNK 2* went on to become a hardcore favourite, appearing in tournaments well over a decade after its release. At the time, it sold well enough to justify a sequel.

→   HIDEAKI ITSUNO
     Capcom vs. SNK 2 director, Capcom Japan

Shortly after we finished *Capcom vs. SNK 2*, we started working on a 3D version of 'Capcom vs. SNK 3' for the PS2. 'CvS3' was meant to be the last [2D fighting game], but then it ended up becoming a 3D game along the way, and then SNK folded and that project got cancelled too.

[Ed. note]   In 2003, following an acquisition and bankruptcy filing, a new incarnation of SNK – under the name Playmore – went on to release their take on the crossover arcade fighting game concept: *SVC Chaos*. The game redrew many of Capcom's characters in the King of Fighters style and featured a deep roster, but reviewed poorly and arrived too late to capitalize on the crossover buzz.

In 2007, the company – by then, SNK Playmore – followed with *SNK vs. Capcom: Card Fighters DS*, which also disappointed critics. Nishiyama left SNK well before either of those games were released, but when asked about the overall success of the crossover series, he sums it up as a modest success.

→ TAKASHI NISHIYAMA
Head of development group, SNK Japan

I don't think we failed in any regard, but I do think that maybe the series wasn't quite as successful as I imagined it could be. I realized that SNK fans and Capcom fans don't have a high level of crossover. Capcom fans have their own preferences; SNK fans have their own preferences. And it didn't quite pan out the way I imagined it would. I don't think it was a failure, though.

CAPCOM FIGHTING ALL-STARS

As SNK went through changes in the early 2000s, their employees spread throughout the industry. Some started new teams, like Nishiyama, who formed development studio Dimps. A group even joined Capcom, bringing things full-circle from when Nishiyama and the *Street Fighter* team had gone to SNK a decade earlier.

→   TOYOHISA TANABE
      Capcom Fighting All-Stars director, Capcom Japan

Basically what happened was, around the year 2000, SNK encountered financial losses, and there was a time when it became a subsidiary of [a pachinko company named] Aruze. So we ended up going to Aruze, but after about a year, Aruze decided that they were going to abandon videogame development. So, unable to see any future with Aruze, I ended up transferring to Capcom thanks to the help of a number of people around me. Someone I knew put me in contact with Yoshiki Okamoto, the head of development at Capcom, and thanks to both of their efforts, Capcom took me in.

It was a team of about 20 people that ended up going to Capcom at the same time. There were more people than that on the team at SNK, but unfortunately, Capcom couldn't bring everybody over, so the number had to be whittled down. So the 20 of us joined Capcom as a single team. I can't deny that there was some of that feeling [of it being a bit strange]. When the 20 of us joined Capcom, I think there were people who thought well of it, but there may also have been people who looked askance and thought, *Who the heck are these guys?* For our part, as a team, we hadn't yet proven ourselves or accomplished anything, so there was a sense of anxiety about how well we'd fit in and what we'd be able to achieve there. Itsuno was really good to us then. I don't get the chance to talk with him much nowadays, but he treated us very well, and the presence of people like him at Capcom was a huge help for us.

[Ed. note] The team's first and only project under their new roof was 'Capcom Fighting All-Stars', a 3D fighting game that brought together characters from Street Fighter and other Capcom franchises including Strider and 3D fighting series Rival Schools. Capcom ended up cancelling the project before Tanabe's team finished it.

There was a lot going on there. [...] When we joined Capcom, there were two plans put forward for the kind of game we could develop. We had a lot of people on our team with experience developing fighting games, so our first idea was to make our own fighting game. However, creating a fighting game from scratch, with a new gameplay system, would have been very time-consuming, and as a new team at Capcom, we felt we had to contribute something to the company as quickly as possible.

So instead, we went with our second idea, which was to use Capcom's pre-existing assets as the foundation for a new project. And that game, well, I can't really talk about too much, but ... that's how 'Capcom Fighting All-Stars" development began. Unfortunately, we just weren't able to work it up into something interesting. Partly due to my own inexperience, in the end, even though our staff did their best, the game never made it to release.

→ JAMES CHEN
  Street Fighter series commentator

I mean, everybody saw the footage of 'Capcom Fighting All-Stars', and it was kind of – even though it was their first official attempt to go 3D [as an internally developed game using Street Fighter characters] – a lot of people looked at it and [were disappointed].

I think that kind of contributed to the whole feeling that Capcom wasn't really going to make a lot of quality fighting games at that point in time, and people were just kind of resigned to say, 'Yeah, OK, whatever.' Capcom wasn't the best anymore at making fighting games. They just weren't, and that expectation wasn't there.

I remember when 'Capcom Fighting All-Stars' first started showing up with footage from game magazines and Japanese game sites. People just looked at it and were like, 'This looks kind of bad', you know? And so when it was cancelled, I still kind of remember people just being like, 'Yeah, it's probably for the better.'

→   TOYOHISA TANABE
        Capcom Fighting All-Stars director, Capcom Japan

Right after 'Capcom Fighting All-Stars' was cancelled, Capcom, as a whole, underwent an organizational change, and I ended up leaving Capcom and joining its subsidiary Flagship. I worked at Flagship for several years. I wasn't involved with fighting games. I was involved with other titles that were in development in the studio at the time.

CHAPTER 17

MOVING ON

By the time they cancelled 'Capcom Fighting All-Stars' in 2003, Capcom had been slowing their fighting game output for years, dropping their custom CPS-3 hardware, cancelling games such as a fourth entry in the Street Fighter III series, and pulling resources away from their arcade division. They continued to port existing titles to consoles, and snuck out a couple of new games with *Hyper Street Fighter II* and *Capcom Fighting Jam* – both built to capitalize on existing games and assets – but the genre was on borrowed time.

Throughout the 1990s, Capcom had pushed their arcade fighting game concepts into nearly every conceivable format. They had defined the genre. Spun off upgrades. Gone back in time. Created new worlds. Negotiated key licences. Hired external studios. Tried new art styles. Shifted hardware. Combined franchises. Twisted their brands into other genres. Joined forces with their enemies. And built some of the best videogames of the decade.

At a certain point, it was time to say goodbye.

Chapter 17 → Moving on

END OF AN ERA

No one we spoke to for this book remembers a specific meeting, memo or formal decision where Capcom put a policy in place. It happened more gradually, many say. But by the early 2000s, everyone knew Capcom was moving away from fighting games.

→   AKIRA YASUDA
           Street Fighter series illustrator, Capcom Japan

I think around the year 2000, [Capcom Japan general producer Noritaka] Funamizu told people who were working on fighting games to basically stop working on fighting games: 'Let's make something original, and it doesn't matter if it sells or not. We should do it anyway.' This is obviously talk from a long time ago, but you know *Resident Evil*, right? Tokuro Fujiwara, who had made *Resident Evil*, had at the same time also made a bunch of other relatively uninteresting games. But I think the reason why those games were made was because Fujiwara wanted to challenge his staff. I think Funamizu wanted to do something similar. Now that the old way of doing things was no longer working, I think he wanted to find a new style, a new way forward, by challenging his staff. And it did provide some hints to the company's direction, in a number of different ways.

I think there were also people in the lower levels of the staff saying that 'Street Fighter is no longer selling, so we want to make something else that's not a fighting game.' The Street Fighter Alpha series had been going on for a while and everyone was bored of that – and it didn't sell very well either – so I think this felt like the moment to try something new, and go after a new challenge. Funamizu was also a big fan of [Nintendo simulation game] *Animal Crossing,* so I think he wanted to make something similar to *Animal Crossing,* which some way or another ended up becoming *Monster Hunter.*

→   NORITAKA FUNAMIZU
      General producer, Capcom Japan

I don't know if I want to talk about it ... By [the late 1990s], I was in charge of the arcade game division, but we knew there really wasn't a future in it going forward. And basically, it was just a question of: How viable could this business remain in the foreseeable future? If you compared Capcom to Sega, Namco and Taito, we were smaller than them, and they had other related businesses. They were major arcade game makers, but we were pretty much just a videogame company at that point. So it felt like there was no future there.

But then we heard about the Sega Dreamcast and the NAOMI board, and we got along with the folks at Sega surprisingly well. And we at Capcom, too, wanted to focus on consumer games. With the Dreamcast and NAOMI, you could develop the arcade game and the console port concurrently – you could complete a console port in just one month, amazingly. So almost all of our projects became joint arcade/console projects, and gradually our development focus shifted to console-friendly games.

→   HIDEAKI ITSUNO
      Capcom vs. SNK 2 director, Capcom Japan

In terms of the environment at the time, the arcade business was starting to shrink. In terms of technology, the arcade version of a game had always been the higher form, the more technologically advanced version. But around this time, the roles started to get reversed, and the technology on home console games started to surpass that of arcade games. So there was less of a need to focus on arcade games. We also had the emergence of platforms like the Dreamcast, where we needed to simultaneously release the game on both home console and arcade. So, the combination led to the dwindling of the dominance of arcade games.

And on top that, you had Resident Evil selling incredibly well; it was a huge success, and so it was a combination of, here's a non-fighting game that's incredibly successful, and then you have the arcade environment shrinking – there's not as much demand for it – so all of that combined kind of created this shift. There wasn't as much of a demand or much of a business benefit just focusing on fighting games. There was more of a shift that was like, *We should spread ourselves out and test the waters elsewhere.*

→ TOYOHISA TANABE
Capcom Fighting All-Stars director, Capcom Japan

I think fighting games had slowly evolved into something for advanced players and pros. It felt like the future of fighting games had become very uncertain. And Capcom kept putting out games like Monster Hunter and Resident Evil, games that didn't depend on Capcom's fighting game franchises. So yeah, we got the sense that the times were changing. Something similar had happened before with shooting games, which became more and more difficult to the point that only advanced players could enjoy them. It felt like we were at a turning point with fighting games, too.

→ SHINICHIRO OBATA
Street Fighter Ⅲ planner, Capcom Japan

I think the reason why fighting games stopped coming out around that time is because they pretty much stopped selling and even the arcade market itself had declined to an extent. I think also it had something to do with the fact that [former Mega Man producer Keiji] Inafune became the most prestigious producer in the company, and it was under his direction that the company focused more on console games like Resident Evil and Mega Man. Of the arcade games Capcom developed, only the [mech combat] Gundam games were hits, and that's why they kept making those. All the arcade developers were told to join the profitable console lines – games like Monster Hunter, Resident Evil and Mega Man. Monster Hunter continues to be a big hit even today, but that game was created by people from the arcade game division.

→ MATT ATWOOD
   Capcom vs. SNK 2 public relations manager, Capcom USA

To some degree, you can't tell the arcade story without talking about what else was going on at Capcom, and there was a lot of experimentation. [Cel-shaded racing game] *Auto Modellista* was completely out of the blue. [...] You had stuff like [mech simulator] *Steel Battalion* and [historial action game] *Onimusha* and [dinosaur horror game] *Dino Crisis*, and they were getting into bass [fishing] games. *Devil May Cry* was one that may have signified – so, it's interesting, because *Devil May Cry* and its success may have sort of cemented the idea that the direction should be on other things. I think that was the first time they saw something beyond Res. Evil that was like, *Oh my god, this is really different and we have the ability to create [things that are] so stylish and so different*. I think all of the internal studios took notice, and I think that the resources were shifted there.

→ JAMES CHEN
   Street Fighter series commentator

At that point in time, it was just one of those things that, as a fan of the games, you just kind of accepted that it was dead. I remember when *Capcom Fighting Jam* first showed up at E3, a lot of people were surprised. They're like, 'Wow, they're making a new game?' And then everyone looked at me. I was like, 'Why does this game look so darn ugly?'

And that was such a prevailing feeling. *Capcom Fighting Jam* came out and was at E3, and everybody was like, 'Oh'. Even then, nobody seemed like they were really hype about it. It just didn't feel like there was any hype for it. I just don't recall anyone seeing *Capcom Fighting Jam* and being like, 'Oh my god, I can't wait to go to the arcade and try this out', and all that stuff. Literally, I just think everybody was like, 'Whatever.' At this point, we had all kind of just given up on hoping for more quality Capcom fighting games, really.

→   TOYOHISA TANABE
        Capcom Fighting All-Stars director, Capcom Japan

I don't know if I would use the word 'disappointed' to describe that generational change. But in terms of the feelings that I experienced at the time, with fighting games slowly winding down, I wondered, would the game industry itself begin to change over time? And how would we, as fighting game developers, weather this change? There was a sense of danger, but also of excitement. I also acknowledged that you can't expect a genre to continue on in the same way forever, right? But as someone who had experienced the energy and excitement of the fighting game boom firsthand, which players of all skill levels took part in, I did think it was a bit sad that it was finally winding down.

→   HIDEAKI ITSUNO
        Capcom vs. SNK 2 director, Capcom Japan

I wasn't sad at all. I felt like I did everything that I wanted to do in the 2D space. And then you had the emergence of new games like *Monster Hunter, Auto Modellista, Devil May Cry 2*, the [JoJo's Bizarre Adventure fighting games, and online horror game] *Resident Evil Outbreak*. I was personally working on an RPG that eventually became *Dragon's Dogma*. I was excited to be working on an action RPG. [... I also was] able to take all of the knowledge that I had built up in the fighting game space and throw it into *Devil May Cry 3*. I realized that all the knowledge I had built up could be expanded into the action game genre as well.

THREE FIGURES LEAVING

Around the time Capcom shifted away from fighting games, three of their highest-profile employees – Yoshiki Okamoto, Funamizu and Yasuda – left the company. None of them say that Capcom's pivot had anything to do with them leaving, but as the three remaining figureheads from the 1990s Street Fighter arcade era, their departures signified a changing of the guard.

Okamoto and Funamizu went on to start independent development studios – Game Republic and Crafts & Meister, respectively – similar to Akira Nishitani leaving Capcom and forming Arika, and Takashi Nishiyama leaving SNK and forming Dimps. Yasuda, meanwhile, pursued a freelance illustration career.

→   KATSUYA AKITOMO
       Marvel games artist and advisor, Capcom Japan

When Okamoto left, I realized how profound his influence had been on creating a relaxed working environment at Capcom. Without him there, I was worried the workplace he had created was about to become a lot less fun. I stayed at Capcom for another year or two after his departure, but as I feared, I started to feel like the workflow was getting worse. In the meantime, things were on track with Okamoto and his new company, and he said it was looking like he could pay my salary, and he invited me to join him at Game Republic.

→   NORITAKA FUNAMIZU
       General producer, Capcom Japan

There were a lot of reasons why I left. I guess the first would be the change in what [Capcom] sought from its creators. Back in the day, it really felt like we were 'creators', always trying to come up with something new. Nishitani was always talking and theorizing about gameplay, and so many people at Capcom then had that strong desire to create something new and interesting. Unfortunately, by the time I quit, Capcom had become a company full of uncreative people. For that reason, I guess it felt like Capcom was becoming a place I no longer found exciting. And I think another big reason for me was that Okamoto had left the company.

> I knew there was no one left at Capcom with good judgement, but yeah, back then, the game I was working on, *Monster Hunter*, nobody thought it would sell and there were very low expectations for it. The only one who thought it would be successful was me.

My relationship with Kenzo Tsujimoto soured a bit too. Every time we would meet, he would complain about *Monster Hunter* and ask what we were going to do about it. It got to the point where I was like, 'Are you asking me to quit?' Okamoto, who had already quit by then, was also asking me to join his company. Though I never said I would.

> You see, Okamoto himself was complaining about *Monster Hunter* a lot too. I didn't want to go somewhere, whether it was Okamoto's company or Capcom, where no one would allow me to make what I wanted. So, basically it just became really hard and unbearable for me to be in an environment like that where people were constantly complaining. Whether I stayed at Capcom, whether I ended up having to go to Okamoto's company, none of those options seemed very appealing. The negativity of it all was very exhausting to me, and I simply lost my will to go on.

My idea was to make *Monster Hunter* the best game ever, and then quit after that. Although, looking back now, maybe I should have just given up and quit in the middle of it. I'm kidding, of course.

HOW TIMES HAVE CHANGED

By the mid-2000s, fighting games were in Capcom's rearview. Priorities had shifted. Key figures like Okamoto and Funamizu had left. Capcom Japan had even sold the Street Fighter IP to Capcom USA.

> It marked a clean break, at least until 2008, when Capcom rebooted the series with *Street Fighter IV* – developed by Nishiyama's team at Dimps. Thanks to a break in the schedule and a focus on what made the series popular in the first place, *Street Fighter IV* and *V* went on to revitalize the brand for a new generation of players, showing that Street Fighter could be a significant ongoing presence in the game industry, rather than a series that flared up and died out in the 1990s.

→   `HIDEAKI ITSUNO`
                 `Devil May Cry 5 director, Capcom Japan`

I think Capcom has changed a lot [since I started there]. People at Capcom today see me as the kind of director who truly loves games, someone with a 'craftsman' mentality – but when I joined Capcom, all the people there were way, way crazier than me. Compared to them, I was one of the 'regular' guys, in fact. In that sense, I think there are more 'normal' people at Capcom today. There were just way more crazy people then. People who basically lived at the office 24/7. I remember being shocked at seeing their desks, with these piles of CDs stacked up everywhere, and scratched to all hell. As long as they created good games, all that sloppiness was tolerated. But I think there are fewer of those kinds of people at Capcom today. The times have changed, you know? [...]

> I do like that I can actually go home now most days. And there's less working on vacations, holidays, and weekends

now, which of course is good. But I didn't exactly hate the way things used to be, either. How can I put it ... back then, there was a certain hunger, a drive – we felt like if we didn't work as hard as salarymen, this whole thing would go belly up. But today it's easier to rest on your laurels and not work that hard, and be relaxed, which has its downsides as well.

→ MOTOHIDE ESHIRO
Street Fighter II programmer, Capcom Japan

Certainly, there are far more people in the company now. And the environment we were operating in, the way the market was set up, was much different back then. Arcades were still super strong; the Super NES hadn't even come out yet in those early days, so it was just such a different landscape.

→ SCOTT MAXWELL
Street Fighter 2010: The Final Fight translator, Capcom Japan

The company grew tremendously while I was there. When I got there in 1988, there were 200 people, I think, in Osaka, which was the main office. And when I left six and a half years later, I believe we had 1,200 people.

→ BRIAN DUKE
Street Fighter series director of national sales, Capcom USA

It kind of grew from being a nice little family-feeling operation to being a major corporation within a short period of time. [...] It was incredible. I'll tell you – that was probably the best time in my videogame career. [...] When things are selling well, life is good. And a lot of times you think that's gonna happen for the rest of your life, and then you work at other companies and you find out that doesn't happen.

→   Yoko Shimomura
                    Street Fighter II composer, Capcom Japan

Street Fighter II changed my life and was my big breakthrough at work. [...] It's a big part of me.

→   KEN WILLIAMS
                    Assistant editor, Electronic Gaming Monthly magazine

Street Fighter has always had a nice little place in my heart. I mean, I haven't even played *Street Fighter V* yet. I just haven't had time. Life kind of catches up with you, especially as you get older and you've got families and you have a different job now. I just don't have time. It's the type of thing that if I start playing it, I'm gonna want to keep playing it all the time. [*laughs*] I've got responsibilities now and that kinda sucks. But it was a very fun way to spend my youth.

→   NORITAKA FUNAMIZU
                    General producer, Capcom Japan

I would say Street Fighter helped develop me as a creator because I spent most of the first half of my twenties on that franchise. Yeah, it's a cliché, but Street Fighter was my life. Looking back, it was a series I worked very hard on, and I invested a lot of my personal feelings into it. I like to think that comes across to players – and if we hadn't worked as hard as we did, I don't think the games would have been so interesting.

→   MONTE SINGMAN
                    Final Fight Revenge senior producer, Capcom Digital Studios

Nothing I do now can ever be as cool as [working at Capcom]. I don't know if that's why John Glenn failed after he came back to Earth, after the few seconds that he was in outer space. My wife asked me, 'Why would people interview you about your Capcom days? They were so long ago.' I said, 'Hey, to some people, this was a moon landing.'

BIO-GRAPHIES

FEATURED SPEAKERS

Like a Hurricane

KATSUYA AKITOMO

Starting at Capcom Japan in the early 1990s as a pixel artist, Akitomo quickly made his mark by talking up Marvel comics and translating them for co-workers, earning a reputation as a Marvel evangelist around the office. That made him a natural fit to work on Capcom's X-Men: Children of the Atom and Marvel Super Heroes fighting games, on which he helped brainstorm character choices and served as a liaison with Marvel.

Before work on those games got underway, he also put together a pitch document for the game that became Darkstalkers, and many credit him with the initial idea for that franchise.

Akitomo ended up staying at Capcom for over a decade, doing various art, translation and interpretation jobs, such as serving as a ghostwriter for Yoshiki Okamoto's Gamest column and helping localize games like Diablo II, which Capcom released in Japan. He eventually followed Okamoto to work at Game Republic, then went on to professionally translate American comics into Japanese and write books on how to assemble model figures.

BRIAN DUKE

Working in arcade sales at Capcom USA, Duke joined Capcom from Nintendo and Universal, where he had worked with the Mr. Do! series. He arrived at Capcom shortly before Street Fighter II launched, and describes selling the game and Champion Edition as the most profitable time in his career.

After a few years of riding that wave, Duke left Capcom for a short period, then he returned a couple of years later and continued to sell Street Fighter games, though in smaller quantities at that point.

He left Capcom for a second time in the late 1990s, going on to a variety of roles in the amusement business, working on virtual roller coasters and cotton candy machines, among other products.

ALDO DONNALOIA

One of Capcom USA's first coin-op sales reps, Donnaloia joined Capcom as part of a skeleton crew working in the office when the original Street Fighter came around. He helped coordinate plans with Atari Games to design the game's unique arcade cabinet, and peddled that cabinet with coin-op sales head Bill Cravens, then left Capcom before Street Fighter II came out.

He says leaving Capcom was 'the biggest mistake of my life', because Capcom went public shortly after he left. 'It made millionaires of a lot of people and I could have been one,' he says. Instead, he joined Double Dragon publisher Technos.

In the mid-1990s, he also helped Incredible Technologies get golfer Peter Jacobsen's name on the Golden Tee golf series.

As a young programmer working at Capcom Japan on Street Fighter II, Eshiro handled, among other things, the character Guile - and felt terrible when players discovered a number of glitches associated with the character. That speed-bump aside, he was able to establish himself as a reliable figure at the company.

Following his work on Street Fighter II, Eshiro went on to have a long career at Capcom, staying there more than three decades and moving up the ranks to become a producer on games in the Onimusha, Okami, Devil May Cry and Phoenix Wright series. He also directed Onimusha 2 and Capcom's 2005 action game Shadow of Rome.

HARUMI FUJITA

One of SNK's earliest composers, Fujita found herself in a corporate tug-of-war when she moved to Capcom in the mid-1980s, caught between two companies and a growing rivalry. But she quickly settled in at Capcom, contributing to platformers like Ghosts 'n Goblins and Bionic Commando and taking part in the company's in-house band Alph Lyla.

A bit of work on side-scrolling brawler Final Fight marked her closest connection to the Street Fighter series while at Capcom, as she left in 1990 - the year before Street Fighter II shipped to arcades.

In the years that followed, Fujita worked on a little of everything, composing music for Neo Geo shooter Pulstar, PlayStation platformer Tomba! (developed by former Capcom console division head Tokuro Fujiwara), and - years later - brawler revival Streets of Rage 4. She also composed a song for this book, offered on vinyl as part of our Kickstarter funding campaign.

NORITAKA FUNAMIZU

Starting at Capcom Japan in the mid-1980s, Funamizu initially helped design arcade shooters, but quickly established himself as Yoshiki Okamoto's right-hand man, producing and overseeing games developed by Okamoto's team. As a result, he played a small role in the development of Street Fighter II, but took over the series in a leadership position starting with Street Fighter II Turbo: Hyper Fighting and stuck with it for about five years, often serving as Capcom's public face of the series.

Meanwhile, he became a general producer at Capcom, earning him credits on more than a dozen franchises ranging from Resident Evil to The Legend of Zelda. For his final project at Capcom, he led development of Monster Hunter.

In 2004, he left Capcom and formed independent studio Crafts & Meister, where he worked for many years on franchises such as Dragon Ball and Gundam, before heading up mobile developer Indigo Game Studios.

JAMES GODDARD

Joining Capcom USA shortly after
Street Fighter II's release, Goddard
helped test and gather feedback on
a variety of games, with his work
on Street Fighter defining his time
there. Serving as the voice of
Western players, he regularly played
fighting games in local arcades and
passed along notes to the development
group in Japan, which at times led
to breakthroughs and at times led to
frustration.

Goddard played a key role in the
design of Street Fighter II Turbo:
Hyper Fighting and contributed to
Super Street Fighter II before leaving
Capcom to join publisher Namco, where
he went on to design hardcore 2D
fighting game WeaponLord.

In the years that followed, he
moved between game industry jobs
at companies including Atari, The
Collective and Microsoft, often
working on combat systems rooted in
Street Fighter-style mechanics.

ELAINE HODGSON

→

After working as an industrial chemist
at the Kennedy Space Center, Hodgson
co-founded game studio Incredible
Technologies in 1985 and proceeded to
run the company for more than three
decades as president and CEO, finding
success along the way with trackball
franchise Golden Tee Golf.

Selling more than 100,000 units across
more than a dozen versions, Golden
Tee became one of the most successful
arcade game franchises of all time,
allowing the company to experiment and
survive in the late 1990s and 2000s
while much of the amusement industry
struggled, and establishing Incredible
Technologies as a brand.

Yet for a period in the early-to-mid-
1990s, the company set up an alternate
label, Strata, which released a mix
of bowling, golf and fighting games
- including two of the most violent
games on the market, Time Killers
and BloodStorm. As one of their
last projects under the Strata name,
Hodgson's team developed the arcade
version of Street Fighter: The Movie.

426   Like a Hurricane

ZENJI ISHII

Serving as the editor of Gamest
- Japan's biggest coin-op game
magazine in the 1990s - Ishii had a
front row seat to Street Fighter II's
public rollout, covering the game,
interviewing the people behind it,
keeping it in regular rotation on the
magazine's cover, and working closely
with Capcom to find various ways to
promote it.

Those promotions sometimes extended
beyond the magazine itself, and
Gamest helped organize tournaments
in Japan, as well. For one of
Capcom's first large official Street
Fighter II exhibitions, Ishii hosted
the event while dressed as Ryu.

According to Noritaka Funamizu, Ishii
knows Street Fighter history better
than anyone.

HIDEAKI ITSUNO

Joining Capcom Japan as a game designer in the early 1990s, Itsuno started out working on a pair of quiz games and hadn't been there long when Noritaka Funamizu invited him to work on Street Fighter Alpha, altering the course of his career. Itsuno spent the next decade working on all sorts of fighting games. Following Alpha, he directed multiple 3D fighters, including Star Gladiator, Rival Schools: United by Fate and Power Stone, while having a hand in 2D games such as Capcom vs. SNK 2.

Around the turn of the century, Itsuno shifted from primarily working on fighting games to primarily working in other genres, directing cel-shaded racing game Auto Modellista, overseeing the Devil May Cry series and creating action RPG franchise Dragon's Dogma. At the time of publication, he's been at Capcom for more than 30 years.

ALEX JIMENEZ

As Capcom struggled with a Dungeons & Dragons project in the early 1990s, Jimenez came in to help, offering his perspective as a hardcore D&D fan and serving as a middleman between the development team in Japan and the licence holders in the US. That work resulted in Dungeons & Dragons: Tower of Doom, a side-scrolling brawler with role-playing elements that attracted a loyal following.

Jimenez went on to work closely with James Goddard and the Capcom USA design support group, writing and giving feedback on games such as Alien vs. Predator, Darkstalkers, X-Men: Children of the Atom, Marvel Super Heroes and Street Fighter Ⅲ.

After leaving Capcom in the mid-1990s, he bounced between a variety of game industry jobs, and in 2014 he formed Heavily Medicated Games, a tabletop publisher working on titles such as DayLight, a party game designed to help players with issues surrounding mental health.

→

CHRIS KRAMER

Starting at Capcom USA as a game counsellor in 1993, Kramer took calls and gave advice to players while assisting multiple departments. On his first day, he says he asked his boss why there wasn't a Mega Man game on Super Nintendo — at which point that boss grabbed an early copy of Mega Man X and told him to write about it.

Over the next couple years, Kramer transitioned to a public relations role, working on games such as Street Fighter Alpha. He left Capcom in 1996 and spent a decade working for companies such as Sony Online Entertainment, then ended up returning to Capcom to head up PR, corporate communications and community, launching Street Fighter IV.

After leaving Capcom a second time, he took jobs at PR agency Fortyseven Communications and tech giant Tencent.

HIROSHI MATSUMOTO

While Takashi Nishiyama thought up the idea for Street Fighter and gets much of the public credit for it, Matsumoto served as his partner through the process, overseeing the bulk of the game's development. Nishiyama took on high-level tasks, generating many of the big-picture concepts behind the game, while Matsumoto led the day-to-day charge, handling specific gameplay and tuning choices.

As it turned out, Nishiyama and Matsumoto's work at Capcom led to a partnership spanning more than three decades. When Nishiyama left Capcom to join SNK, Matsumoto followed. When Nishiyama left SNK to start Dimps, Matsumoto stood by his side. And when Nishiyama signed a deal with Capcom to return to the Street Fighter series with Street Fighter IV, Matsumoto showed up once again, with the two sharing executive producer credits.

In between all of that, Matsumoto contributed to the Sonic the Hedgehog and Dragon Ball franchises.

→

The art director on Incredible Technologies' Street Fighter: The Movie arcade game, Melgosa came to the franchise without a lot of experience on fighting games, and spent much of his time on it attempting to compete with Midway and their work on Mortal Kombat. Melgosa was one of five people from the studio to fly to the Street Fighter movie set and capture images of the actors to use in the game, where he was fascinated by the prop design work and less fascinated by Jean-Claude Van Damme.

In the years following his work on the game, Melgosa left Incredible Technologies briefly before returning, and went on to a long career there working on arcade games like Silver Strike Bowling and Target Toss Pro, eventually moving into the company's casino games division.

DANA MORESHEAD

Working for Marvel's creative services
group throughout the 1990s, Moreshead
contributed to everything from
marketing to style guides to theme
parks, including licensing deals for
products such as Capcom's X-Men and
Marvel fighting games. Specifically,
that meant collaborating with Capcom
staff such as Takeshi Tezuka and
Katsuya Akitomo to approve character
choices, artwork, and anything
considered a creative concern for the
comic publisher.

Moreshead left Marvel in 1998 and
went on to work for comic legend Stan
Lee before starting his own creative
agency under the name Fishbrain.
Decades later, he joined Disney Parks.

JOE MORICI

One of Capcom USA's earliest
employees, Morici helped establish
the company in the West, handling
licensing agreements with companies
like Disney and overseeing the U.S.
console division through the 1980s
and early 1990s. For a period of
time, Morici wrote and signed letters
that appeared at the beginning of
each of Capcom's instruction manuals,
thanking players for their support
of Capcom's games.

Towards the end of his run at Capcom,
Morici also took over their U.S.
arcade group, before moving on to
roles at game publishers such as
Metro3D and Eidos.

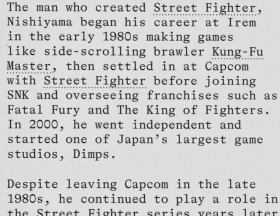

TAKASHI NISHIYAMA

The man who created Street Fighter,
Nishiyama began his career at Irem
in the early 1980s making games
like side-scrolling brawler Kung-Fu
Master, then settled in at Capcom
with Street Fighter before joining
SNK and overseeing franchises such as
Fatal Fury and The King of Fighters.
In 2000, he went independent and
started one of Japan's largest game
studios, Dimps.

Despite leaving Capcom in the late
1980s, he continued to play a role in
the Street Fighter series years later,
setting up deals for Capcom crossover
games at SNK and development work on
Street Fighter Ⅳ and Ⅴ at Dimps.

Describing himself as someone who
likes to oversee games rather than
dig into the finer nuts and bolts,
Nishiyama generally avoids making
public appearances, saying he doesn't
like doing interviews and that he
thinks Dimps' culture is reflected in
that sense of privacy. 'That said,'
he adds, 'I do think there is room to
become more open-minded and maybe we
should be a little bit more open about
what we do. Maybe that will happen
when the next president steps in.'

SHINICHIRO OBATA

Working at Capcom Japan for more than a decade, Obata played key design roles in a variety of fighting games, working on the Darkstalkers and JoJo's Bizarre Adventure series, as well as Street Fighter III: New Generation, helping to pull the game together following years of development struggles.

In 2008, he founded independent studio Byking, working on games in the Gundam and My Hero Academia franchises, as well as Square Enix's arcade-shooter/action-game mash-up Gunslinger Stratos. In a 2014 interview with website Tech in Asia, he said he left Capcom because he thought it would take too long to accomplish his goals if he stayed. 'For creators who have real ability and are energetic, a safe, large company is dangerous,' he said.

SEIJI OKADA

As a young programmer at Capcom Japan in the early 1990s, Okada worked on Street Fighter II under the nickname 'Marina' and stuck with the series through many of its follow-ups, contributing to the initial Super Nintendo port and the Street Fighter Alpha series, among others. He also worked on the Darkstalkers, Marvel vs. Capcom, and Capcom vs. SNK brands, having a hand in most of Capcom's fighting game franchises.

Okada stayed at Capcom for more than a decade, and ended up continuing to work with Noritaka Funamizu at mobile development team Indigo Game Studios.

IAN ROSE

As Capcom USA's first general counsel, Rose dealt with a wide range of legal issues in the early-to-mid 1990s. Those often consisted of day-to-day licensing agreements and approvals, but also included larger projects such as Capcom's lawsuit targeting Data East and their game Fighter's History, and countering the proliferation of counterfeit Street Fighter arcade boards.

After leaving Capcom in 1995, Rose joined game publisher Mindscape for a few years, then moved into a variety of tech-focused legal roles at companies such as Dolby, EcoTensil, and TrueKat Digital.

Street Fighter II's lead composer,
Shimomura only worked at Capcom for
around five years, but contributed
to more than a dozen soundtracks
including Ghosts 'n Goblins spinoff
Gargoyle's Quest, brawlers Final Fight
and The Punisher and role-playing game
Breath of Fire.

After leaving Capcom, Shimomura spent
about a decade at Final Fantasy
publisher Square, primarily composing
music for role-playing games like
Super Mario RPG, Parasite Eve and
Kingdom Hearts.

Post-Square, she moved into a
freelance career, contributing to
some of the biggest franchises in the
game industry, from Final Fantasy to
Kingdom Hearts to Smash Bros., as well
as a long list of smaller projects -
and even some work outside of games.
She also composed the theme song for
this book, offered on vinyl as part of
our Kickstarter funding campaign.

TOM SHIRAIWA

A longtime game industry localization manager, Shiraiwa oversaw translation and localization work for many of Capcom's fighting games in the 1990s, and served as a middleman between Capcom Japan and Capcom USA for many of the biggest discussions and debates between the two offices.

After leaving Capcom in the early 2000s, he went on to roles with Mighty No. 9 development studio Comcept and Guilty Gear development studio Arc System Works, among others. In game credits, he is often listed under his birth name 'Takuya' rather than his adopted name 'Tom'.

SCOTT SMITH

Working as a product manager at Capcom USA, Smith started the summer before Street Fighter II hit arcades and witnessed the series transform Capcom as it became more and more successful. His role included everything from developing marketing plans to answering fan phone calls to giving feedback on games.

In one particular case, that feedback led to a name change that has become an established part of Street Fighter lore – he gets credit for thinking of 'Akuma' as a Western name for Super Street Fighter II Turbo boss Gouki. Smith left Capcom in 1996.

TOYOHISA TANABE

Working at SNK for just over a decade, Tanabe spent years contributing to the King of Fighters series and directed what many consider the series' best entry, The King of Fighters '98. After leaving SNK in the early 2000s, he joined Capcom for a short time and worked on cancelled 3D fighting game 'Capcom Fighting All-Stars', then joined Yoshiki Okamoto's narrative and design-focused studio Flagship.

Prior to King of Fighters, Tanabe worked on Neo Geo favourite Baseball Stars Professional. After leaving Capcom, he worked on the Kirby and Fire Emblem series, among others.

Though not an official Street Fighter
II team member, Tezuka sat next to
planner Akira Nishitani during the
game's development and had a front
row seat to its production, giving
occasional feedback and helping test
the arcade board. As a result, he was
one of the first people outside of the
development team who saw how special
the game was turning out to be, and he
knew he wanted to work with Nishitani
in the years following.

His wish came true when he joined
Nishitani as a planner on X-Men:
Children of the Atom, before leading
development on Marvel Super Heroes
and going on to produce 3D fighting
game Power Stone. Towards the end
of his run at Capcom, he oversaw
the company's mobile game lineup
and produced the mobile version of
Street Fighter IV.

In 2014, he left Capcom and started
his own company, Mugen Combo,
designing mobile games with the goal
of making them accessible to everyone,
not just hardcore players.

Street Fighter II's lead programmer,
Ueyama worked as a coder on many
of Capcom's biggest arcade games
of the late 1980s and early 1990s,
contributing to Ghouls 'n Ghosts and
Final Fight before taking a lead role
on SFII and working on multiple Street
Fighter games.

As the Street Fighter series evolved
in the mid-1990s, Ueyama turned his
attention to Capcom's online efforts,
working on network programming
challenges for a wide swath of
fighting games as well as other titles
like cel-shaded racer Auto Modellista
and cooperative horror experiment
Resident Evil: Outbreak.

After more than a decade at Capcom,
he moved on to reunite with
Yoshiki Okamoto at Game Republic
and later, Noritaka Funamizu at
Indigo Game Studios.

JEFF WALKER

Head of arcade sales at Capcom USA
in the early 1990s, Walker came from
roles at Atari, Nintendo, Gottlieb
Pinball, and Data East, and oversaw
Street Fighter II and Champion Edition
sales at the peak of the fighting
game boom. He stuck around at Capcom
for the launch of Hyper Fighting, and
then moved on to work with distributor
Betson, manufacturer Interactive
Light, amusement chain GameWorks,
and others.

Years later, he co-founded the
Mantiques Network, selling vintage
memorabilia and appearing on The
History Channel's show Pawn Stars.

A former editor at GamePro magazine, Winstead joined Capcom USA during the development of Street Fighter II Turbo: Hyper Fighting and played a design support role on Hyper Fighting and Super Street Fighter II, among other games, working closely with James Goddard.

Winstead left Capcom before the release of Super Street Fighter II Turbo, and went on to work with Goddard at multiple companies — first at Namco on WeaponLord, and later at Atari Games (Tenth Degree), The Collective (Buffy the Vampire Slayer), and Crunchtime Games (Shred Nebula). The two also worked on the 2013 reboot of 1994 Street Fighter competitor Killer Instinct, with Goddard on the publishing side at Microsoft and Winstead on the development side at Double Helix.

AKIRA YASUDA

Known for his iconic art and his controversial statements, Yasuda started at Capcom in the mid-1980s, working as a background artist on the side-scrolling shooter Side Arms, but his career took off a couple of years later when Capcom paired him with game designer Akira Nishitani. Together, the pair oversaw two of the biggest hits of the era: Final Fight and Street Fighter II.

Many credit Yasuda both for his illustration and pixel art abilities, noting that he played a key role in defining the look of Capcom's late-1980s/early-1990s arcade games.

Yasuda stayed with Capcom for almost two decades, contributing to fighting games like Darkstalkers and Star Gladiator, and he even moved to California to work on Red Dead Revolver after fighting game boom came to an end. In 2003, he left Capcom for a freelance illustration career.

GUEST SPEAKERS

MATT ATWOOD

→

Working at Capcom USA in the late 1990s and early 2000s, Atwood handled public relations for games such as Street Fighter Alpha 3 and Marvel vs. Capcom. Following his time at Capcom, he went on to do PR for 2K, Nintendo, Electronic Arts and Reverb Communications.

JUSTIN BERENBAUM

→

Working at Capcom USA in the mid-1990s, Berenbaum took on a variety of different roles - from helping with retail chain G&G Software to managing mail-order sales to working in customer support. After leaving Capcom, he went on to a number of business development roles in the game industry, working for companies such as Activision and 505 Games.

PETER BETTI

Eventually settling in as CEO and chairman of H. Betti Industries - the company behind distributor Betson - Betti held various positions in the family distribution business over the years, and worked closely with Capcom USA sales head Jeff Walker as Street Fighter II and Champion Edition took off in the early 1990s.

SATINDER BHUTANI

A popular figure at Capcom USA, Bhutani started at Capcom in 1991 and spent almost a decade there, first working with Bert Kitade on the company's controversial route business (where they cut out the middleman and operated arcade games themselves), and later working as a salesman handling a handful of Street Fighter titles. After leaving Capcom, he joined coin-op manufacturer Andamiro USA, where he went on to become president before retiring in 2020.

JAMES CHEN

→

Tournament player turned commentator,
Chen grew up with fighting games and
became one of the most popular figures
in the fighting game community,
referring to himself as a fanboy,
commentator and historian. He also
wrote this book's foreword.

RYAN CRAVENS

→

Son of well-known Capcom salesman Bill
Cravens, Ryan has built his own career
in the amusement business, working
on sales and marketing for companies
including Incredible Technologies and
Stern Pinball.

TODD CRAVENS

→

Bill Cravens' other son, Todd, has also spent his career in the amusement business, working in sales with his father, then moving to companies such as distributor Betson and casino game company Galaxy Gaming.

STEPHEN FROST

→

As an editor at PlayStation magazine PSM in the late 1990s and early 2000s, Frost covered Capcom's fighting games - and then years later, while working as a producer at game studio Digital Eclipse, he joined forces with Capcom to develop the Street Fighter 30th Anniversary Collection.

JOE GANIS

→

A tester at Capcom USA in the early 1990s, Ganis discovered bugs in games like Street Fighter II and supplied feedback to the development team in Japan, offering suggestions for the series and working closely with James Goddard.

BILL GARDNER

→

Head of Capcom USA in the late 1990s and early 2000s, Gardner arrived as Street Fighter's popularity was fading and console franchises like Resident Evil were the new stars. Prior to joining Capcom, he worked at Panasonic where he helped oversee software for the 3DO console. After leaving Capcom, he founded publisher 0~3 and later ran Eidos' North American office.

JOHN GILLIN

→

Head of Capcom USA's marketing department in the early-to-mid-1990s, Gillin arrived just a few months before Street Fighter II hit consoles, showing up in time to see Capcom's consumer sales explode. He came from Del Monte Foods and stayed until 1994, at which point he took over marketing at Sega of America.

SETH KILLIAN

→

Street Fighter tournament player turned Capcom USA community manager, Killian worked as a special combat advisor on Street Fighter IV, offering the development team player feedback and getting a character named after himself: Shadaloo Intimidation Network CEO (and final boss) Seth.

SCOTT MAXWELL

A rare Western engineer working at Capcom Japan, Maxwell started in third-party development at Capcom USA in 1988, and soon after, went to Japan for three months to learn 'the Capcom process'. As it turned out, three months turned into more than three years, as he stayed in Japan doing various programming and translation tasks before returning to Capcom USA in the mid-1990s. Prior to joining Capcom, Maxwell worked as a programmer for Pacific Dataworks International, an independent studio that developed the Commodore 64 version of Street Fighter, though he wasn't deeply involved with the game.

JUSTIN MCCORMACK

Overseeing Marvel game licensing in the mid-1990s, McCormack worked with Capcom on their X-Men and Marvel fighting game series, and also had a hand in Marvel's clothing, toy, restaurant and theme park business.

MICK MCGINTY

The artist behind Street Fighter II's Western box art, McGinty worked for decades as a freelance illustrator, contributing promotional artwork for a variety of games in the 1990s and focusing on landscape and still-life pieces over time. He revisited his Street Fighter II box art for the Polygon story that inspired this book in 2014. McGinty died in 2021.

TATSUYA MINAMI

Starting at Capcom Japan in the late 1980s, Minami stayed there for almost two decades, producing many of the company's console games, including ports of various Street Fighter titles. After leaving Capcom in 2006, he headed up independent studio PlatinumGames, which he oversaw until 2016.

MONTE SINGMAN

→

Working as a producer at Capcom's US development studio in the mid-1990s, Singman helped with early concepts for Final Fight Revenge, a competitive fighting game that brought back the Final Fight brand in 3D. The game shipped on Sega's underpowered ST-V arcade board in 1999, and failed to take off next to high-end 3D series like Virtua Fighter and Tekken.

CLAUDE STERN

→

Representing Data East in the trial over similarities between Street Fighter II and Fighter's History, Stern went home victorious, though Fighter's History never achieved the same level of success as Street Fighter (despite a sequel appearing on SNK's Neo Geo hardware).

TOMOTAKA SUZUKI

→

A content creator well before YouTube and Twitch came around, Suzuki - who goes by the name TZW (and declines to say what the name means) - built a name for himself in the early 1990s by producing fanzines and VHS tapes that showed advanced Street Fighter combos and techniques. His videos ended up getting copied many times over and sent around the world, with all the tracking errors and fuzzy visuals you'd expect from bootleg tapes.

CHRIS TANG

→

A Street Fighter II tournament player, Tang joined Atari Games early in his career and helped design a few fighting games including Primal Rage. He then made his way to Capcom, serving in a design support role on games such as Street Fighter III. After leaving Capcom in the early 2000s, Tang joined Capcom co-worker Erik Suzuki at a new studio, Geneaza.

LAURIE THORNTON

→

A public relations manager at Capcom USA in the early 1990s, Thornton worked on Street Fighter II as it became one of the biggest games in the world, as well as many of Capcom's other games and corporate communications efforts. She went on to found independent public relations firm Radiate PR, and helped launch networking site LinkedIn.

COREY TRESIDDER

→

Working for Capcom USA in the mid-1990s, Tresidder started in customer service, handling calls from players who needed help with games, and moved into a marketing role over time, writing copy and cleaning up translated text for Capcom's English instruction manuals.

PAUL WIEDERAENDERS

Working in arcade sales for Capcom
USA as Street Fighter II took off,
Wiederaenders worked closely with
Bill Cravens and pushed Capcom's CPS
arcade hardware, letting clients know
about the benefits of being able to
swap out games.

DARRYL WILLIAMS

As a technical service manager at
Romstar in the 1980s and early 1990s,
Williams worked with both SNK and
Capcom in different capacities. And
after leaving Romstar, those roots led
him to jobs at Capcom Coin-Op
and SNK's US office, before he
eventually settled in at mobile game
network Playphone.

KEN WILLIAMS

An editor at Electronic Gaming Monthly, Williams wrote under the name Sushi-X and came up with the magazine's infamous 1992 April Fool's joke revealing a hidden Street Fighter II character named Sheng Long. Decades later, his email signature still includes the quote, 'You must defeat Sheng Long to stand a chance.'

KAZUNORI YAMADA

A composer at Capcom Japan in the 1990s, Yamada contributed sound effects to the console versions of Super Street Fighter II and Super Street Fighter II Turbo, but is best known for his work on the Mega Man series, spanning multiple decades.

REPORTING
NOTES

→   MATT LEONE
     Author

This book is an edited and expanded collection of articles that appeared on Vox Media's games and entertainment website *Polygon* in 2014, 2020 and 2021.

While the book tells the story of Capcom's fighting game boom centring around the release of *Street Fighter II*, it is not a comprehensive account of the creative and business decisions throughout the company at the time.

Capcom's corporate history is expansive and messy, filled with politics, cultural differences, handshake deals, egos, sensitive topics and the personal dynamics of hundreds of people over multiple decades. We left some leeway for detours in the book, but weren't able to touch on many related business decisions, such as the company's real-estate ventures, their work to go public, their retail aspirations, their arcade locations and route business, their US development efforts, their European offices, Kenzo Tsujimoto's northern California winery, various lawsuits, and the successes and failures of more than 100 other games.

We spent years researching this story and are acutely aware of how much there is left to report. How many holes there are because we were only able to talk to three of the four people in a room, or because two of them disagree on a key point, or because the third misunderstood what the first was saying at the time. We went to great lengths to track down as many relevant people as possible, fact-check what they said, and find those who disagree with them or remember situations differently. But inevitably, we were unable to account for all interpretations of every story told.

As ever, history is told by those willing to speak, which puts a slant on things. We attempted to include voices from all over the world wherever possible, but for logistical reasons and because of who was willing to talk, the word count favours those who spoke English – which is not ideal for a book about a series developed primarily in Japan.

We conducted interviews with 27 Japanese speakers for the book. For each of these, we used a live interpreter and a separate post-interview translator to fact-check and re-translate quotes for accuracy.

Given the oral history format and the challenges inherent with establishing tone when dealing with translated quotes, we spent hundreds of hours editing the text with proper context as our primary goal – which sometimes included editing paragraphs out of the order they were originally spoken.

We have changed certain game, system, and character names throughout this book to reflect their English versions and reduce confusion. Job titles reflect past roles relevant to the topics discussed, and in some cases represent internal roles rather than listed credits in shipped games.

Thank you to everyone who read or otherwise supported this book. It's been a pleasure.

END MATTER

Special thanks:
Jason Andersen
Frank Cifaldi
Harumi Fujita
Chris Grant
Adam Laatz
Ashley Leone
Emily Leone
Tracy Leone
Greg McLemore
Maddy Myers
Ingrid Milkes
Chris Plante
Jimmy Pon
Mike Rougeau
Samit Sarkar
Yoko Shimomura
Chelsea Stark
Alex Zabava

Interpreters and
  translators:
Alex Aniel
David Crislip
Alex Highsmith
Jean Pierre
  Kellams
Hiroko Minamoto

Benefactors:
Carl Thomas Aarum
Izzy Abdus-Sabur
Merwan Achibet
Daniel Adams
Zach Adams
Ben Ahmady
Andy Ahn
Xabier
  Akordagoitia
Jorge Alfaro
  Porras
R Ali
Hussain Alj
Drew Allen
Jason Allen
Thomas Alvarez
Toys Amemiya
Andrew
Adelaide Andrews
Evan Anger
Alexander Aniel
W Paul Apel
Arcade Dream Team
Mark Argent
Hamza Arif Jaka
Arkotype
Tom Armitage
Benjamin Arnault
Adrian Arnese
Art
Tyler Ashcraft
Stephen Ashworth
Nick Atkins
Paul Audino
Dale Austin
Boghos Avetikian
Josef Axner
Collin Ayers
Mat Azel
Andrew Babiuk
Rusty Bailey
Chad 'Bornliar'
  Baker
Paul J Baker
Geoffrey Bakker
Vijay Bal
Chris 'Banthug'
  Bannon
Corbett Baratta
James Bareham
David Barnett
Paul Barnett

Alfredo Barraza
Chase Barrette
Dwight Barthelman
Thom Bartley
Samuel Bass
Bauble Clock
Stefan Bautista
Aziz Bawany
Jeff Baxter
Christopher Beal
Matt Bednarik
Bob Bedore
Alex Beech
Josh Bell
Icilio Bellanima
Kate Bender
Caroline Bennett
David Bennett
Scott Bennett
Ian Benneyworth
James Bentley
Laszlo Benyi
Tim Berry
Jimmy Bertelsen
Manu Bertolus
David Bettencourt
Jag Bhachu
Leon Biddulph
Mark Biggs
Design Bisch
Kelvin Bivins
Euan Blackledge
Justin Blakely
Blanka Blankowsky
Mathew
  Bleasdale-Clews
Kim André Bøe
Kirk Bokesch
Jon Bonilla
Matthew Booy
Keith Albion
  Borgholthaus
Joseph Bosner
Jake Botterell
Davide Bottino
Luke Boulerice
Scott Boulet
DS Boyce
Gareth Bradley
Kristopher Bradney
Aidan Braniff
Jeremy Brewer
Mike Brewer

Dean 'Citypoppu'
  Brown
Nigel Brown
Ken Bruno
Michael Buckler
Ron Buckman
Rocco Buffalino
Bugula
Kevin Bunch
Catherine Byng
Emil Caillaux
Abe Cajudo
David Cameron
Jason Camp
André Campos
Jeremy Canceko
Robin 'Ken' Cane
Brendan Canney
Captain Chaos
Mario Carballo
  Zama
Lucas Cardoso
Mattia Carletti
Brian Carr
Filipe Carvalho
Garry Casey
Mark Cassar
Nick Castellina
Mauro 'mrz' Catena
Brian Catton
Matthew Cawley
Chris Ceglia
Marco Celia
Aaron Cerny
Andy Chalkey
Joseph
  Chamberlain
Rex-Hilaire
  Chamberlain
Jerry Chan
David Chanza
  Tellez
Gilbert Chaparro
Isaac Chappell
Paul Charlton
Jeff Chee
Jared Cherup
Nick Chester
Tsoek 'Chockles'
  Cheung
Marc Chima
Shau Bing Chin
James Chivers

Adrien Cho
Jason Choi
Noyon Choudhury
Nicholas Chow
Lawrence Chu
Ping Chu
Keegan Chua
Eric 'eOn' Chung
Iain Clark
Thierry Clavel
Peter Clay
Stefan Claypool
Tom Cleaver
Nicolas Clement
Hamish Clift
Blake Coglianese
Michele Colombo
Chris Comeau
Chris Conroy
Dyl Cook
Adam Cooperman
Eli Coronado
Steve Correa
Derek Correia
Gilbert Cortes
  Guzman
Ian Craig
Matthew Cranor
Alex Cross
Ben Cross
Joseph Cross
Dennis 'Banana
  Ken' Crowley
Lee Cullen
Jon Cunnane
Caitlyn Cykala
Peter Czegledy
Joshy D
D13TZ13
Mattias Dahlberg
Agostino Damiano
Carolyn Dao
Arseniy Dashevskiy
Dav
Steven David
Patrick Davidson
Ben Davis
Kevin Davis
Keith Day
Elmar de Koning
Guillermo
  Deagustin
Joe Dean

Iker Del Campo
  Saiz
Tara Sibel Demren
Joseph
  deNiverville
Gurvir Singh Deol
Rigo DeSantiago
Michael Di Natale
Ian Dick
Joshua Dickens
Peter Dijkstra
Brent Disbrow
Preston Do
Cody Dolan
Nick Dominguez
Alexander
  Donaldson
Ben Dornis
Aleks Dorohovich
Kevin Doyle
Phil Doyle
Marcus Drakken
Jean-Charles Drost
Kevin Ducoff
Kevin Duffy
Andi Duncan
Carl Dungca
Barry Dwyer
Andreas Edlinger
Henrik Edlund
Justin Edmund
Sadat Edroos
Bloopers Edwards
Tarek Elbanhawy
Tom Eldon
Gino Elias
John Ellenich
Joseph
  Elliott-Coleman
David Elstob
Greg Elward
Alex Engel
BJ Enriquez
Jordi Escobar
  Bonet
Ethan
Felix Evangelista
Matt Evans
Nick Evans
Steven Evans
Filippo Facchetti
Adam Fahy
Esteban Fajardo

Lorenzo Fantoni
Mauricio Farah
Alan Farrell
Sean Feeley
Diamond Feit
Juan Fernandez
Murilo Ferreira
Jérémie Fesson
Steven Feurer
Thomas Finnerup
Andrew Fisher
Ben Fisher
Matthew Fisher
Brian Fishman
Casey Fitzgerald
Sean Flannigan
David Fleming
Mark Flemmich
Luis Flores
Steve Flores
Tate Flowers
Fluxcore
James Foley
Max Folkman
Nick Folkman
Bruno Fonseca
Adrian Ford
Jason Ford
Klemens Franz
Dave Frear
Brett Freeman
Cameron Friend
Francisco Furtado
Melanie
  Fussenegger
Manu Gabaldon
JF Gagné
Luke Galambos
Ryan Gallagher
Ian Gander
Joao Carlos
  Garcia Arias
Rodrigo García
  Carmona
Clay Gardner
Michael Gargano
Ricardo Garza
Geeklifepaca
Eilonwy
  George-Wallis
Peter Gerena
Joachim Germain
Luigino Gigante

Brice Gilbert
Jonathan Glover
Stu Gollan
Philip Golobish
Claudio Gomboli
Jesyel Gonzalez
Oscar González
 Cabo
Joshua Gooden
Dave Patrick
 Goodfellow
Sebastien Goutal
Jesper Granmyr
Christopher Grant
Oliver Grant
Richard 'Lard'
 Gray
Ryan Gray
David Green
James E Greenhorn
Dave Gregal
Griff
Blake Gross
Felix Grundmann
Miguel Guerreiro
Olivier
 Guillemette
Christopher Gunn
Jim Gunning
Giovanny Gutierrez
Gilbert Guttmann
Mathew Guy
Guybrush
 Threepwood
Jessica H
Jonny H
Matt H
Terry Hale
Anthony Hall
Nathan Hallett
Johnnie Hamn
E Hanby
John Hanold
Michael Hansen
Alan Harding
Dominic Harman
Justin Harman
Oliver Harper
Amanda Harris
Patrick Harris
G Hartman
Jarett Hartman
Robert Harvey

Shaun Harvey
Brendan Harwood
Shehzad Hasan
Lasse Hassing
Vegard Sandanger
 Hauso
Phillip Haydon
Andrew Hayward
Seppo Helava
Patrick Deric
 Jack Henderson
Ross Hendry
Heiko Henke
Gastón Hernández
 Hernández
Blake Hester
Tony Heugh
Dave Hicks
Kenji Higa
Jonathan
 Hildebrandt
Tobias Hildesheim
Andrew Hill
Jason Hill
Jimmy Hillis
Jacob Hinrichsen
Billy Hinzo
Ravi Hiranand
Toni Ho
ZY Ho
Rick Hoadley
Kimson Hoang
Lucien Hoare
Justin Hochella
Paul Hodgeson
Micah Hodosh
Gregory Hogan
Terje Høiback
JJ Holder
David Holdsworth
Richard Holt
OE Homol
Sinclair Hong
Neil Hood
DC Hopkins
Martin 'Hoppy'
 Hopkins, Rand,
 Anjy and MJ
Ian Hosler
Brandon House
Maxwell House
Ken Houston
Luciano Howard

Howard The Duck
Andy Howell
Andrew Hsieh
Joseph Hsieh
Anthony Hubbs
Lee Huggett
Derek Huie
Ira Humphrey
Quentin Humphrey
Max Humphries
Nicoll Hunt
Richard Hunton
Alex Hutchinson
Kaiser Hwang
Tyler Hymanson
Zuber Ibrahim
Yoshihiro Ikuta
Jonathon
 Imperiosi
Christian Iñiguez
Göran Isacson
Stefan Isaksson
David Isherwood
Jean-Philippe
 Issaly
Alejandro Izuel
 Vinue
Lee Jackson
Shareef Jackson
Jonas Jacobsson
Jaime
Ahmed Jameel
Hardip Jasser
Chris Jessee
Andrés Jiménez
 Guerra
JJc14
Gareth John
JohnDoe
Aaron Johnson
Hari Johnson
Walter Johnson
Lamont Jones
Mike Jones
Adam S Jordan
Jim Jordan
Jamaine Josephs
Julius Viloria
Ed Junco
Michael
 Jusenius
Angelo Kanaris
Jonny Kanaris

Aliaksandr
 Kanaukou
Max Kappes
Jay Kay
Kamran Keenan
Darren Keig
Sean Kelley
Chris Kelly
Michael Keough
Mark Kerr Jr
Neil Khambhaita
Richard Kho
Michael Kibedi
Romain Killian
Jonathan
 'Persona' Kim
Hawken King
Patrick King
Ray King
Kayla Kinnunen
Christian
 Kirkegaard
Aaron Kirkham
Ryan Klaverweide
Vaughan Knight
Felipe Knorr Kuhn
Turgut Kocer
Justin Koh
Marcin Kosman
Josip Kovac
Miodrag Kovachevic
Riley Kruger
Eleisha Kubale
Roman Kudryashov
Oleg Kuznetsov
Alex Kyriacou
Gregorios
 Kythreotis
Nick Lachica
Kitty Lam
Ben Lambert
Kenneth Lamont
Kai Lancaster
Jared Lance
Gregory Landegger
Kris Lane
Josh Langford
Brandon Langley
Jordan Lapio
Peter LaPrade
David Laranjeira
Andrew Lashinsky
Frederik Lauridsen

Ugo Laviano
Zach Lay
John Learned
A Lee
Adrian Lee
Andrew Lee
George Lee
Josh Lee
Maik Leenards
Ethan Lego
Bjorn Lehmann
Jarkko Lehtola
Joonas Lehtovaara
Warren Leigh
Thiago 'Dvincent'
  Leite
Matt LeMay
Rick Lemon
Ryan Lenau
Joe Leonard
Barbara Leone
Bill Leone
Tracy Leone
William Leone
Vincenzo Lettera
Marc Letzmann
Michael Levesque
Aaron Levin
Derek Lewinski
Jeffrey Lewis
Matt Lewis
Ryan H Lewis
Christoph Licht
Paul Liggett
Eric Lindholm
William Linn
Elvin Liow
John Lipari
Sky Liu
Sebastian Lizon
Phillip Loeb
Youri Loedts
Tony Loiseleur
Alain Lok
Phoenix Lombardi
John Loner
Nicholas Long
Nick Long
Stephen Long
Mun Keat Looi
Alexander Lopatin
Daniel Lopes Alves
Thomas Lotito

Alun Lower
Mathew Lucas
LuckyDaniel'
  Lehmann
Benedikt Ludwig
Sebastiaan Luiten
Patrick Lum
Tom Lynch
Brandon Ma
Brian MacCarthy
Carmine Macchia III
Bruno Machado
  Brandao
Kenny Mack
Roberto Macken
Shirley Mackintosh
Tim Macneil
Andrea Maderna
Tam Mageean
Alan Maguire
Devendra Mahendran
James Mai
Hammad Malik
Rick Mallen
Kate Malloy
Kris Maloy
Stephen Maluck
George C Manis
Jesse Mann
Matthew Manning
Juan Marable
Charlie Maragna
Marc
Philippe Marcelino
Koldo Aingeru
  Marcos
Ryan Markel
Edgar Marques
Eric Marrs
Fabien Marsaud
Edward Marshall
Geoffrey Martin
James Martin
Matthew Martin
Rob Martin
Samuel Martin
Esteban Martinez
David Martinez Jr
Xavier Martinez
  Palau
Leonardus Martins
Lee Massie
Beatrice Matarazzo

Michael Mateyko
Frank Matzke
Joe Mazzanti
Angelo Alessio
  Mazzeo
Dylan McArdle
Jared McCannon
Nick McCarthy
Michael McCartney
Alex McConnell
Kev McCullagh
Frank McDonald
Ben McGrath
David McGreavy
Shaun McIlroy
Skye McIntyre
John McKee
Adam McNicol
Stephen McVay
Matthew Meacham
Alan Meades
James Medd
Diego A Medina
Didem Turker Melek
Nick Mellish
Frédéric Ménétrier
Phil Merricks
John Meschisen
Raja Miah
Midwinter Minis
Luis Miguel Mayor
  Ortega
Ichirou Mihara
Kazuteru Mikami
Mike 'Zangief U
  of O'
Evan Miller
Jared Miller
K and K Miller
Matt Miller
Connor Mills
Andrius Mitkus
Aaron Moe
Piero Molino
Devin Monnens
Marc Monticelli
John Moody
Jacob Moore
Michael 'Mocha'
  Moreno
Jerrod Morgan
Joel Morgan
Peter Morgan

Robert Morgan
Andrew Morley
David Morley
Maximillian Morris
John Henry Mostyn
Nima Mottacki
Patrick Mullen
A Murder of Crows
Joe Musso
Francesco Muzzi
Logan Myers
Chris 'Devilotx'
  Nabinger
Nai and Pedri
Ruben Naour
Yousif Nash
Harrison
  Nathaniel-Wurie
Leland Navarro
Maxwell
  Neely-Cohen
Jason Neifeld
Christopher Neil
NES Jumpman
MC Nguyen
T Evan Nichols
James Nicholson
Andrew Nicklin
Chris Niedringhaus
Trent Nix
Salil Nizar
Adam Noah
Glen Nogami
Kieran Nolan
Koen Nomden
Matt North
Jimmy Norville
Nostalgia_Chaser
Ross 'Marty Sucks'
  Nover
Gareth Noyce
Jérémy Noyé
Alex Núñez
Magnus Viktor
  Nystrom
John O'Connell
Peter O'Flynn
James B O'Neill
Hamilton O'Toole
Damian Ogden
Samuel Older
Craig Oldham
Simon Olliver

Phil Olsen
Ubaka Onyechi
Ying-San Ooi
Efrem Orizzonte
Ivan Ortega
Ichiro Ota
Kyle Overby
Eric Overton
Leonard Owen
Daniel Page
Anthony Palmieri
Renato Silvio
  Papucci
Ashley Pardbuck
David Parrett
Rob Pascocello
Ryan Patterson
Pete Pearce
Kynan Pearson
Erik Pede
Fabrizio
  Pedrazzini
Braden Pemberton
Matt Penna III
Robby Perdue
Andrew Perea
Mathieu Perreault
Steve Perriam
Russ Perry Jr
Bruno Pešec
Joseph Peterson
Joe Petrancosta
Guillermo Agustín
  Peyrano
Drew W Pfefferle
Chad Philip
Raymond Alexander
  Pickwoad
Mark Pienpakdee
Felix Pietsch
Adam Pigford
Sebastian Pinaud
Jason Pinon
Pixelate
Ed Plager
J Playtis
Douglas Pleger
Martijn Poels
Mike Polce
Patrick Polk
Bryan Pope
Aaron Poppleton
Ryan Porter

Tim Porter
Marcello Portolan
Charles Pratt
Stuart Preece
Nicholas Preuster
Christopher Price
Arlen Pringle
Earl Prusak
Adrian Purser
Dean Pyke
Pierre-Olivier
  Racette
Casey Rain
Todd Ramsey
Alex Rasmussen
Casey Rathunde
Erik Ravaglia
Alexander Ravajy
Mattia 'Zave'
  Ravanelli
Joseph Recla
Jon Redshaw
Nicolai Reichert
Dylan Reiff
Arthur Reinders
  Folmer
Frank Reno
William Reser
Sascha-Manuel
  Reuter
Josef Reyes
Gabriel Richard
Gustavo Richieri
Eleven Rico
Oasis Rim
Summer Ring
Paul-Matthieu
  Riolacci
Derrick Ritchie
Michael Rivero
Benjamin Rivers
RKasa
Danny Roberts
Ed Roberts
Jarrad Roberts
Jeff Roberts
M Roberts
Nathan Roberts
Shaun Lee Roberts
Jeff Robertson
Josh Robinson
Crawford Robson
Mark Robson

Rockabilly Joe
Cesar Rodrigo
  Rodarte
Jim Rodis
E-Man Rodriguez
Andrew Rooney
Wade Rosen
Jordan Rosenberg
Zach Rosenberg
Neil Ross
Luis Ruano
Alex Rudolph
Danny Russell
Rick Rust
Ryan
Nick Sadler
Joe Saint
Esteban Saiz
Rena Sakaguchi
Haru Sakai
Ahmed Salama
Esteban Salazar
Dom Salvia
Evan MR Sampson
Mike Samy
JP Sanchez
David Sanger
Fabio Santana
Brian Santos
Abhilash Sarhadi
Cabel Sasser
Anthony Saunders
Andy Savage
Matt Scarpulla
Rolf Scheimann
Lucas Schippers
Rob Schmuck
Magnus Schönfeldt
Alexander Schulz
Eric Schwarzkopf
Joseph Scott
Brian Scott Walker
Mike Scuderi
Peter Semple
Alex Severson
Justin Severson
Greg Sewart
Yifat Shaik
Mahmood Shaikh
Craig Shaw
Pete Shaw
Jim Shepard
David Sheppard

Shervyn
Dave Shevlin
Clifford A
  Shoemaker
Sean Sicher
Mathew Signaigo
Esteban Gaspar
  Silva
Dan Silverstone
  (Pica)
Simone
Ian Skeen
Skymap Games
Adam Small
Joshua Smalley
Colby and Finley
  Smith
Craig Smith
David Smith
Graham Smith
Jason Smith
Max Smith
Peter Smith
Tessandra Smith
Tom Smith
David Sneed
Håvard Sommervoll
Oluseyi Sonaiya
Sebastian Sonntag
Audi Sorlie
Jan T Sott
Terrence Spearman
Elijah Spector
Greg Spenser
Tom Spindlow
Dennis Spreen
David Springate
SQ YB
Alexander
  Stafford-
  Williams
Kyle Starr
Nicholas Starrett
Michael Steber
Michael Steffes
Moshe Leib Steiner
Jim Stirrup
Tanner Strom
Stephen Strome
James Sturgeon
Mark Stuttard
Biran Su
Mika Suikkanen

Dean Sullivan
Louis Sullivan
Eric Sunalp
SuperVGA
Chris Suzuki
Hiroyuki Suzuki
Tomotaka Suzuki
Ange Suzzoni
Mackenzie
  Swearengen
Sylvain Swimer
Alex Synge
Samantha T
Andreas Tabak
Tabmok99
James Tackett
Mohammed Taher
Iain Tait
Kentaro Takahashi
Wing Ping Tam
Drew Tan
Karen Tan
David Tang
Ezra Tassone
James Taylor
Patrick Tenney
David 'DDT' Teo
Rick Thiher
Alastair Thomas
John Thomas
David Thompson
Francis Thompson
Andrew Thomson
Ian 'Sho-Ryu-
  Ken80' Thornley
Maxim Titkov
Matt Tom
Matthew Tominey
Luis Torres
Pascal Tran Binh
Thomas Treptow
Joe Trigg
Michael Trinder
Chad Trotter
Alex Tsai
James Turnbull
Tzenes
Carl Urban
Herbert Urban
Johnny Utah
Gavin Valdez
Chris Valentine
Melissa Valentine

Petteri Valkonen
Kevin Valliere
Ramon van
  Barneveld
Vincent Van De
  Velde
Brad Van Orman
Harold and Hans
  Vancol
David
  Vanderstreaten
Vans
Richard Varall
Remy Varannes
Jennie L Vasquez
VC
Albert Vegers
Olaf Veldkamp
David Velez
Nic Velissaris
Rune Vendler
Rolf Venema
Ash Versus
Marc Viger
Andrea Vigogna
Alex Vissaridis
Cristian Viver
Sebastien
  Vizzacchero
Sam Von Ehren
Jamie Voto
Long Vu
Ferdinand Vykoukal
Paul W
Shu W
Berno Walch
Jon Waldman
Michael Wall
Dave Wallace
Sam Waller
Gemma Walsh
Nick Walton
Michael Walz
Ben Wander
Jamie Ward
Trey Washington
Anicorn Watches
Keith Watt
Thomas Webber
Paul Webster
Benjamin Weetman
Brian Weisberg
Mike Weissberg

Robert
  'Weaselspoon'
  Wells
Qu Wenhao
William
  Wentworth-
  Sheilds
Glen West
Steven Westburg
Nick Westin
Danny WF
Richard Whalley
Matt Whan
Michael Wheldon
Isaiah Whisner
Conlett White
Dave White
Nick Whiting
Aaron Lloyd
  Whitmore
Marcin Wichary
Adrian Widera
Jeff Wiggins
Crossman Wilkins
Daniel Willey
Joey Williams
Ross 'Seiromem'
  Williams
Stu J Williamson
Jake Willis
Nick Wilson
Randall Wilson
Robert Wilson
Simon Wilson
Konni Winkler
Joe Winn
Peter Winnberg
Adam Winstanley
Simon Wistow
Steven
  Wojciechowski
Wolf
Joseph Wolfenden-
  Williams
Stephen Wood
Kevin Wray
Adam Wright
David Wright
Nigel Wright
Steven 'Fight'
  Wright
Dan Wu
Tony Wu

Daniel Wysling
XS
Tim Xumsai
The Yabs
Chris Yang
Benny Yau
Jared Yee
Brian Young
Simon Young
Yancy Young
Derek Yu
Damjan Zamaklar
Alessandro Zampini
Darko 'Dachaz'
  Zelić
Zork Zeno
Chen Zhiming
Kim Zhu
Dirk Ziegert
Oliver Gabriel
  Zimmermann
Luka Zlatic
Zubaz Zubaz
Lucas Ezequiel
  Zubeldía

First published in the UK in 2022 by Read-Only
Memory, an imprint of Thames & Hudson

This edition published in the United Kingdom
in 2023 by Thames & Hudson Ltd,
181A High Holborn, London WC1V 7QX

First published in the United States
of America in 2023 by Thames & Hudson Inc.,
500 Fifth Avenue, New York, New York 10110

Like a Hurricane: An Unofficial
Oral History of Street Fighter II
© 2023 Thames & Hudson Ltd, London

Foreword © 2023 James Chen
Text © 2023 Matt Leone
Illustrations © 2023 Tyrell Cannon

Designed by Callin Mackintosh

British Library Cataloguing-in-Publication Data
A catalogue record for this book is available
from the British Library

Library of Congress Control Number 2022936116

ISBN 978-0-500-02593-2

Printed in China by RR Donnelley

FSC
www.fsc.org
MIX
Paper from
responsible sources
FSC® C144853

Be the first to know about our new releases,
exclusive content and author events by visiting
thamesandhudson.com
thamesandhudsonusa.com
thamesandhudson.com.au